I0828092

IMAGES
of America

LAKE CHARLES

On the Cover: This photograph shows one of the floats in the Rice Day Carnival, which occurred on the opening day of the Calcasieu Parish Fair in the early 1920s. At the time, Southwest Louisiana was the top producer of rice in the nation, and Lake Charles was dubbed "Rice City." The industry declined later in the decade and the Rice Day Carnival did not continue. See chapter six for more Rice Day Carnival photographs and information. (Courtesy David H. Levingston collection and Jeanne L. Owens of Vintage Arts.)

IMAGES
of America

LAKE CHARLES

Janet Allured, Jessica Hutchings,
and Debbie Johnson-Houston

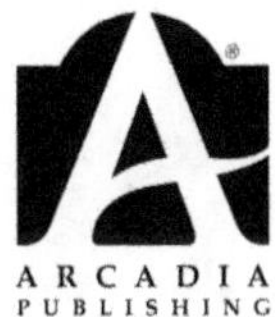

ISBN 978-1-5316-6140-3

Published by Arcadia Publishing
Charleston, South Carolina

Library of Congress Control Number: 2011931814

For all general information, please contact Arcadia Publishing:
Telephone 843-853-2070
Fax 843-853-0044
E-mail sales@arcadiapublishing.com
For customer service and orders:
Toll-Free 1-888-313-2665

Visit us on the Internet at www.arcadiapublishing.com

To the photographers, amateur and professional, whose work made this book possible, and to the archivists at McNeese State University who preserve photographs for public use.

Contents

ACKNOWLEDGMENTS

First and foremost, we wish to thank the dedicated and professional staff at the McNeese State University Frazar Memorial Library archives—Pati Threatt, Chelsea Bryant, and Sue Cormier. They dealt with our incessant requests promptly and with a smile. Without them, this book would not exist. Unless otherwise noted, all photographs appear courtesy of the McNeese State University archives. A portion of the proceeds from this book will be donated to the archives to help support its ongoing mission to preserve and protect southwest Louisiana's history.

We are also indebted to the many people in our community who responded to our requests for information or who answered our call for photographs and worked with us, sometimes for hours, to locate appropriate images, to identify the people, places, and dates of the photographs, and to help ensure historical accuracy of the text. They are: Jeanne Owens of Vintage Arts, Thomas D. Watson, Stella Miller of the Black Heritage Festival, Emma DiCarlo-Vincent, Steven Burrow, Frances Paret Walker, Lawrence "Gumbo" Morrow of *Gumbeaux Magazine*, Cheryl Kirk-Duggan, Marcus J. Combre of Combre Funeral Home, Daniel Ieyoub, Robert G. and Sarah Quinn Jones, W.T. "Billy" and Kay Krause Blake, Reginald Ball Jr. of Reggie Ball's Cajun Foods, Cissie Clark, Lake Charles Civic Ballet, and others who are credited throughout the book. Last but not at all least, we are grateful to amateur photographer Dennis Thibodeaux, a CITGO reliability engineer and 1981 McNeese engineering graduate, who graciously donated many of the recent images. His stunning photographs may be viewed at flickr.com.

We thank our families for putting up with our extended late-night hours and long absences while we worked on this project. Finally, we must acknowledge the expert guidance and always-prompt and professional support from Amy Perryman at Arcadia Publishing. She has been exceedingly patient and gently but firmly managed to prod us toward meeting our deadline tactfully and with good cheer. We thank her for making this a positive experience for us all.

INTRODUCTION

Lacking deepwater connections to the Gulf or a railroad before the Civil War, southwest Louisiana was cut off from much of the outside world and thus had few permanent settlers in the antebellum era. Lake Charles was little more than a village of 500 people when it incorporated in 1867. The town grew rapidly after the Civil War primarily because the cheap land and untouched forests of longleaf yellow pine attracted those seeking a fresh start. Railroads snaked through in the 1880s, and immigrants from Iowa, Kansas, Nebraska, and Michigan—as well as from Europe—brought along the skills, industry, and capital necessary to build an economy based primarily on agriculture and timber. Because reforestation was not practiced, many lumber towns in Louisiana became ghost towns once the timber was depleted. Upon recognizing the problem, a reforestation effort began in western Louisiana and eastern Texas, and business leaders in Lake Charles urged the development of water resources to diversify the economy. When the community voted in bond issues to improve waterways and secured matching state and federal funds to help construct a port, Lake Charles was spared the fate of many other boomtowns that faded into obscurity. Its economy took off in a new direction as the Port of Lake Charles brought in business, particularly the petrochemical industry, along the waterways. After suffering through hurricanes, fires, and floods, the city has learned from each disaster and passed reforms that have allowed it to rebuild stronger than before. Readers will find that history detailed in the following pages.

Among the many treasures of southwest Louisiana is its diverse population. The first few settlers, such as the Salliers, LeBleus, and Ryans, with their servants and slaves, were as likely to speak French as English. Immigration created an ethnic pluralism nearly as great as in New Orleans. Particularly notable was the large number of German immigrants brought over by Daniel Goos and his wife. This multicultural heritage is celebrated today in the area's many festivals, some of which are pictured in these pages. These festivals preserve the musical and cultural heritage of Lake Charles, much of which was nurtured in isolation and emerged from poor neighborhoods. In addition to indigenous artistic traditions, the fine arts have also been important to the community. The Arcade Theater, community bands, orchestras, theater, ballet companies, and choral societies included in chapter seven offer evidence of the people's love of and support for the cultural economy. Indeed, many of the town's most famous "products" are artists, from the late Boozoo Chavis, Lake Charles's famed zydeco musician, to Pulitzer Prize–winning playwright Tony Kushner; their backgrounds could not have been more different. Chavis was born in 1930 in the Dog Hill neighborhood south of Lake Charles. His people were French-speaking Creoles, most likely with Attakapas blood, who bred and trained Cajun racehorses that became part of the foundation breed of the American Quarter Horse Association. In "Uncle Bud," he paid homage to the patriarch of the Creole cowboys, "Uncle" Bud Pete. Chavis's classic hit, "Paper in My Shoe," was released in 1954 on Goldband Records, and he became a sensation.

Though there is much to admire and celebrate in the lake area's heritage, like the rest of the South, it had its time of segregation and disfranchisement of African Americans—that history, too, is told in these pages. Because the area was a backwater before the Civil War, plantation agriculture did not take hold, and there were relatively few people, slave or free, who lived in Lake Charles when the war began in 1861. The African American population was brought in primarily by lumber barons, who needed manual laborers to perform the difficult and dangerous work of logging. Compared to sharecropping, which was the most likely alternative for African Americans elsewhere, working for the lumbermen paid better, and they flocked to take advantage of the opportunity. Logging camps (some of which became permanent, such as Merryville) were typically isolated, owned by the company, heavily male, and sometimes oppressive. Saturday was payday, and the lumberjacks and sawmill hands typically caught a ride into Lake Charles to enjoy the nightlife, which included a legal red light district until 1918. Unlike Storyville, the famous red light district in New Orleans, the one in Lake Charles was not segregated and served both black and white customers. Unfortunately (perhaps), no pictures of the bawdy houses survive.

Legal segregation (known as "Jim Crow"), discrimination, and disfranchisement ended in the 1960s because of the National Association for the Advancement of Colored People (NAACP), the civil rights movement, and federal law. Unlike many other areas of the South that suffered turbulence during those difficult years, Lake Charles quietly underwent integration and the end of the Jim Crow system. There are no pictures of angry, screaming mobs or federal troops occupying school buildings, as in Little Rock, Arkansas. Instead, we tell that story through yearbook pages that depict a few of the first brave black students who broke the color line. The last chapter concentrates on the changes and institutions that mark the emergence of the post–Jim Crow era, when the area shook off that tragic part of its history and emerged into the modern era.

Telling a complete history of our area from photographs is impossible. Natural disasters have destroyed many records over the years, most recently Hurricane Rita in 2005. We have, therefore, relied upon an extant, though incomplete, sampling. To save our history from the next natural disaster (or from an overzealous heir who cleans out the attic by throwing things away), we encourage anyone who has materials related to the history of southwest Louisiana to contact the McNeese State University archives. Without this invaluable resource, begun at the behest of Dr. Robert Hebert in 1980, far more of our history would have been lost. A portion of the proceeds of the book will be donated to the archives. Please contact Pati Threatt at Frazar Memorial Library, Box 91445, Lake Charles, LA 70609; call 337-475-5731; or visit the McNeese website (mcneese.edu) and click on the "library" tab.

McNeese's archive has been invaluable to us in another way—by digitizing information about the history of southwest Louisiana on its website. That website and the *Lake Charles American Press* archives have supplied most of the information contained in these pages. We are grateful to Dr. Thomas D. Watson, retired professor of history at McNeese State University, for reviewing the manuscript and catching many mistakes. We hold ourselves responsible for any errors that may remain.

Because space was limited, we decided to include only a few photographs of McNeese, choosing instead to concentrate on the history of the community. McNeese's faculty has contributed enormously to the community in more ways than can possibly be listed, and it was painful to leave them out. For those interested, we suggest consulting *McNeese State University*, written by Kathie Bordelon and published in 2001 as part of Arcadia Publishing's campus history series. The McNeese archives department has multiple copies available for purchase.

One

FOUNDERS

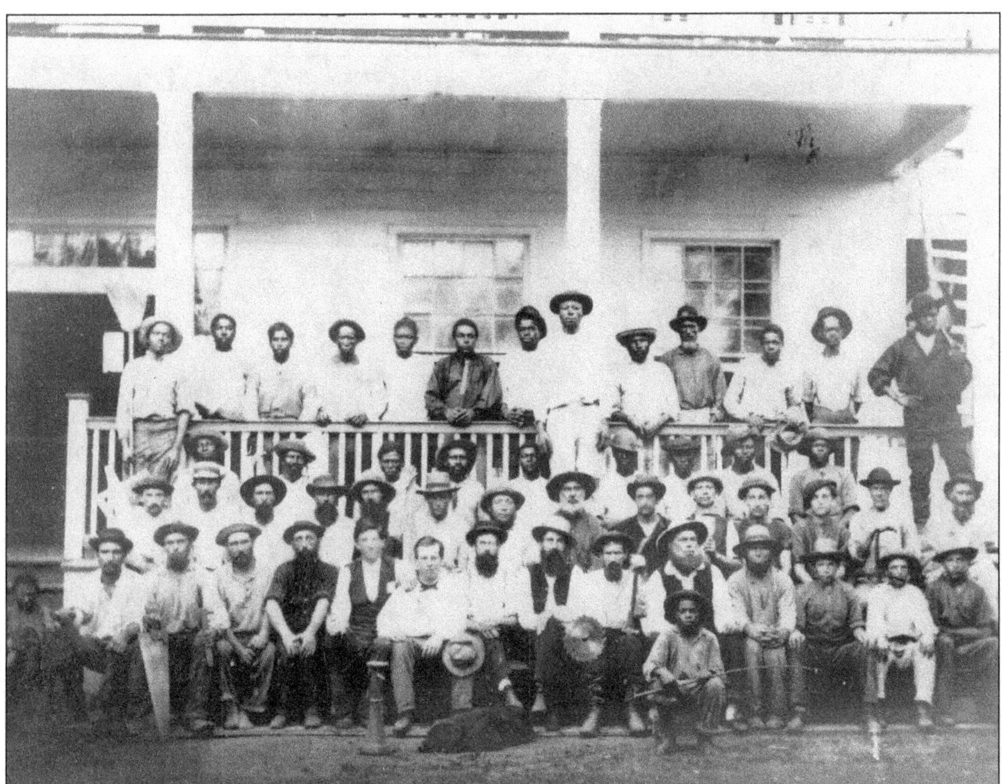

Largely unsettled before the Civil War, Lake Charles grew after the war because of the demand for lumber to rebuild the South. To recruit labor, sawmill owners lured blacks away from sharecropping by promising higher wages. This c. 1890 photograph of Daniel Goos's millworkers shows a racially integrated work force that likely includes Irish and German immigrants as well as local blacks. They are posed on the porch of the Goos family home in Goosport.

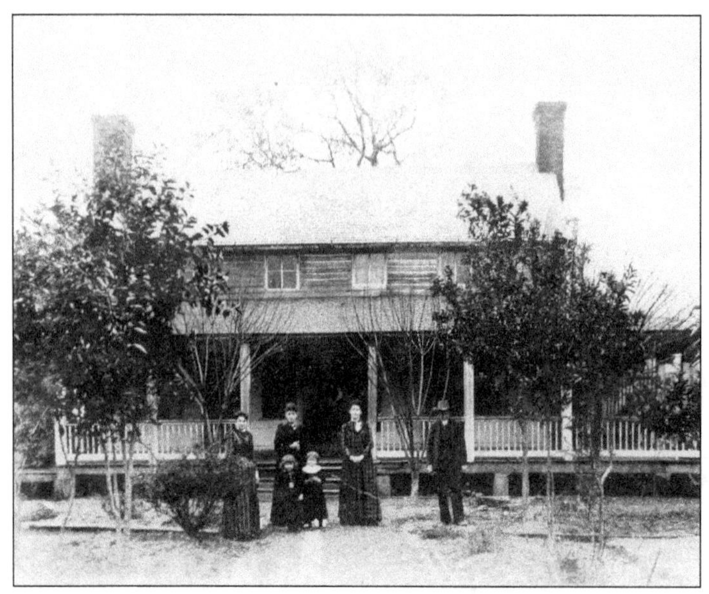

In this c. 1895 image, John Jacob Ryan Jr. (1816–1899), the "Father of Lake Charles," stands in front of his homestead on Broad Street near the lakefront with several of his children. His father, John Jacob Ryan Sr., was one of the first white settlers west of the Calcasieu River, having settled his family here in 1819. Getting into any area first was an advantage, and Ryan acquired large amounts of farmland cheaply and easily. He and A. Henry Moss owned much of what is now downtown Lake Charles.

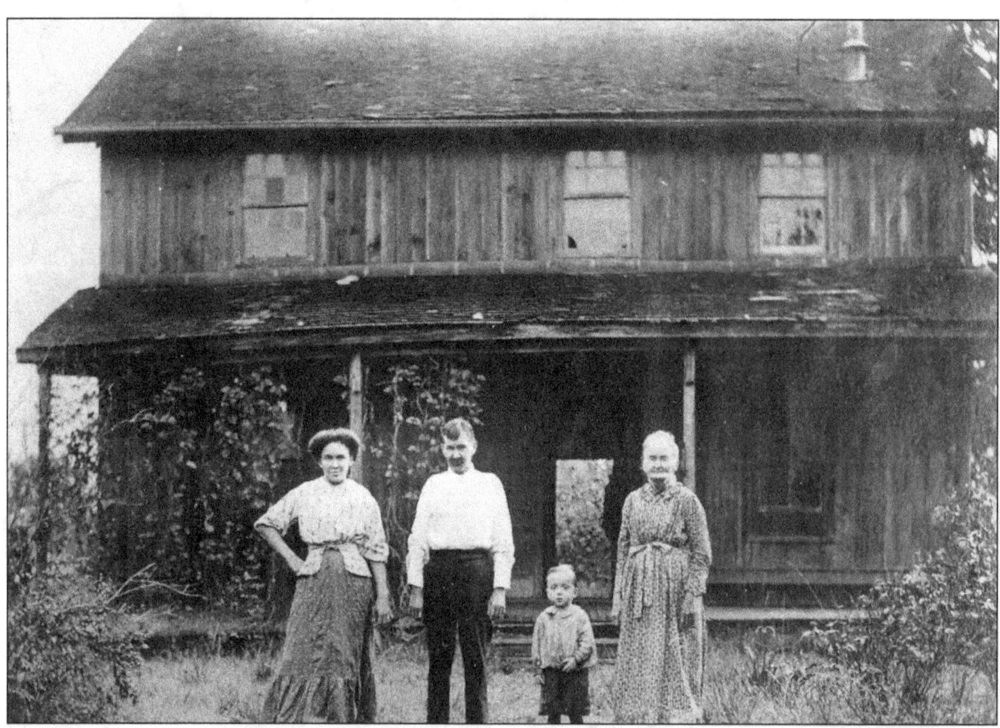

The descendants of Thomas Bilbo stand in front of the family home around 1930. The house began as a fort for the old Camp (Cantonment) Atkinson military outpost, which Bilbo purchased after it was abandoned. Bilbo married Ann Lawrence, and their daughter Rebecca Bilbo married Jacob Ryan Jr. Three downtown streets—Bilbo, Ann, and Lawrence—are named for them. The Bel Lumber Company purchased the home from the heirs, with the exception of the one acre on the lake where the family cemetery is located.

Located on the east end of the downtown Civic Center Lake Front and erected in 1999, this 15-foot-tall bronze statue is the work of Janie Stine LaCroix, a sculptor and direct descendant of John Jacob Ryan Jr., the "Father of Lake Charles" who is buried in the Bilbo Cemetery. The cemetery was acquired by Thomas Bilbo as part of the Bilbo House purchase in 1832. (Courtesy of Dennis Thibodeaux.)

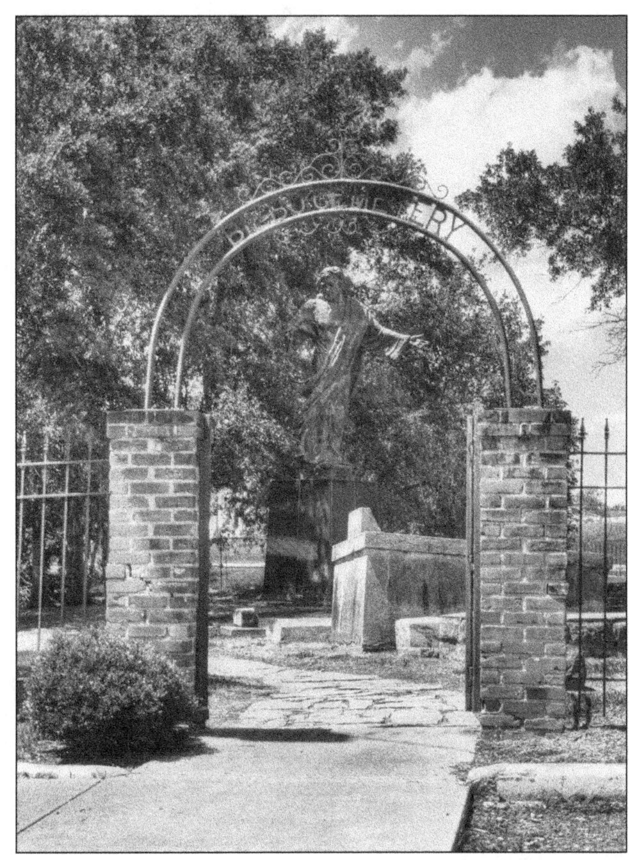

When Daniel Johannes Goos (pronounced "Goss"), an immigrant from Schlesweg-Holstein, and his wife Katherine Moeling (from Germany), arrived in "Charlestown" in 1855, they increased the number of white families from five to six. (The others were Sallier, Ryan, Hodges, Pithon, and Bilbo). They are pictured at their home in Goosport with some of their 15 children.

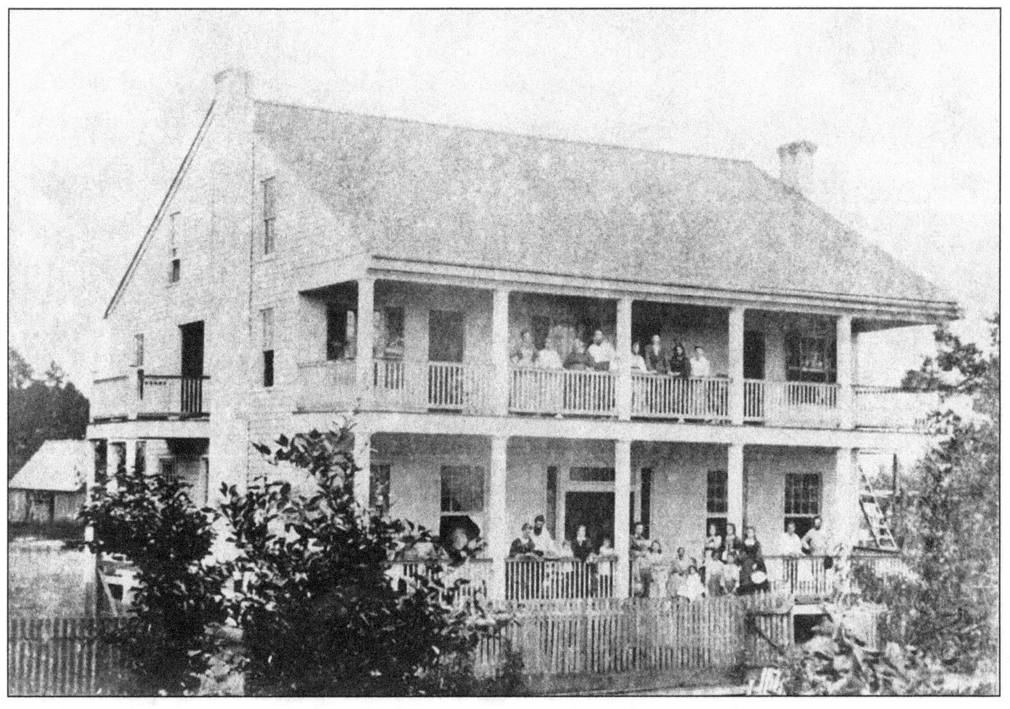

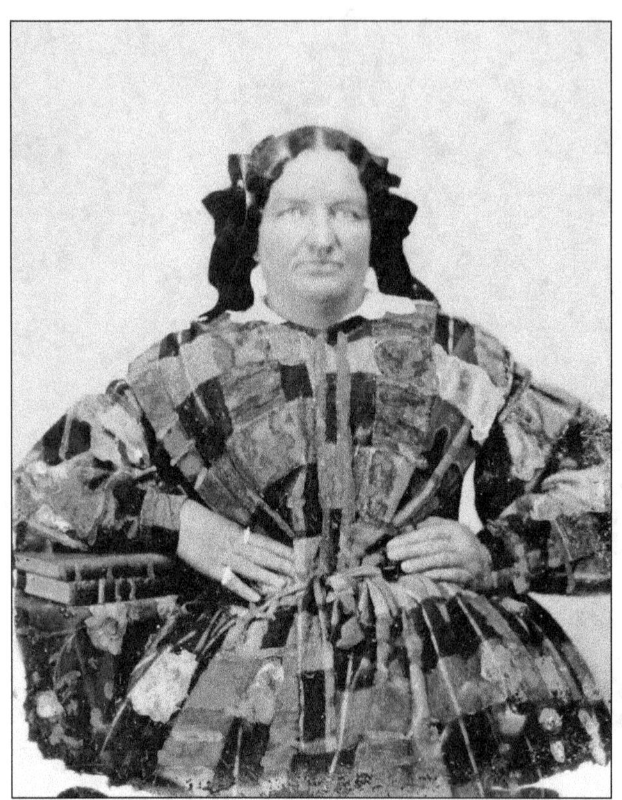

This is the only known picture of Katherine Moeling Goos (1827–1884), wife of Daniel. The Gooses can be considered the founding parents of Lake Charles. Their descendants number in the thousands, and include the Bel, Lock, Paret, Fitzenreiter, Jessen, Perkins, Moss, Krause, and Beatty families. (Courtesy of Billy and Kay Krause Blake.)

The Goos home, mill, and shipyard are visible across the river in this photograph. As Daniel Goos's lumber business boomed, he and his wife recruited relatives and others from Europe to immigrate to the area. They brought capital and skills to manage the mills and to build and operate the fleet of barges and boats necessary to transport the lumber. Others worked in the mills or the shipyards as laborers.

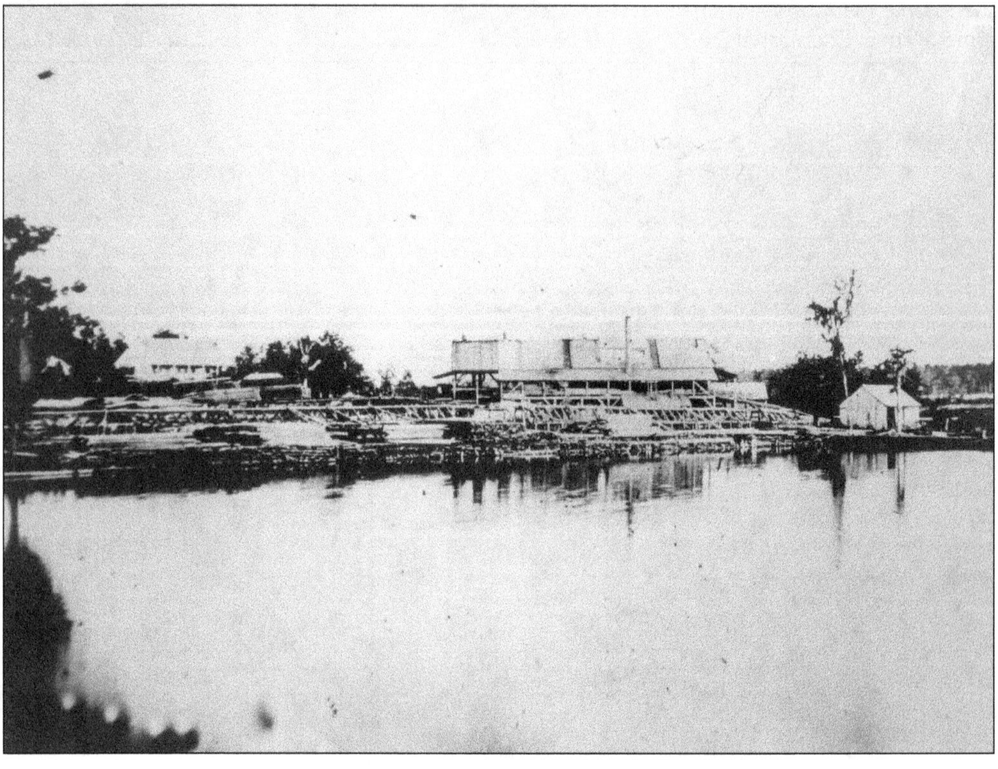

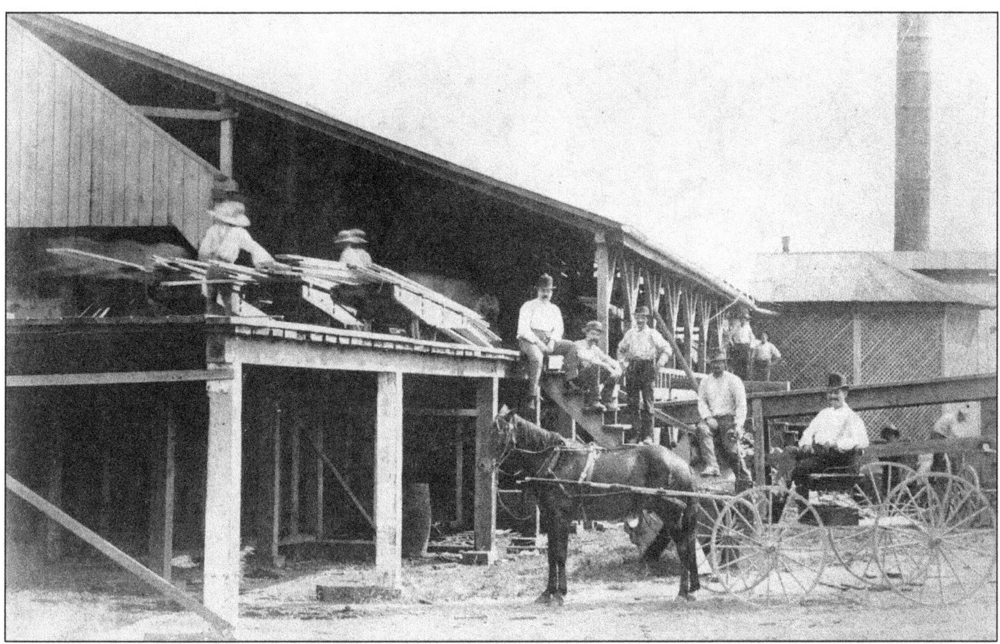

By 1900, at least 10 mills operated within a three-mile radius of the Lake Charles area. The quality of the longleaf timber was so highly rated that it was marketed as "Calcasieu Pine." Streets in old Lake Charles bear witness to the lumber heritage and the families that built it: Moeling, Fitzenreiter, Pine, Mill, Moss, Drew, and Kirby. The lumber companies built communities such as Dry Creek and Ragley to house the workers. Many of the lumber barons came to own tens of thousands of acres of surrounding timberland.

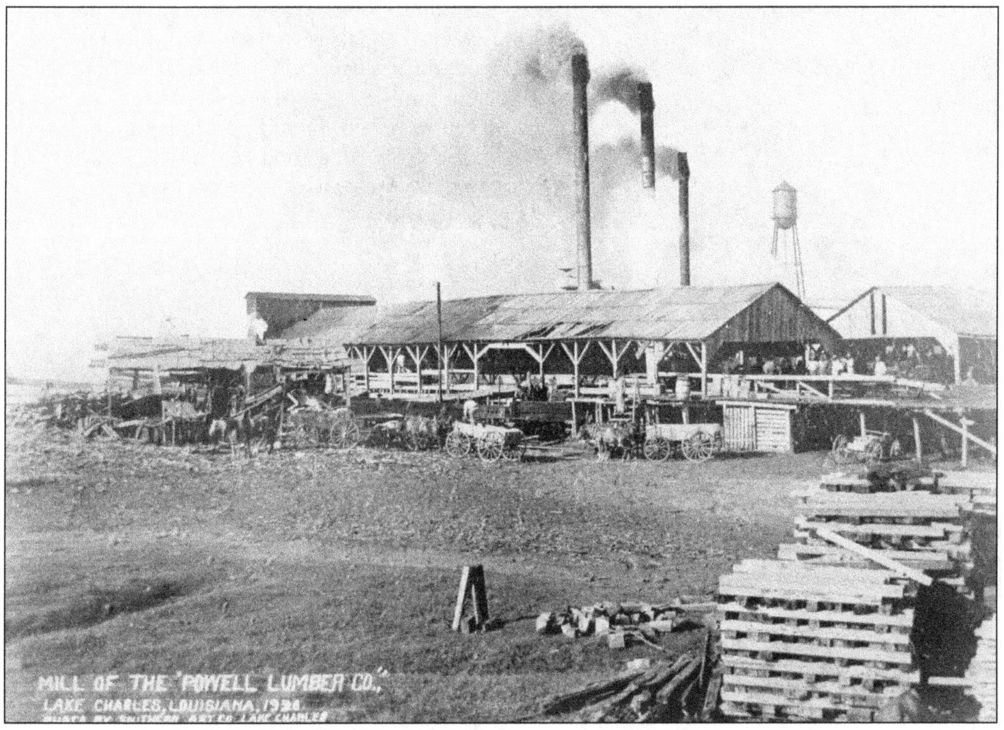

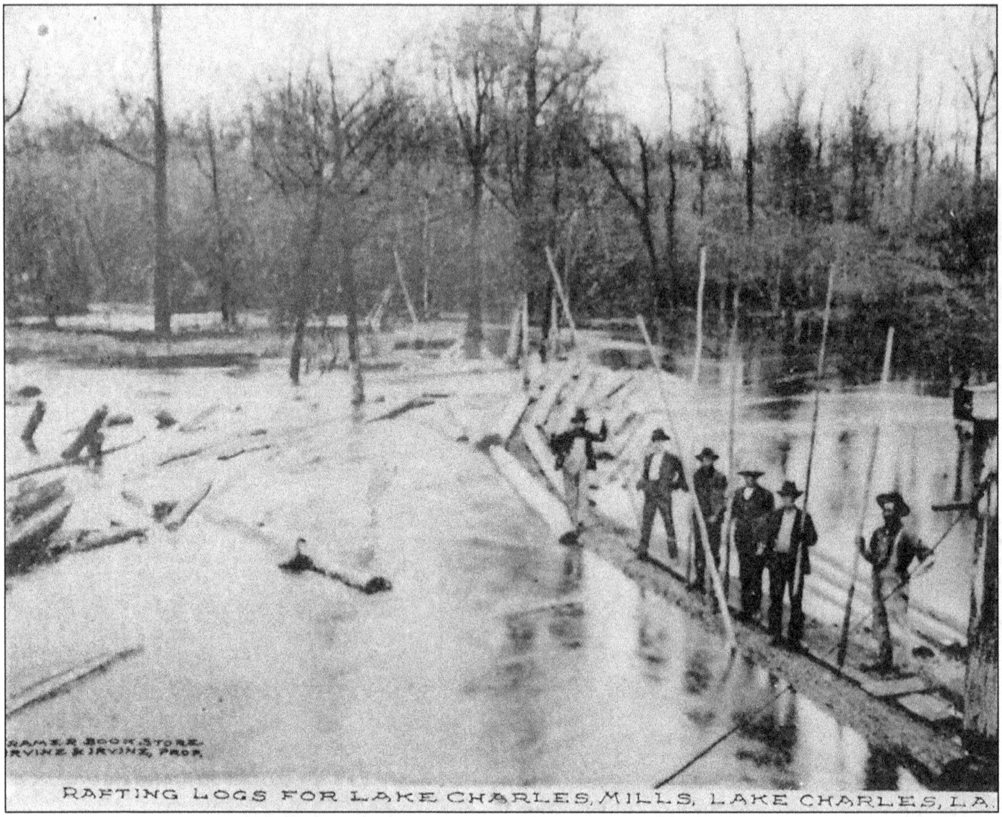

RAFTING LOGS FOR LAKE CHARLES MILLS, LAKE CHARLES, LA.

Before the railroads penetrated the area, logs were brought down the Calcasieu River and rafted in the lake up to the surrounding sawmills. Schooners took the cut lumber out to the Gulf of Mexico and west to Galveston. In addition to being sold throughout the South, a good deal of it went to Mexico to build the railroad network there.

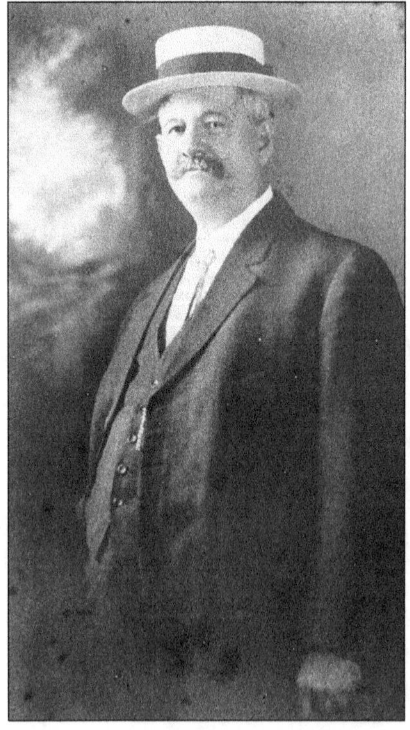

J.A. Bel (1857–1918), born in New Orleans, was the son of John Bel, a native of France, and Della Delphine McLean. He came to Calcasieu Parish at the age of 15 and took a job in George Lock's sawmill on Prien Lake. He soon married one of Daniel Goos's daughters (Della Moeling Goos) and went into the lumber business himself. He acquired thousands of acres of timberland, built sawmills, cofounded the Calcasieu National Bank, and built deepwater tugs to transport the lumber. (Courtesy of Billy and Kay Krause Blake.)

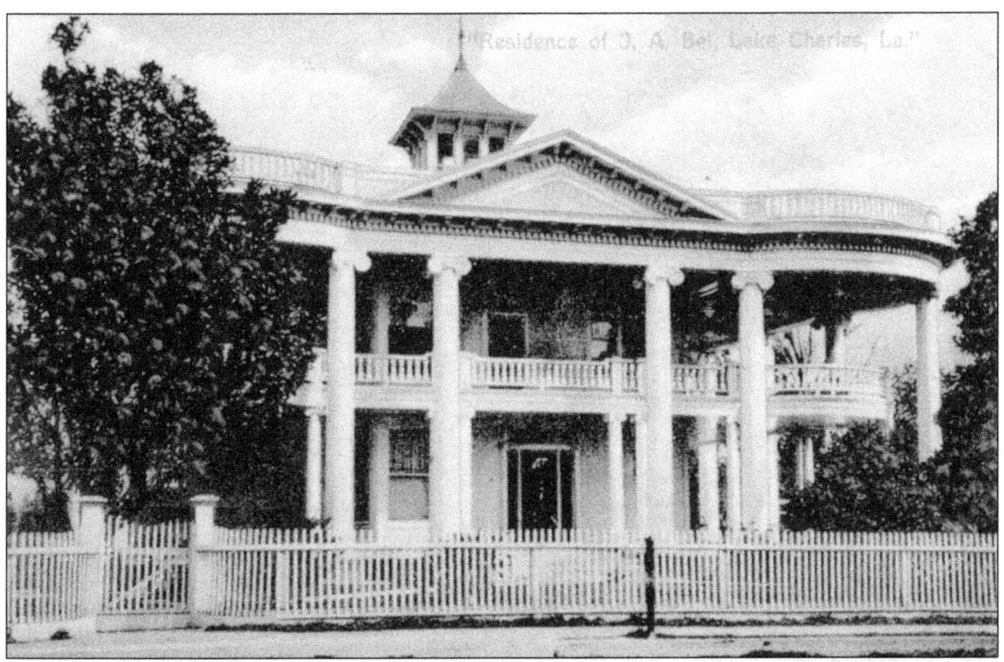

The home of J.A. Bel, like many of the old Lake Charles homes, was built with lumber from his mill. This house, located on the corner of Mill and Moss Streets, was later donated to Boys Village. It was dismantled and, minus its surrounding porches, reconstructed on the site of Boys Village (see chapter five).

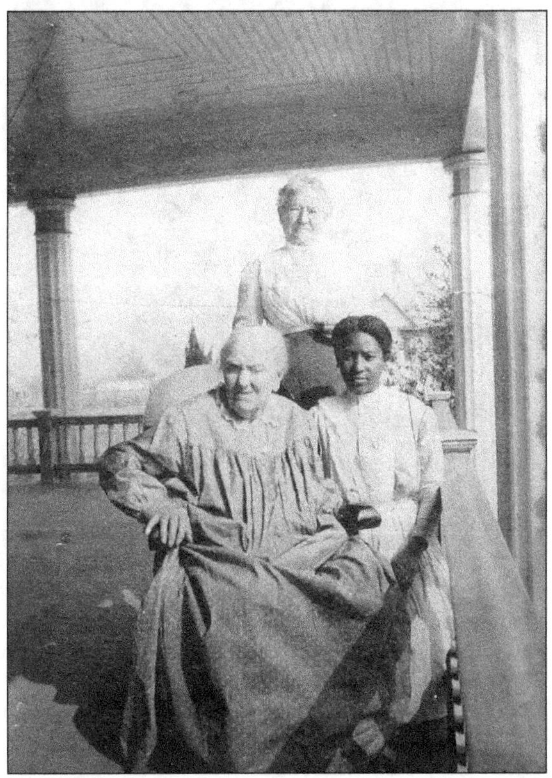

Barbara Katherine Moeling (seated left) was the sister of Katherine Moeling Goos. She was one of many members of the Moeling and Goos families who joined Daniel and Katherine Goos in making Lake Charles their home. Born in Bavaria in the 1820s, in her old age she was looked after by her nieces, Della Moeling Goos Bel and Ellen Goos Lock (1849–1921), standing behind her. The unidentified servant girl was likely Barbara Moeling's caregiver. (Courtesy of Billy and Kay Krause Blake.)

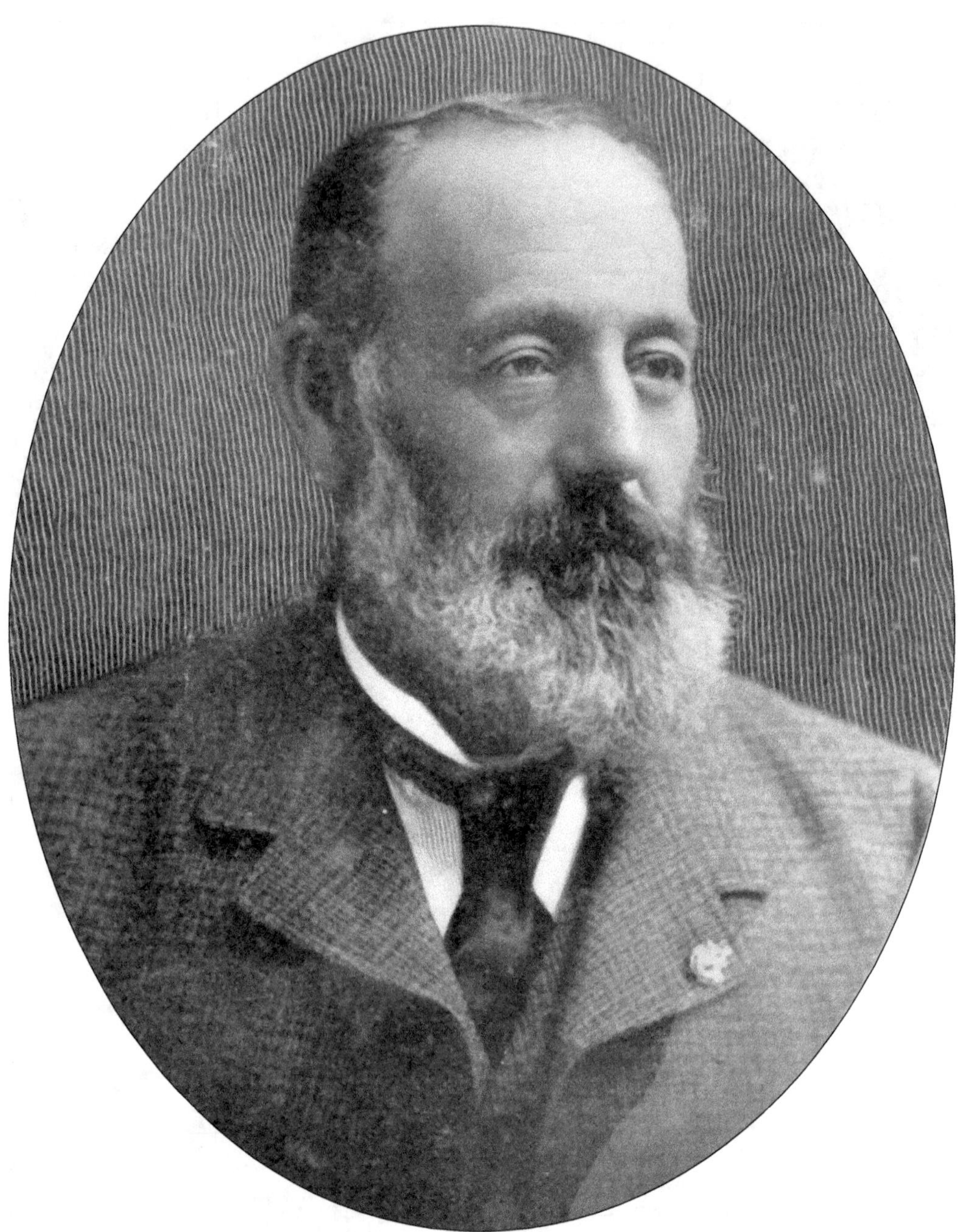

Capt. George T. Lock (1839–1917), a native of England, was a mariner who arrived in Lake Charles in 1868. He built a steam-powered sawmill on Prien Lake and eventually owned a large portion of the east bank of Prien Lake (the present-day Lock Lane area). When that mill burned, he and a partner built another at Lockport, where PPG is today. Lock was a cofounder of First National Bank and Episcopal Church of the Good Shepherd, a Mason, an Elk, and a Grand Snark of the Order of Hoo Hoo (see chapter four). When he died, his widow, Ellen Goos Lock, donated a full block of land at the corner of Ryan Street and Miller Avenue (now Seventh Street) to the city for the creation of Lock Park. Their daughter, Letitia, married Milnor Paret. The entire family is pictured on the next page.

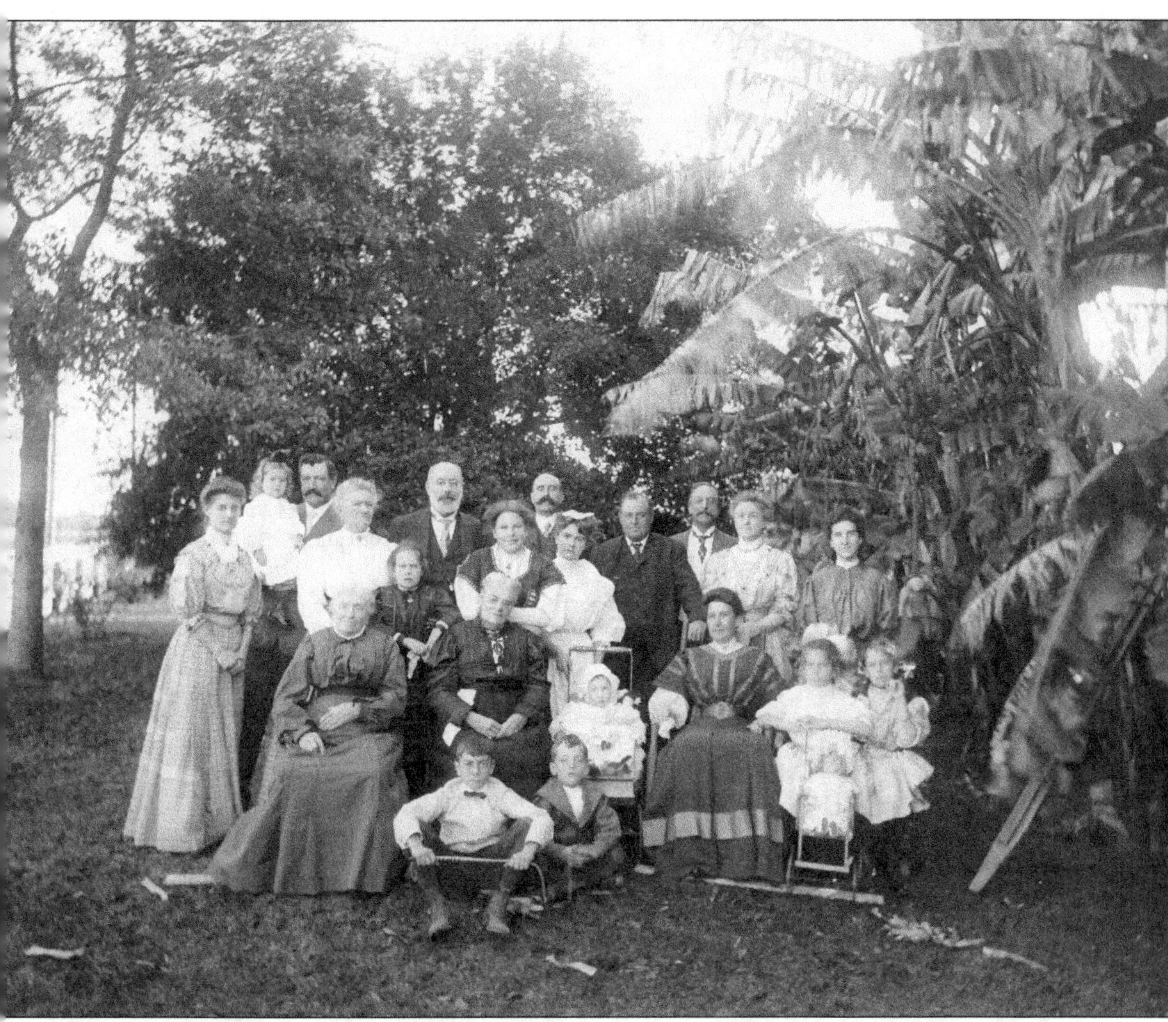

The family of Captain Lock was photographed on the lawn of their home on the northwest corner of Broad and Reid Streets; Broad Street is visible in the background. Pictured from left to right are (on the ground) Milnor Peck Paret Jr. and George Lock Paret Sr.; (seated) unknown, Elizabeth Ann Chorley Edwards Lock Knight, Helen Martha Paret Van Dunk (baby in carriage), Mamie Louise Miller Lock, Irene Moeling Paret Richardson, and unknown; (standing) Delia Joyce Moss Lock, Delia Joyce Lock Preston (baby), George Thomas Lock Sr., Elmina Martha "Ellen" Goos Lock, Selma Miller Lock (child), Captain George Lock (white haired man), Cora Law, George W. Law, Irma Letitia Lock Tieman, Fred Goos Lock, Milnor Peck Paret Sr., and unknown. (Courtesy of Francis Paret Walker.)

In the 1880s and 1890s, northerners flooded into the area, particularly from Kansas, Nebraska, and Iowa. J.B. Watkins, a railroad and land developer from Kansas, hired Seaman A. Knapp (pictured), the president of Iowa Agricultural College, to help develop a commercial crop for the area as a way of enticing settlers to buy Watkins's land. Knapp, the "father of the rice industry," is responsible for establishing the USDA's Agricultural Extension System and children's clubs that were the forerunners of the Four-H clubs.

This home on the corner of Broad and Ford Streets was built by R.H. Nason, one of the "Michigan men" who moved to Lake Charles in the 1880s after the timber resources of their home state were exhausted. They brought valuable capital and experience with them and helped to make Lake Charles a booming lumber town. This house, like many in the historic Charpentier District, was built in a northern architectural style reminiscent of the homes the men had left in Michigan. Nason bought the old Goos mill property and established a sawmill that was later sold to Bradley-Ramsey.

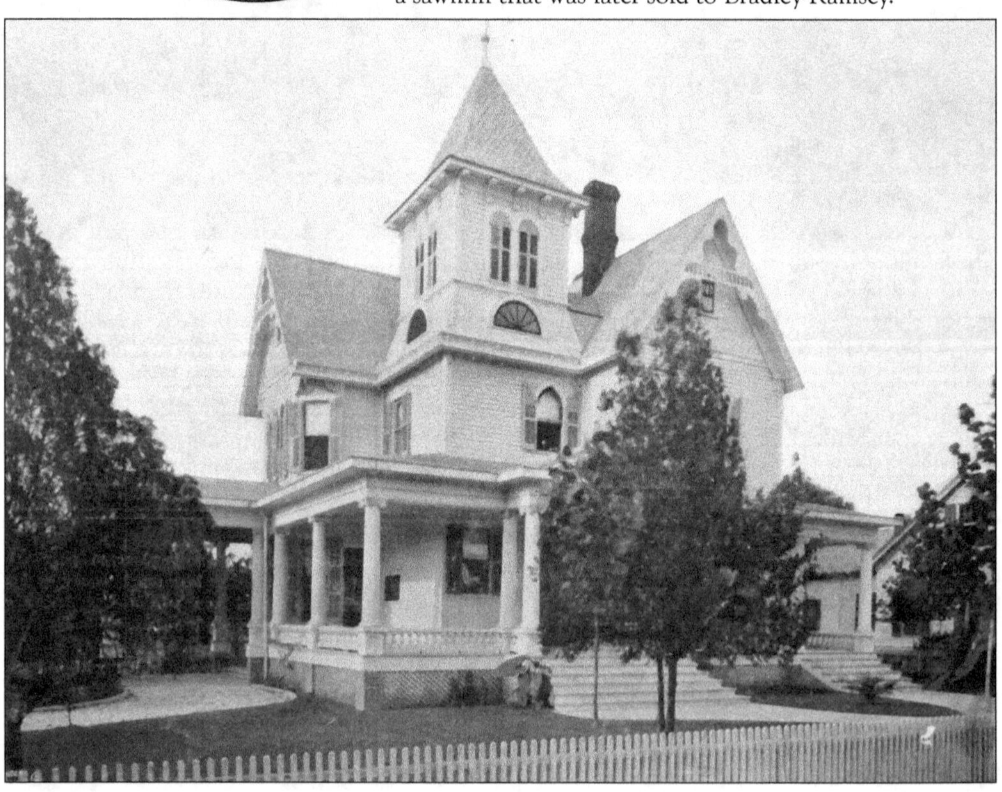

Thad Mayo was a schoolteacher born in New England but reared in Plaquemine Parish. He moved to Calcasieu Parish in 1875. After teaching for a bit, he went to work at the clerk of court and made a set of abstract books for Calcasieu Parish. With his nephew Augustus M. Mayo (who married Minnie Knapp, daughter of Seaman A. Knapp), he founded the oldest abstract company in Calcasieu Parish. Because they were wise enough to keep their abstract records in a fireproof vault, theirs were the only land records to survive the Great Fire of 1910.

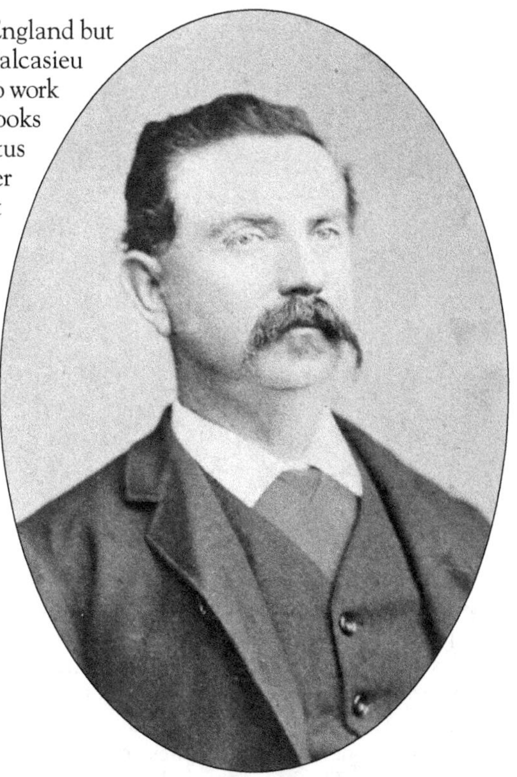

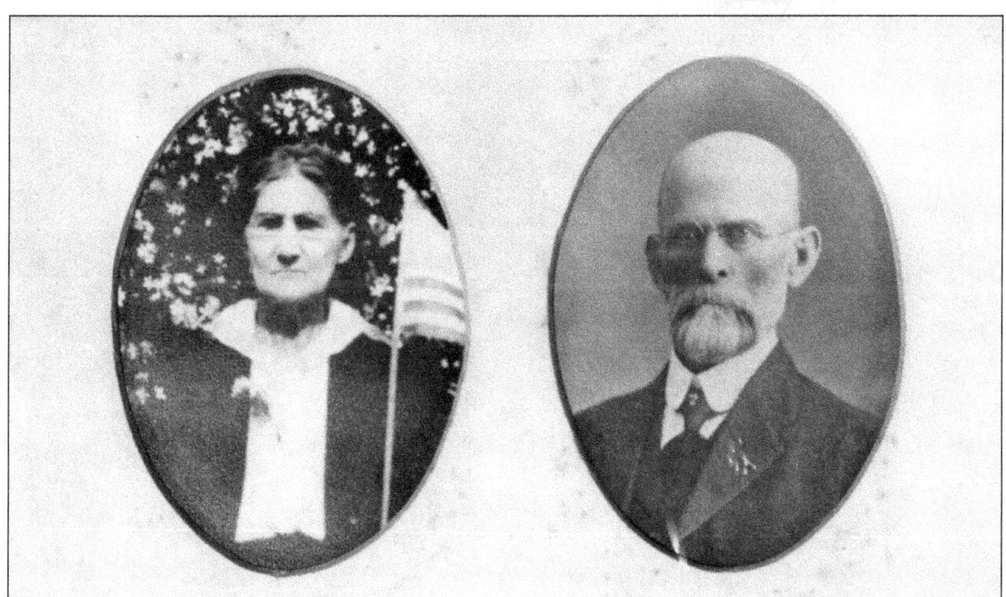

John McNeese (1842–1913), pictured here with his wife, Susan Bilbo McNeese, was also a northerner. Born in New York to Scottish immigrant parents, he served in the Union Army and moved to Texas after the war for health reasons. He had a varied business career and a law degree, but he is best known for working to improve the quality of the schools in the area. Known as "the father of education" in Calcasieu Parish, he served as the first superintendent of schools from 1888 until his death in 1913.

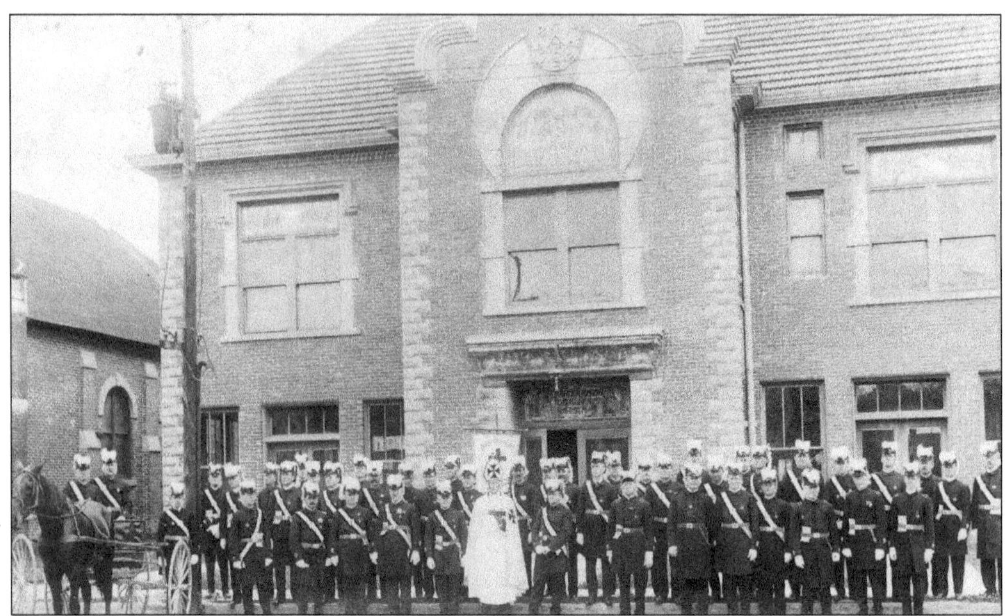

This photograph of the Freemasons in front of their lodge shows the second of three Masonic temples built on this Hodges Street site. The buildings were used as schools, theaters, and venues for town meetings. Lodge No. 165 was founded in 1859 and included most of the city's early developers: Goos, Reid, Ryan, Moeling, Mayo, Pujo, Bel, Lock, Powell, Bilbo, Krause, Kaufman, and Knapp. This building was destroyed in a 1918 hurricane and was replaced by the current stone structure. The Masonic Hall served as a meeting place for all Protestant congregations until they could build their own churches.

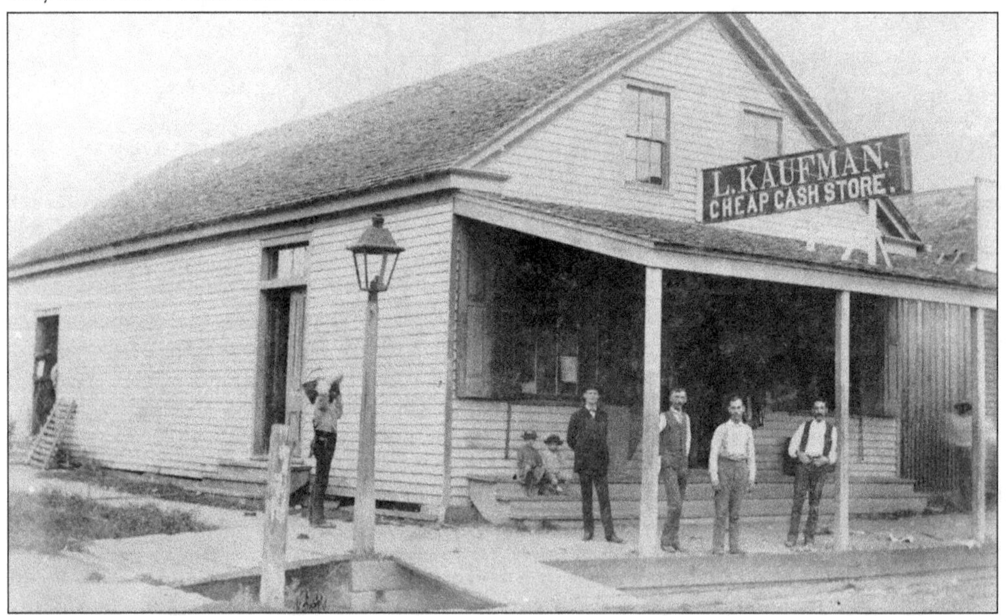

Opened in 1879, Leopold Kaufman's store was located on the corner of Ryan and Broad Streets. Kaufman later started the First National Bank inside the store to aid customers' ability to buy, sell, and trade. The men in the front of the store are, from left to right, George Wells, Will Gayle, John Blanchard, and Leopold Kaufman.

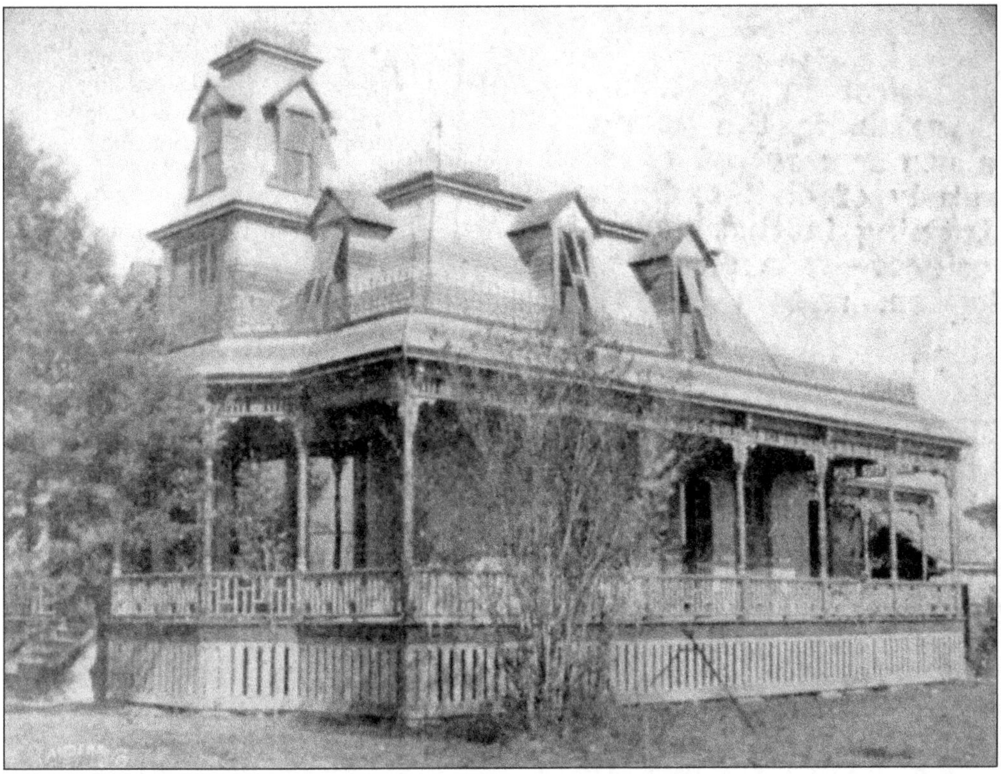

Leopold Kaufman's home on Bilbo Street was built in 1889. Kaufman was one of many Jews who migrated to the area from Alsace-Lorraine, a region of France caught in a tug-of-war with Germany. Fleeing the constant tumult, they found a comfortable niche in southwest Louisiana because they spoke both French and German and could easily do business with the many German-speaking immigrants, such as the Goos family. A successful merchant, Kaufman was an active leader in the civic and cultural affairs of community life and worked especially hard to improve the public school system.

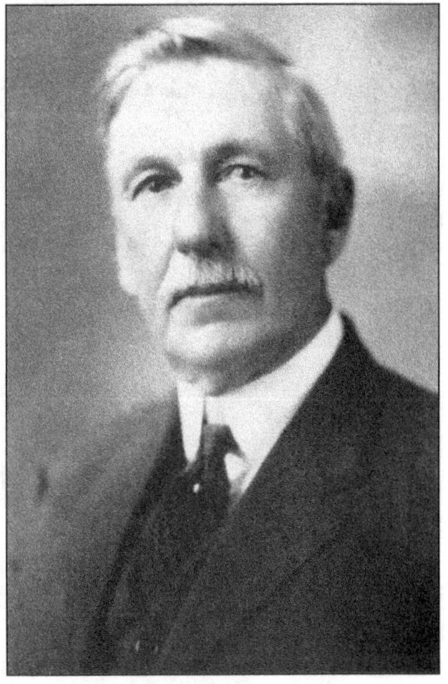

Arsene Paulin Pujo (1861–1939) represented the Seventh Congressional District of Louisiana in the US House of Representatives from 1903 to 1913, supporting many progressive measures. Nationally, he is most famous for investigating the "money trust" and helping to produce recommendations that resulted in the passage of the Federal Reserve Act. While in Congress, he secured appropriations that led to permanent improvement to local waterways. His father was from France; his mother, Eloise LeBleu, was a native of the area. Pujo Street is named for him.

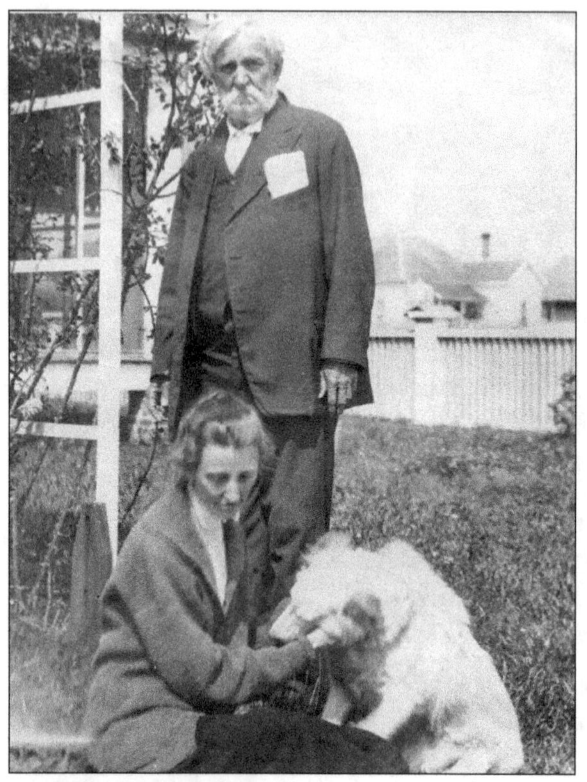

Oilman/rancher John Geddings "Ged" Gray (d. 1921) is pictured with his daughter, Matilda Geddings Gray, on their property in west Calcasieu Parish around 1920. Starting out as a rancher, Ged Gray acquired 30,000 acres from Vinton to the coast. Like many of the first settlers who got in on the ground floor when land was cheap, he ended up with a bonanza when oil was discovered on the land. The Ged Oilfield has been producing since 1912. (Courtesy of Matilda Gray Stream.)

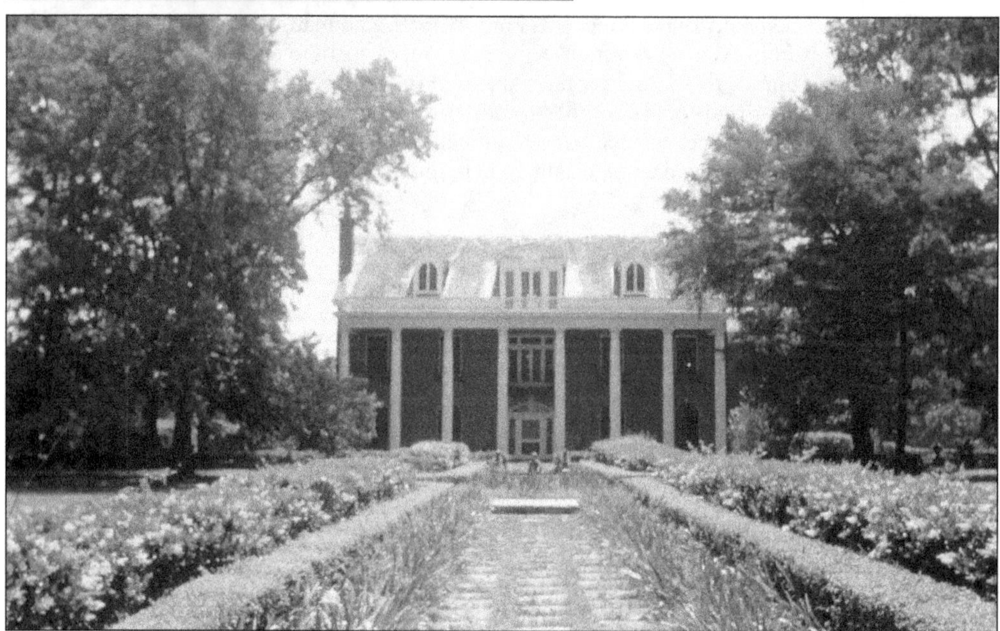

Matilda Geddings Gray (d. 1971) ran the business after her father's retirement and became a trailblazing businesswoman in a "man's world." A major philanthropist and preservationist, she restored a home in New Orleans and the Evergreen Plantation in St. John Parish. The home she built in 1923 at 2417 Shell Beach Drive (pictured) was designed by the famed New Orleans architectural firm Favrot and Livaudais; it now houses the offices of the Stream Companies.

Two

Rise of a City

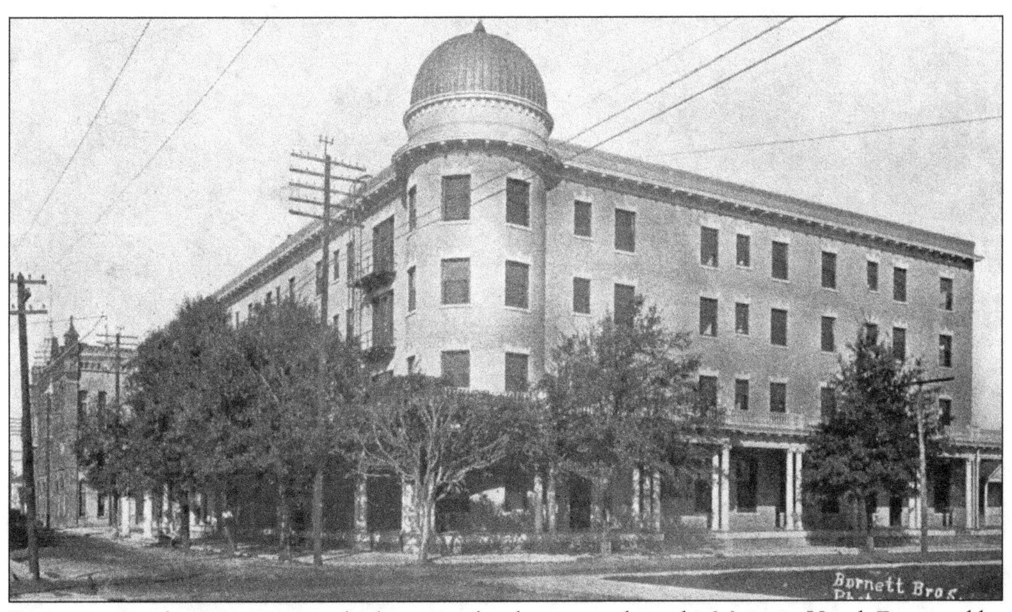

Few structures better represent the booming lumber town than the Majestic Hotel. Financed by wealthy businessmen to help attract convention business, the hotel opened in 1906 on the corner of Pujo and Bilbo Streets. Built entirely of wood, it was spared from the Great Fire of 1910 because it had its own water plant. This symbol of Lake Charles's heyday was demolished in 1965.

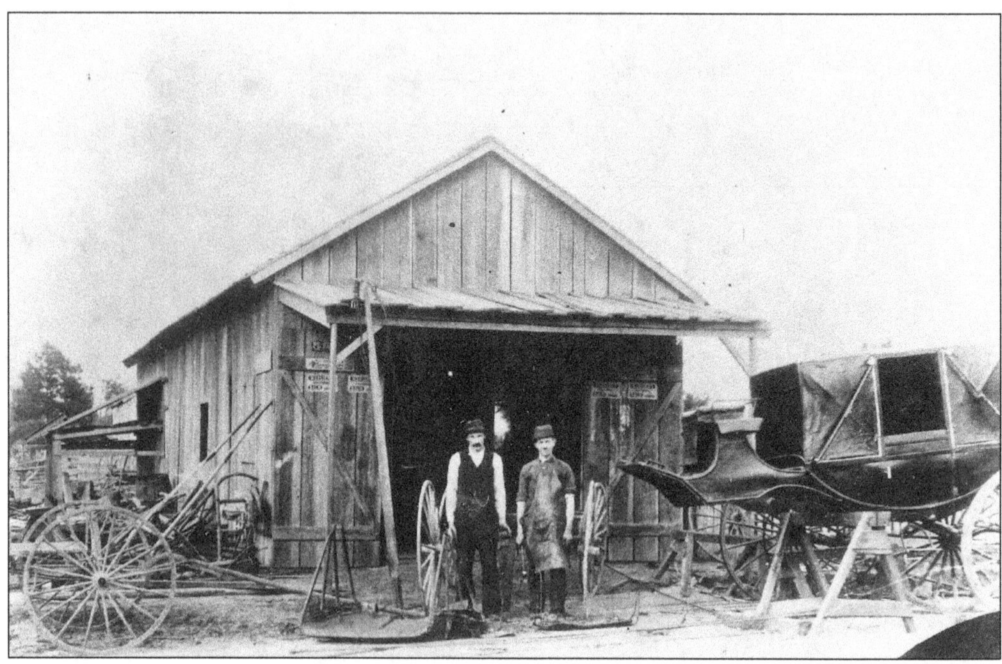

Before electric trolleys provided public transportation, most people walked everywhere unless they could afford to hire a cab like the one being worked on in this blacksmith shop located on Division Street, near Ryan Street, in the 1890s.

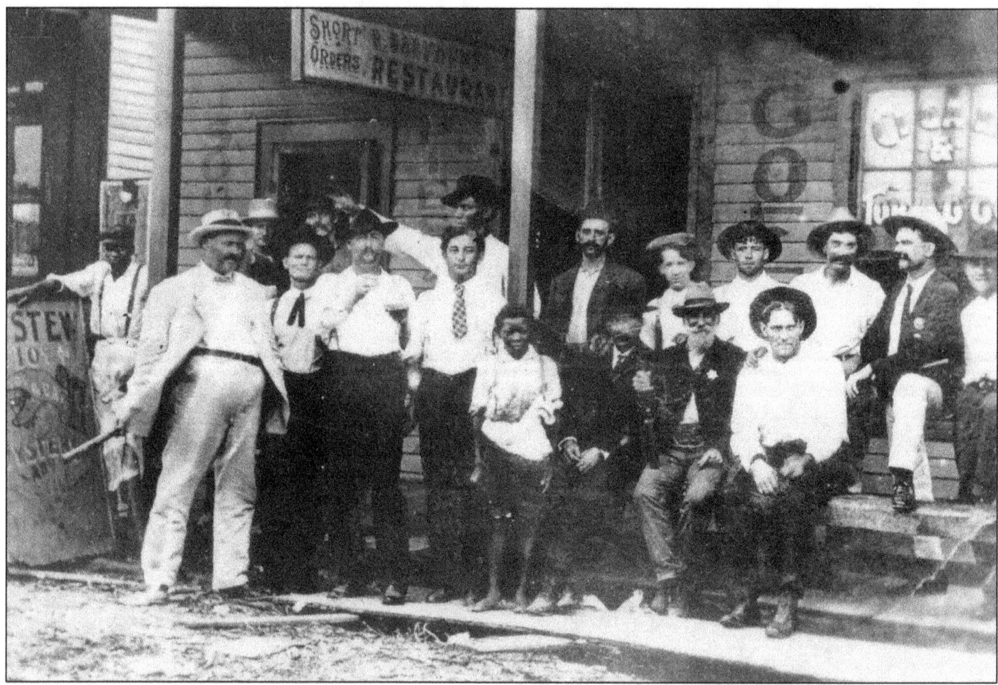

This photograph was taken in front of Richard Sarvaunt's restaurant and bar on Railroad Avenue, between Reid and Kirkman Streets, also called "Battle Row" because of the frequent brawls that spilled out of the saloons lining the streets. The child in the center is an errand boy; one of the men is employed to encourage the workers to enter the saloon. Gambling was common in these places.

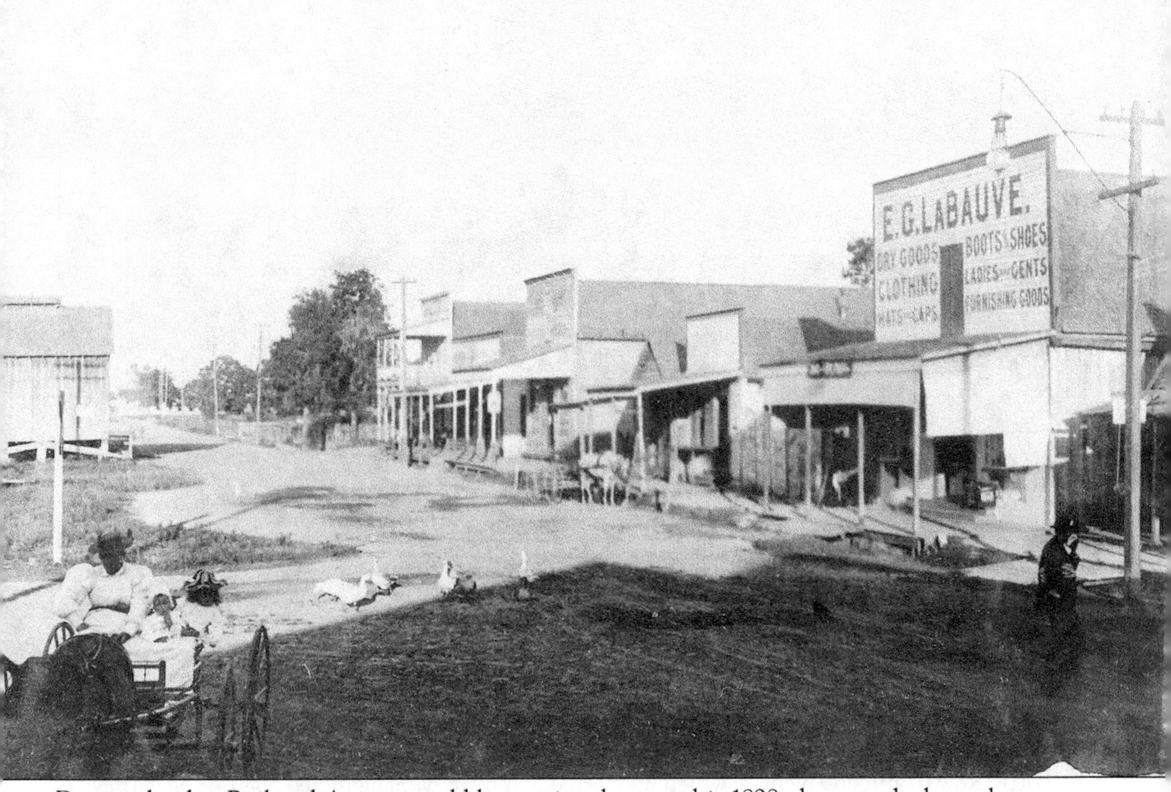

During the day, Railroad Avenue could be a quiet place, as this 1898 photograph shows, but at night, it was a different scene. With a large number of sawmill hands and railroad workers coming into town for weekend entertainment, brothels and saloons proliferated. Lake Charles joined several other cities in Louisiana in creating a "red light district" to confine houses of prostitution to one area of town so that prostitutes would not ply their trade throughout the city. In Lake Charles, the district existed near the intersection of Railroad Avenue and Boulevard Street (later Enterprise Boulevard) until it was ended by city ordinance in 1918.

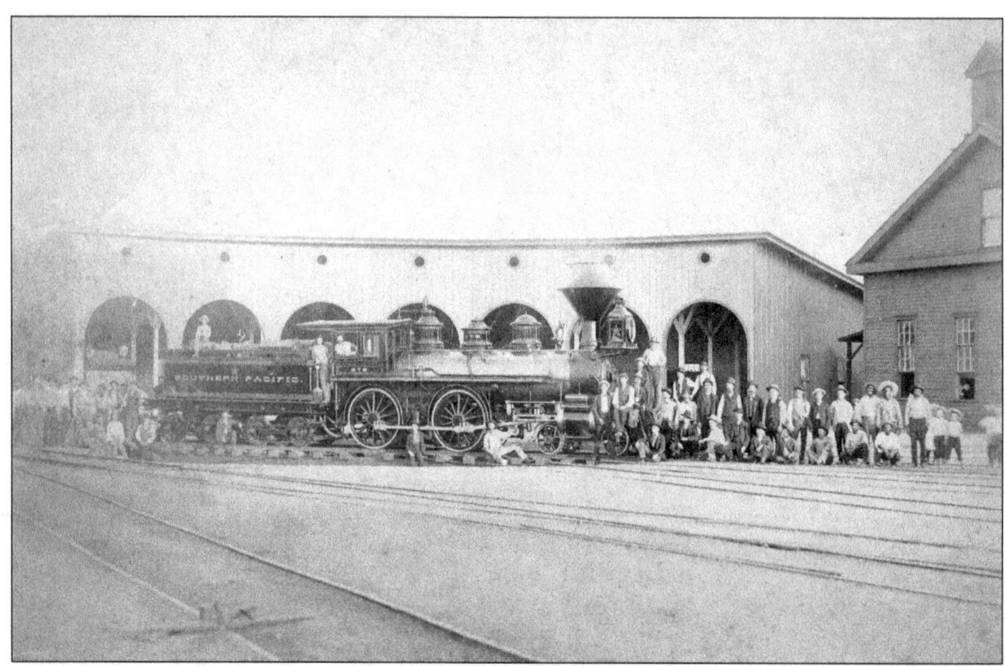

The first train rolled into Lake Charles in 1880, and five railroads serviced the city by 1906, with an annual payroll of $500,000. In the photograph above, the Southern Pacific Railroad proudly shows off its new engine. The Southern Pacific connected Lake Charles to a vast network of lines that extended all over the country. Though paid much less than whites, blacks could find jobs with the railroads and are clearly part of this workforce. Below is the Southern Pacific Depot on Battle Row (Railroad Avenue), which was torn down in 1899. Slaughtered pigs on the cart await delivery. Rigmaiden's Bakery and Saloon was next door.

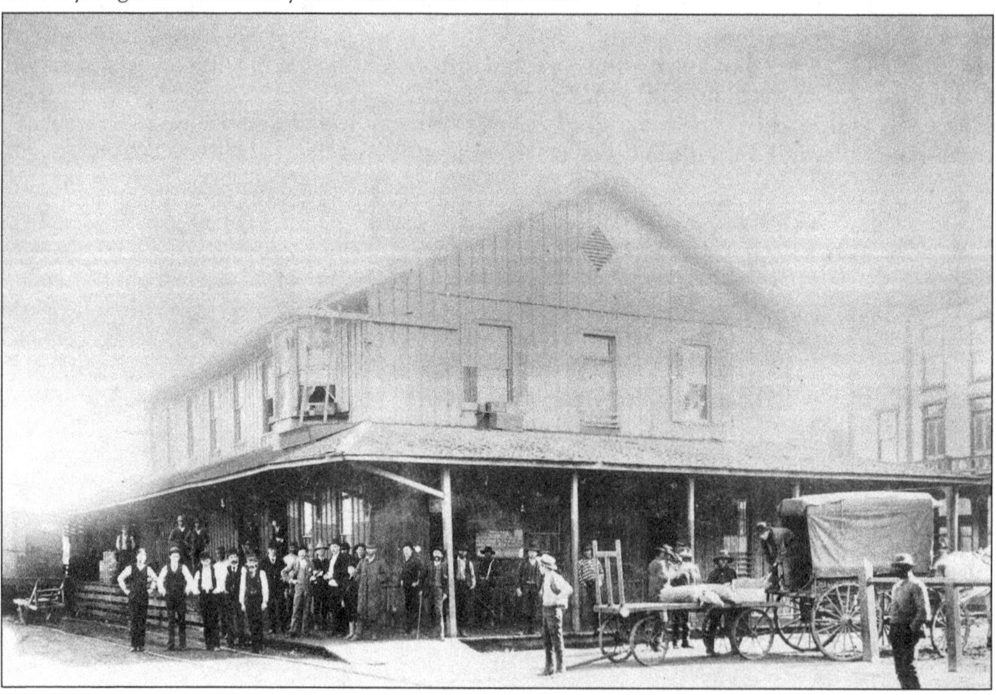

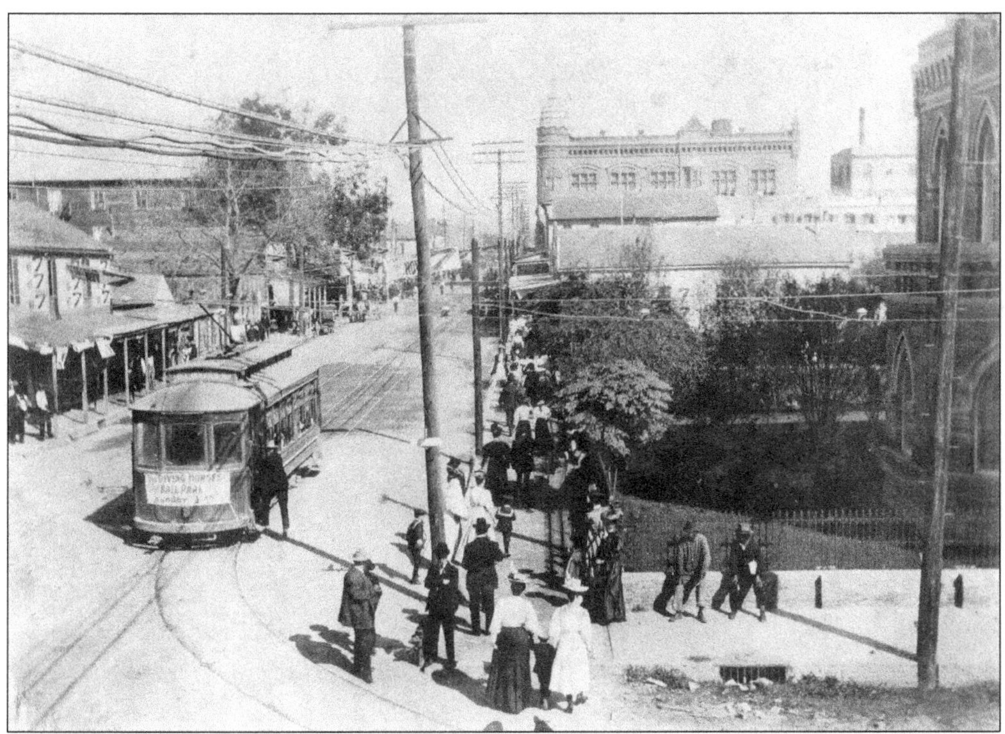

The Lake Charles Street Railway, built in 1906, ran a series of electric trolley tracks on Ryan Street, Shell Beach Drive, Hodges Street, and Kirkman Street that provided public transportation in downtown Lake Charles until 1926. The photograph above, taken in 1907, looks north on Ryan Street from the intersection at Kirby Street. The Catholic church's property is to the right, enclosed by an iron fence. On Saturday night, which was payday for the loggers and mill hands, the town was crowded with male workers, and the trolley company doubled its trolley runs from the Southern Pacific Depot to the red light district. The trolley barn is shown below. (Both courtesy of Jeanne Owens of Vintage Arts; photographs by David H. Levingston.)

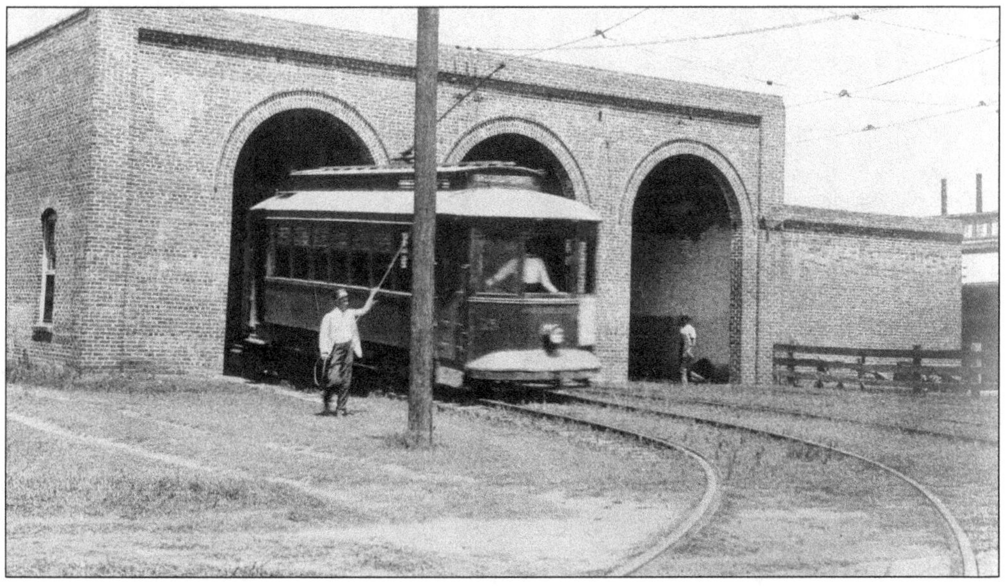

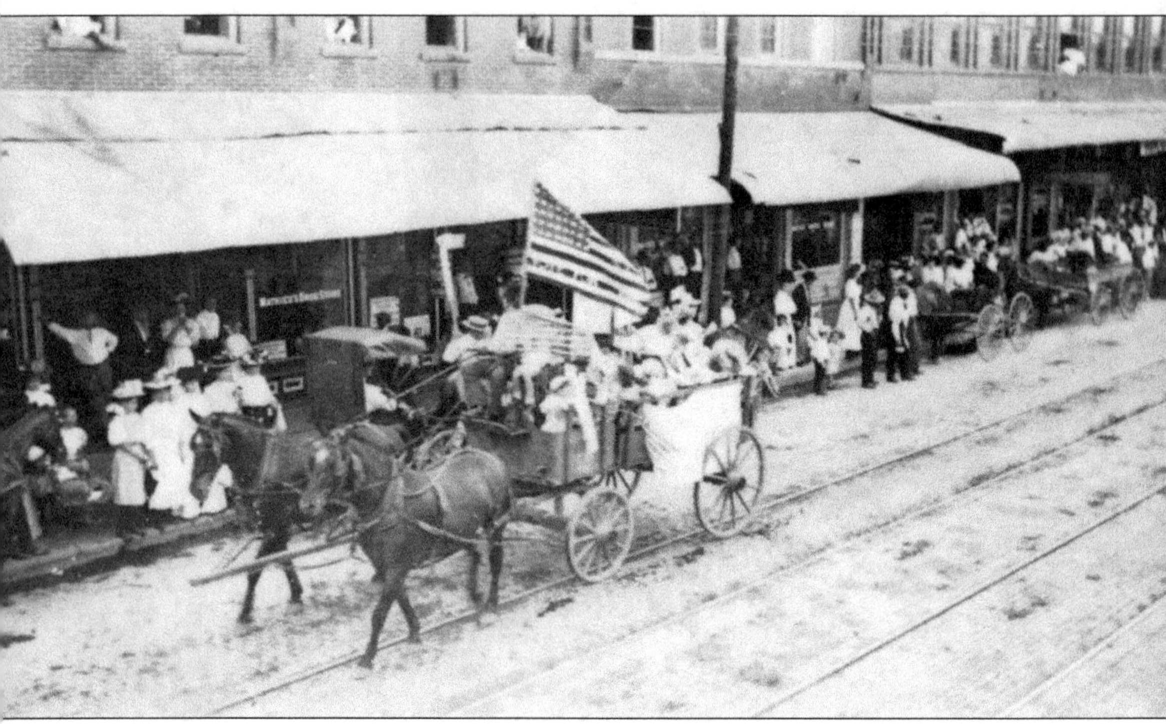

Temperance leagues were popular among evangelical Protestant groups, whose efforts to end sin in the city met with little success. Anti-gambling laws and blue laws were passed but openly flaunted. A parish-wide prohibition went into effect in 1908, but it, too, was largely ineffective. In this photograph, a prohibition parade travels down Ryan Street.

Borealis Rex delivered mail, passengers, and freight between Lake Charles and Cameron. On holidays, it served as a pleasure craft. It docked at the foot of Pujo Street, in the present-day location of the Civic Center. It was retired from service in 1931, put out to pasture by the opening of Highway 27 the same year.

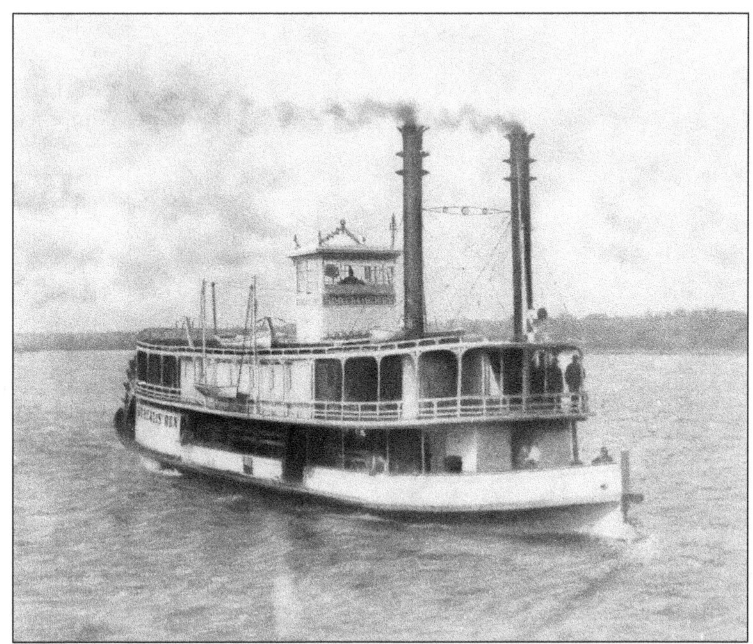

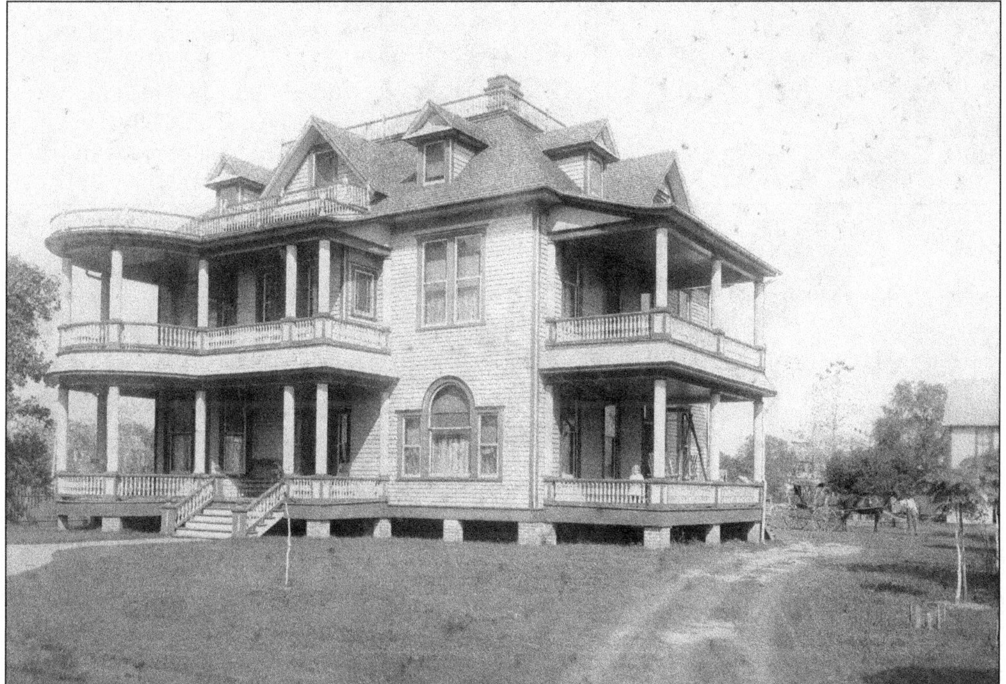

Charvey Barbe built this magnificent home on Shell Beach Drive, which is no longer standing. A native of France, Barbe married Clara Pujo, who also spoke French, and acquired property on the lake when Pujo's aunt, Dalilah LeBleu Sallier, died in 1866. Many of their 10 children invested in Texas land and became wealthy from oil. One daughter, Claudia Marie Barbe, continued to live in her aunt's home on the lake. While undertaking renovations to the old structure, she allegedly discovered the original Sallier cabin within the walls. That home (not pictured) is still owned and occupied by the Barbe family today.

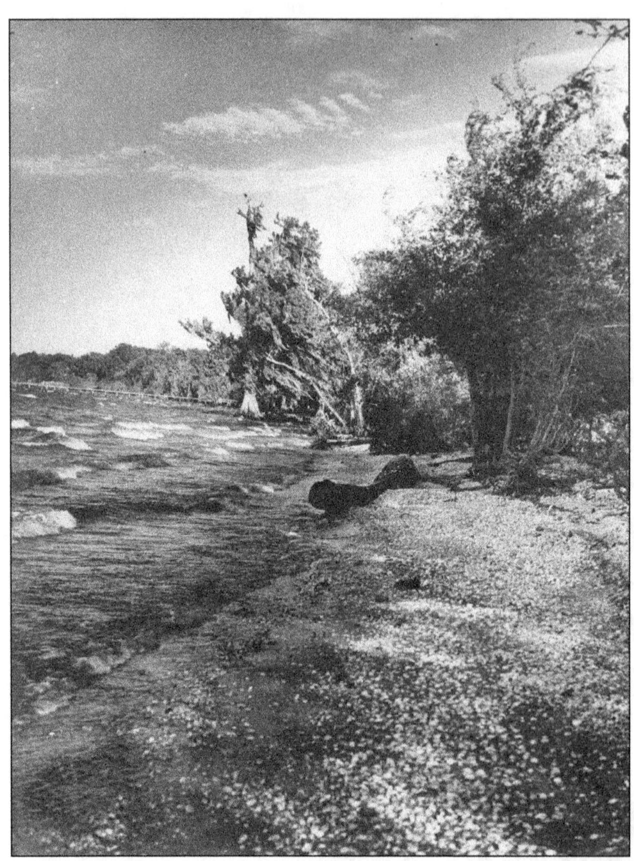

This photograph of Shell Beach Drive shows the ruggedness of the lakefront before improvements were made. The Barbe family built a pleasure pier and pavilion out into the lake, upon which their children played. Barbe Elementary School is on property that the Charvey Barbe heirs sold to the school board. Another descendant, Judge Alfred M. Barbe, as a trustee of the Drew Estate, gave a great deal of money for public education. Barbe High School is named for him.

In this c. 1900 photograph, L. Kreamer, jeweler, sits on one of the three large Indian mounds for which Shell Beach Drive is named. The mounds were created by the Attakapas Indians, who dug clams from the lake and discarded the shells here. The shells were later used to pave roads and driveways around the parish.

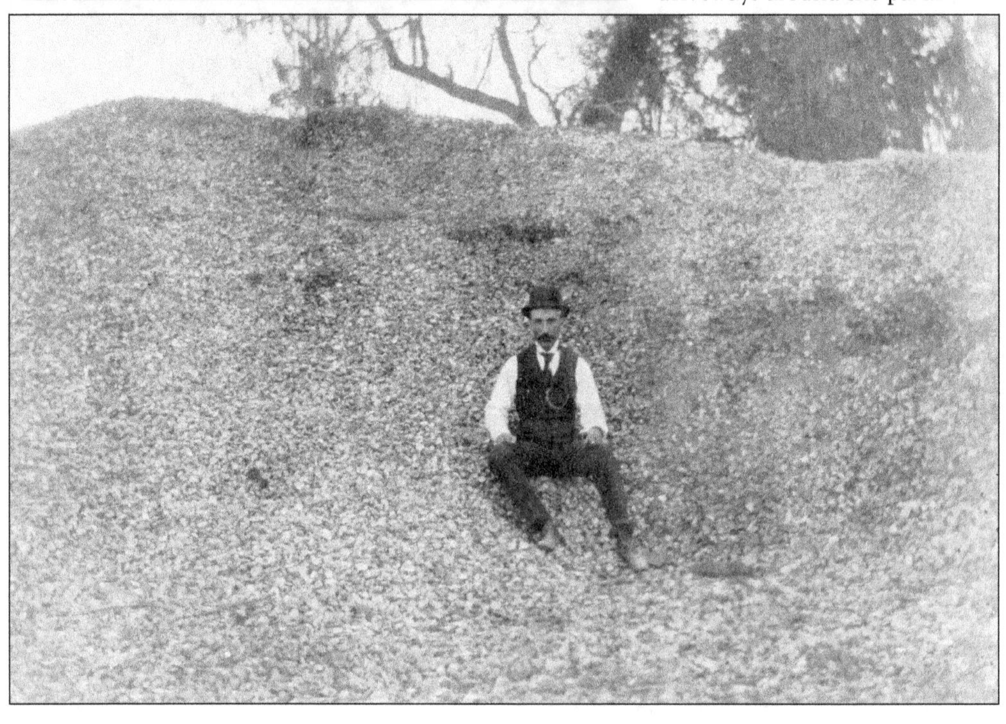

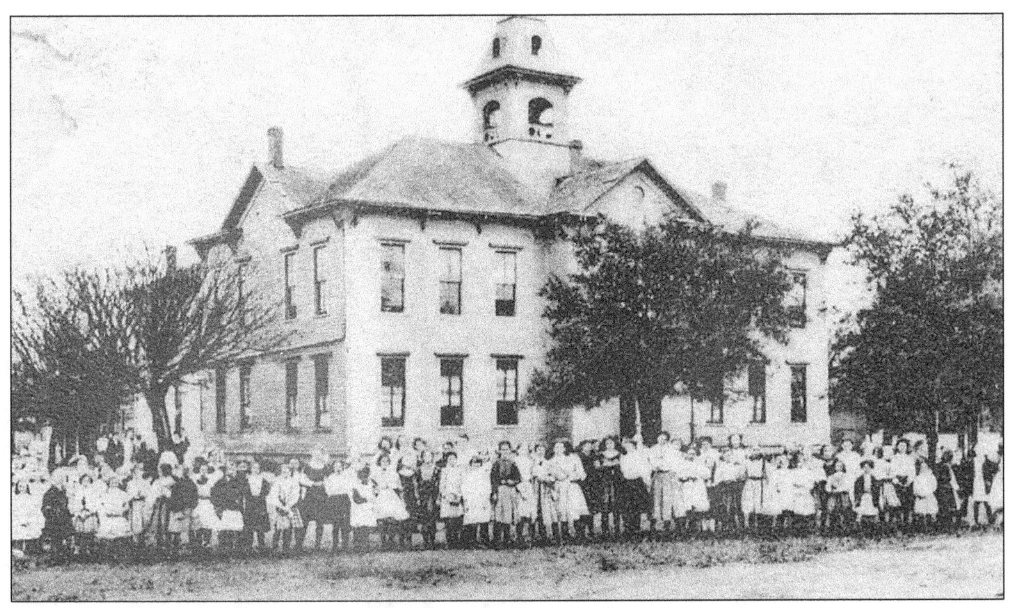

Children gather in 1905 for a group photograph in front of Lake Charles Central and High School, the city's first public school, built in 1890. Because the school educated students of all ages, overcrowding caused superintendent John McNeese to split the two schools in 1893, with the high school students occupying an annex on the grounds. Pictured below is Lake Charles College, established by New England Congregationalists in 1890. The building and the 13 acres around it were purchased by the school board (at the urging of McNeese) in 1903 as Lake Charles High School. Although it is in the present-day city center (and now occupied by Lake Charles-Boston Academy), at the time it was so far out in the country that people complained about the long walk.

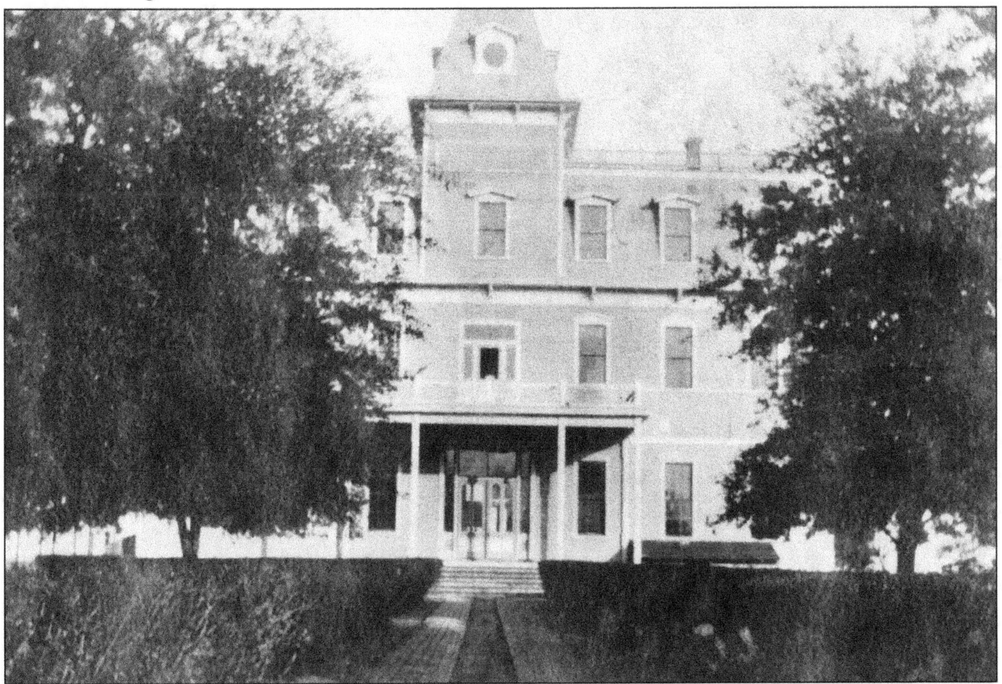

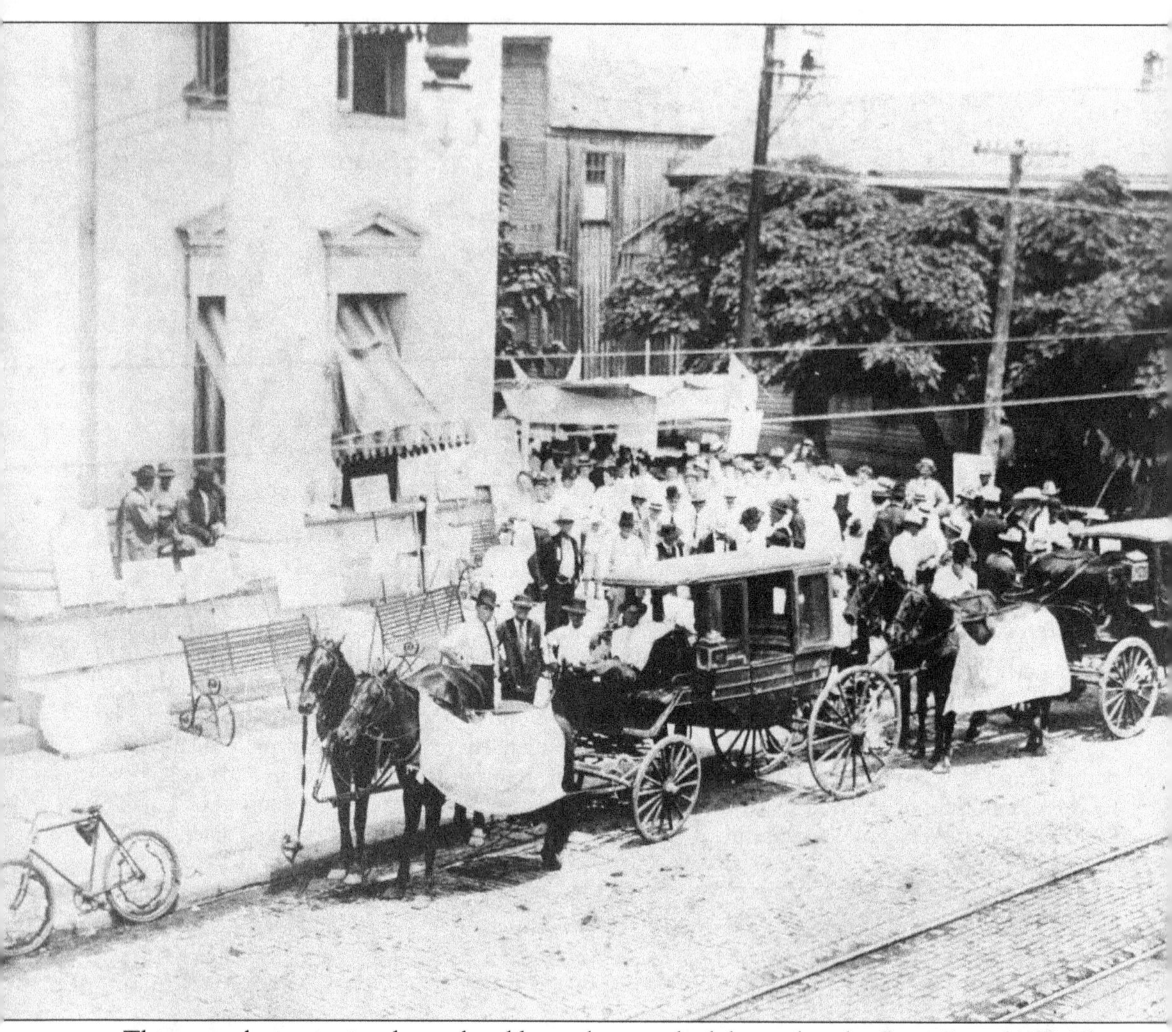

This scene depicts voting day at the old courthouse, which burned in the Great Fire of 1910. The poor quality of the photograph makes it appear as though some of the people are black, but that is not likely; blacks in Louisiana were effectively denied voting rights by the state constitution of 1898, which required voters to pay poll taxes and pass literacy tests before they could vote. Approximately 95 percent of Louisiana's black voters were disfranchised by these provisions, as were about 50 percent of all whites. The state constitution of 1921 created loopholes that allowed many poor whites to vote, but blacks continued to be disfranchised until the civil rights era.

Three

Early Congregations

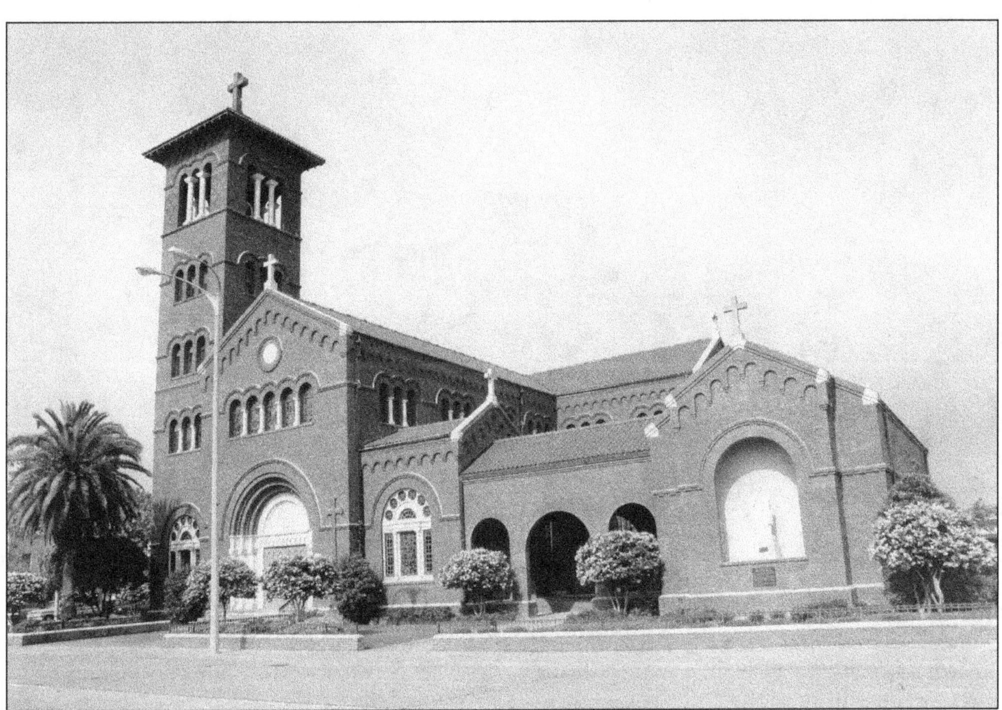

Some of the first settlers in southwest Louisiana were French-speaking Catholics. In 1857, they purchased land at the intersection of Kirby and Ryan Streets and built a small frame church called St. Francis de Sales. A new church with the name Immaculate Conception was completed in 1881, and it grew to include a convent, an academy, and several other facilities, which were all destroyed in the fire of 1910. The current red brick Romanesque building was dedicated in 1913.

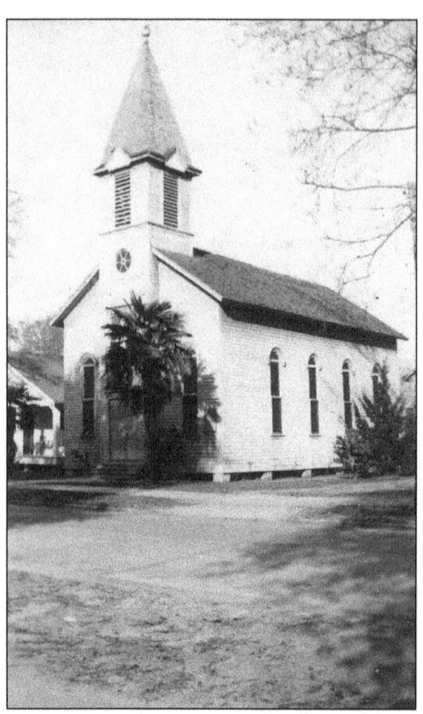

This is the oldest existing church building in Lake Charles. Built in 1888 on Ford Street (originally called German Street because of the high percentage of Germans in the area), it began as St. John Lutheran, founded by Daniel Goos to serve the people he had recruited from Europe. Services were conducted in German until the 1930s. Though damaged in the hurricane of 1918, the little church was rebuilt. Rudolph Krause (of Krause and Managan Lumber Co.) contributed handsomely. When the congregation moved to Enterprise Boulevard in 1955, the building was sold to First Baptist and became Grace Rescue Mission, which still serves people today.

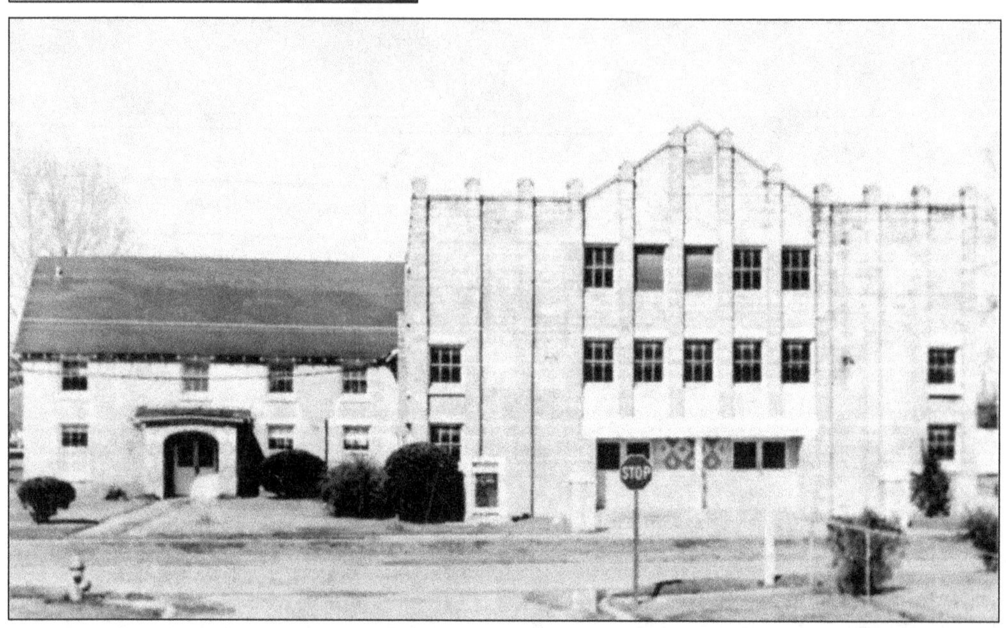

Reeves Colored Methodist Episcopal Church, founded in 1865, is one of the oldest chartered organizations in the state. It is named for Rev. George Reeves, a white Civil War veteran who was sent to minister to the congregation just after the Civil War. They met in brush arbors until funds could be raised for the purchase of property and a building. Church records indicate that the congregation remained integrated for some years, and Reeves remained a member of the church until his death in 1916. The original church building was built in 1877 by "Uncle" George Ryan, the former slave of Jacob Ryan, and was used as the first approved school for blacks in the parish. It was destroyed in the hurricane of 1918.

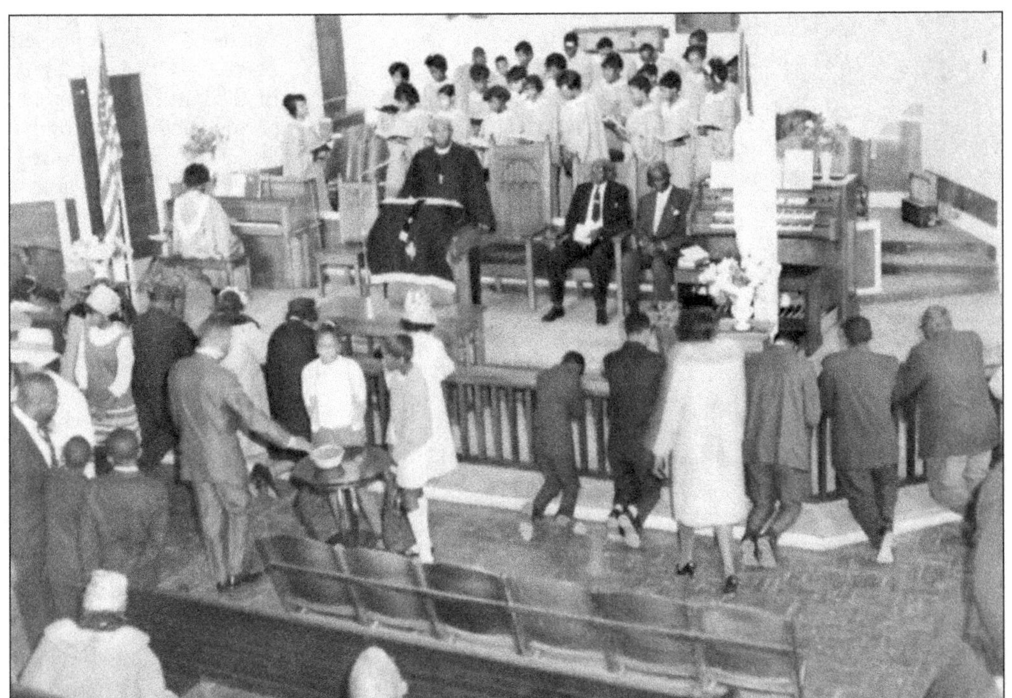

This and the previous image are from a series of 12 photographs printed as postcards featuring Reeves Christian Methodist Episcopal Temple and its members in 1970. By this time, the term "colored" had been dropped from the congregation's name, and the church had several choirs, including the gospel, senior, junior, and youth choirs. Pioneering church leaders championed many social, economic, and educational issues for the congregation. Continuing in this tradition, many Reeves members remain at the forefront of civic and government affairs today.

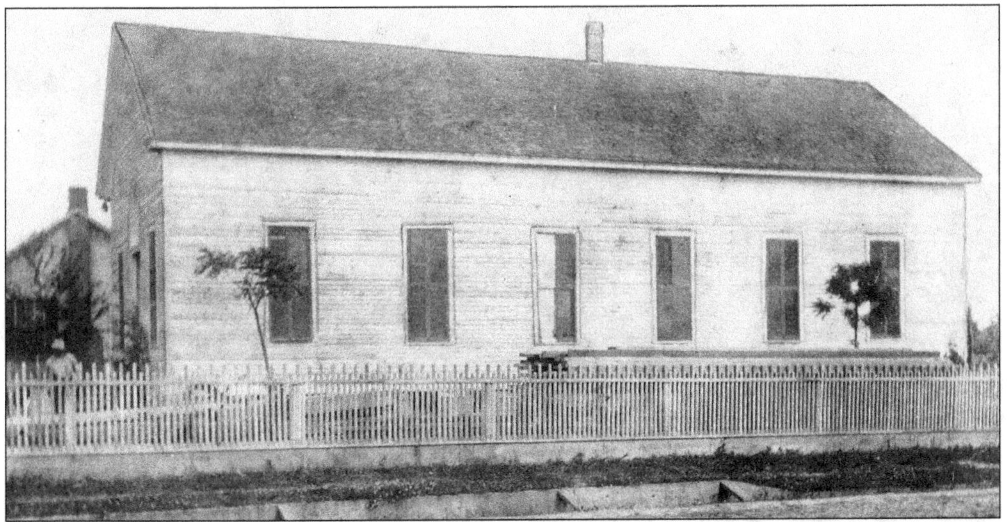

This was the first church building in Lake Charles. Known as Broad Street Methodist, it was built in 1875 at the corner of Broad and Bilbo Streets. The names on its rolls include some of the city's founders: Moss, Ryan, Kirkman, Bilbo, Shattuck, Susan McNeese, and Mims. Seaman A. Knapp was a member, but left to found a northern-affiliated Methodist congregation (which later became Simpson Methodist Episcopal) in 1890.

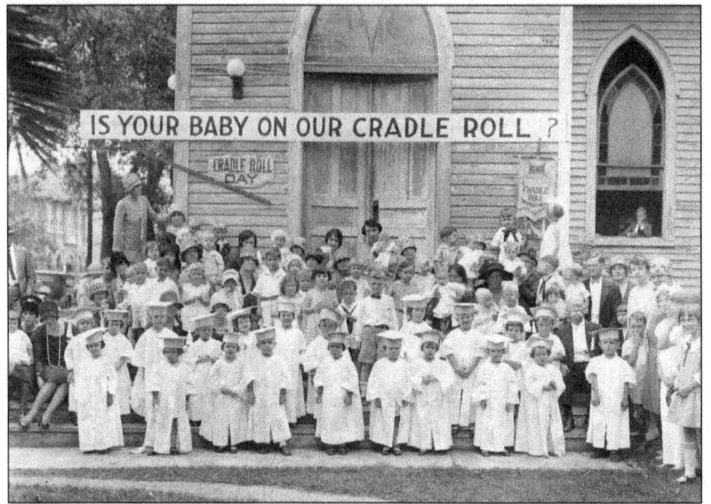

Augustus M. Mayo joined Broad Street Methodist in 1883 and immediately became active in church leadership. He is pictured here in 1927 seated at right, among the crowd of "cradle roll" children in front of the new structure built in 1920 on the corner of Broad and Kirkman Streets. Mayo directed the Sunday school until his death in 1944, when Oscar Maxfield took over as general Sunday school director.

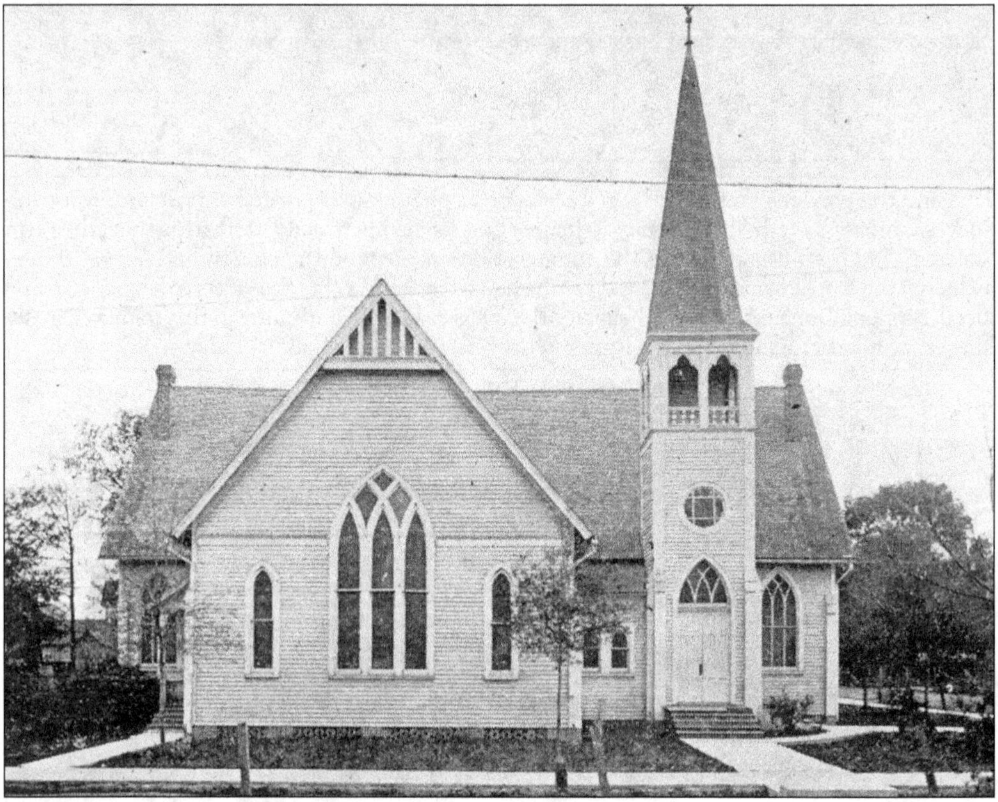

Seaman A. Knapp, C.A. King, D.A. Kelly, and W.P. Weber were among the migrants from the north who founded First Methodist Episcopal Church, part of the northern branch of Methodism, in 1890. They held services in the Masonic Hall until this building was completed in 1898 on the corner of Pujo and Moss Streets. When the Methodist branches united in 1939, the congregation changed its name to Simpson. The church sponsored Troop No. 1, the first Boy Scout unit in the South. Its members were instrumental in establishing the YMCA and McNeese Junior College. The church initiated the first interracial committees in the city and offered meeting space. It moved to Highway 14 in 1954, and merged with St. Luke's Methodist in 1983.

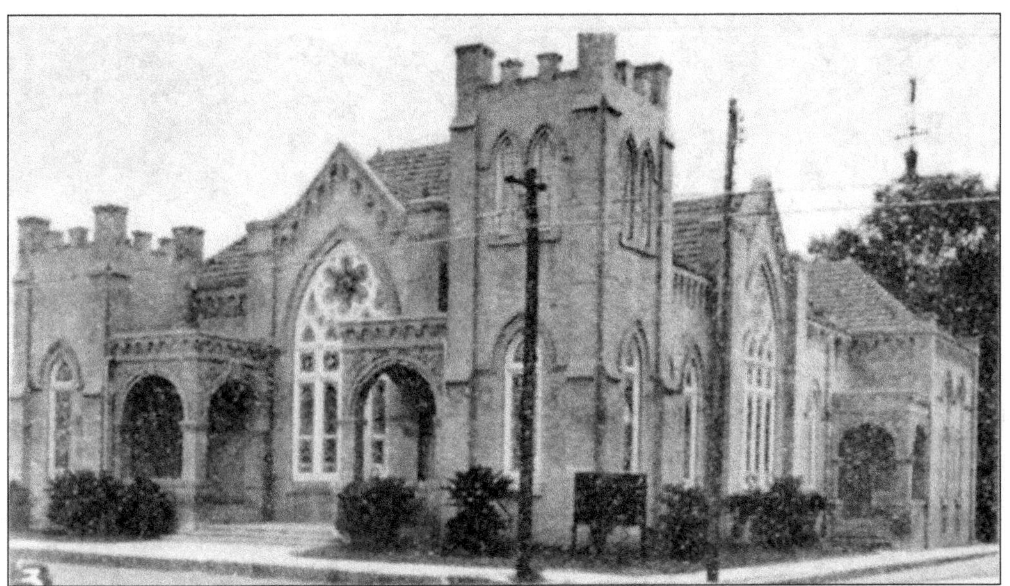

First Baptist Church formally organized in 1880, with 18 members who "were limited in means." By 1910, its numbers had grown sufficiently to build this impressive new structure at the corner of Pujo and Hodges Streets. It was dedicated in 1910, the day after the Great Fire ravaged much of the rest of downtown. This building was demolished in 1957.

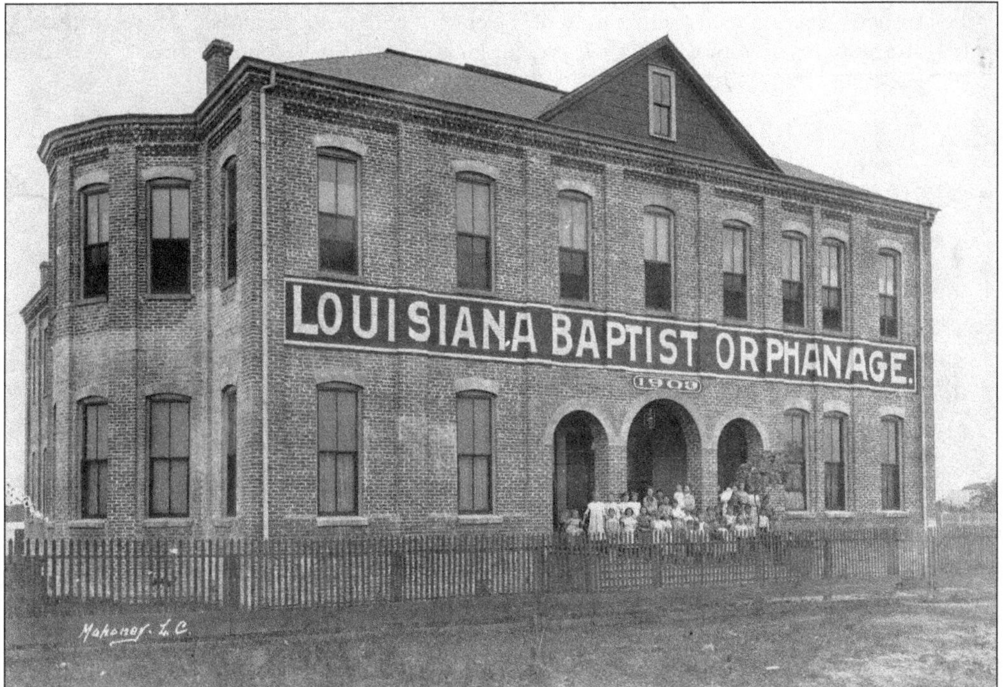

First Baptist Church chartered the Louisiana Baptist Orphanage in 1903. It was the forerunner of the Baptist Children's Home, which moved to Monroe, Louisiana, in 1925. Shortly thereafter, the building and the surrounding 16 acres were purchased by Mrs. J.A. Landry and donated to the Catholic Church. The building became Landry Memorial School for boys, a parochial school run by the Christian Brothers. It was demolished in 1969 to make way for the construction of St. Louis High School.

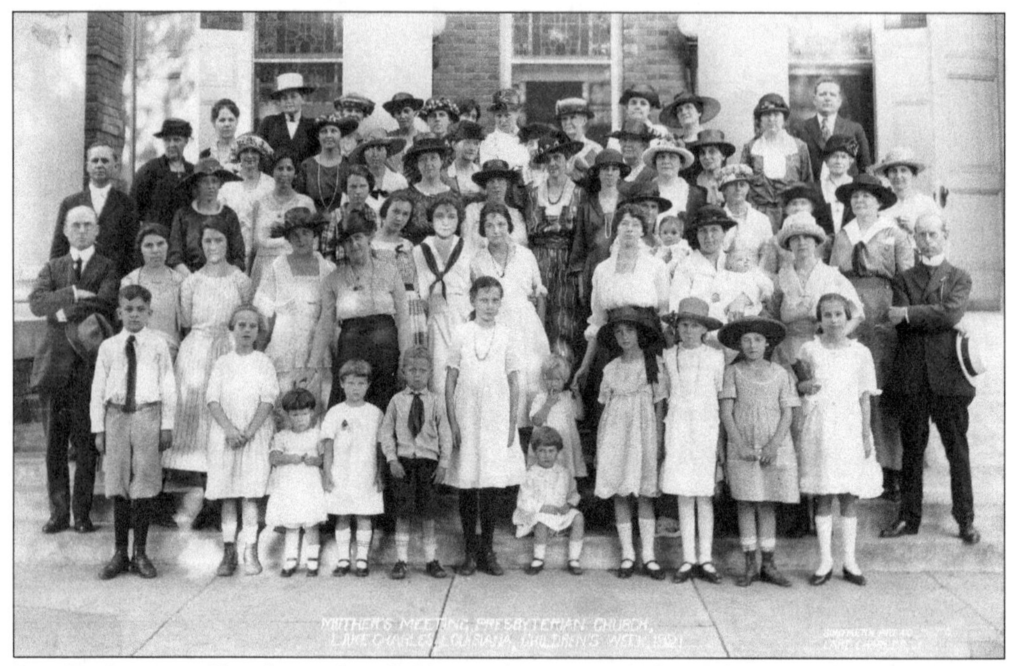

First Presbyterian Church was founded by northerners, including John McNeese, but affiliated with the Southern Assembly. Their first building was dedicated in 1890. This 1921 photograph of the Mothers' Meeting was taken in front of the church built at Broad and Ford Streets in 1919. In 1951, the congregation moved to their present location at 1801 Second Avenue.

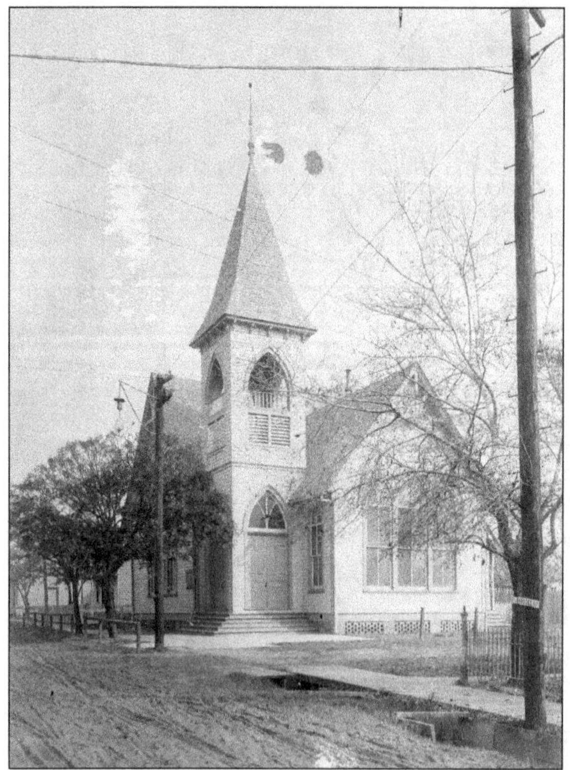

Midwesterners organized First Christian Church in 1894. The Ladies Aid Society held ice cream socials, suppers, cake sales, and quilting bees to raise money for the purchase of the lot at the corner of Hodges and Iris Streets and the construction of this building in 1896. When it burned in the Great Fire of 1910, Jews offered the use of their new synagogue, which the congregation gratefully accepted until a new church could be built.

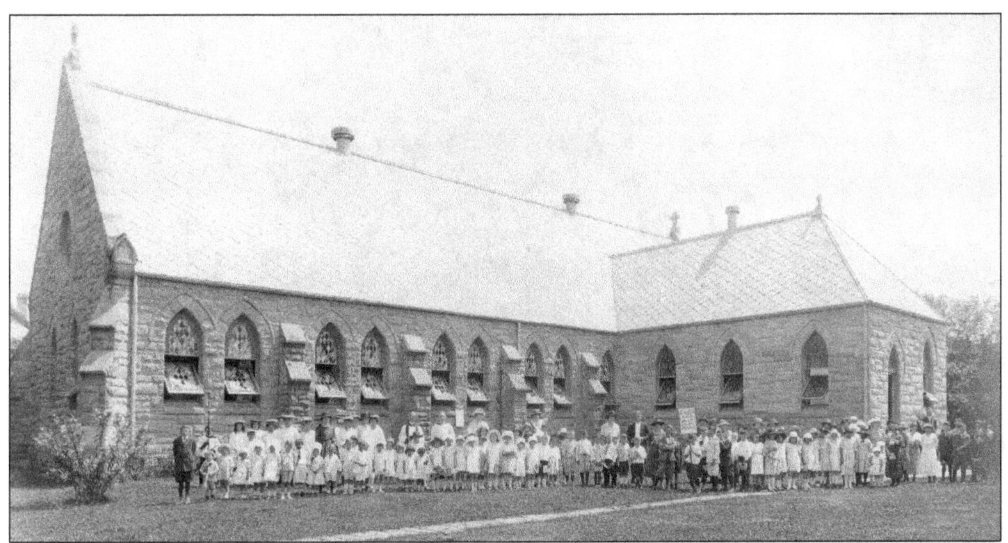

Capt. George Lock (from England), W.A. Knapp, and several northerners established the Episcopal Church of the Good Shepherd in 1885. Starting out in a wooden structure on Hodges Street, the Ladies Guild raised money to purchase property on the corner of Kirkman and Division Streets in 1894 and to construct a stone church reminiscent of those that dotted the countryside in England. This Gothic Revival structure was destroyed in the hurricane of 1918 but was rebuilt as before. It was placed in the National Register of Historic Places in 1984. This photograph shows the new parish hall, constructed in 1926.

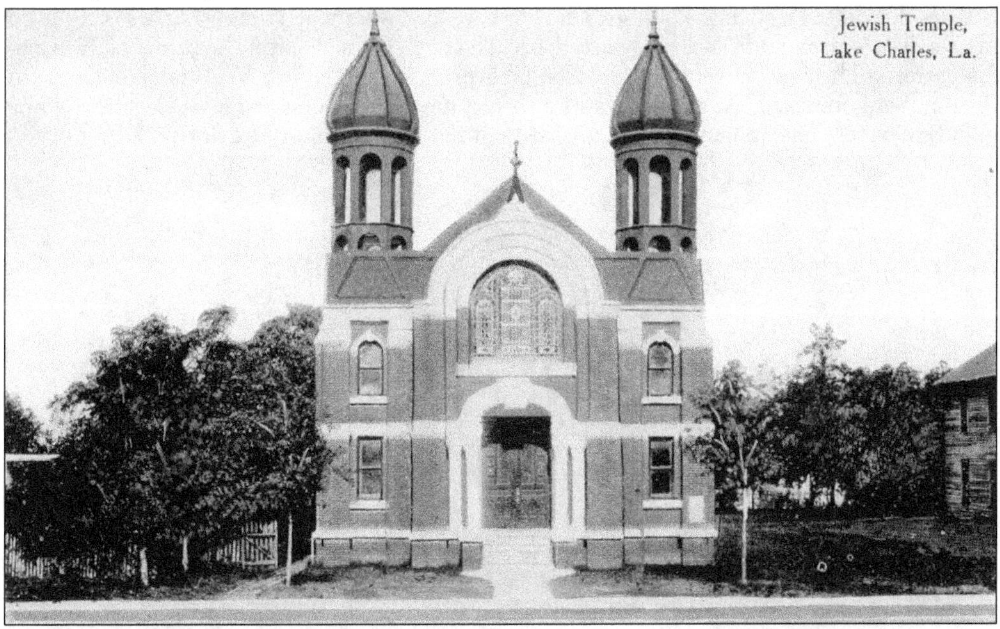

By 1894, enough Jews had migrated to Lake Charles to consecrate a congregation. Many had come from war-torn Alsace-Lorraine and spoke French, and they quickly established many of downtown's first mercantile and retail stores. In 1904, they constructed this Romanesque temple displaying two Byzantine-style onion domes. The domes were destroyed in the 1918 hurricane and were never rebuilt. Today, Temple Sinai is listed in the National Register of Historic Places and continues to be a thriving place of worship for the Jewish community of Lake Charles.

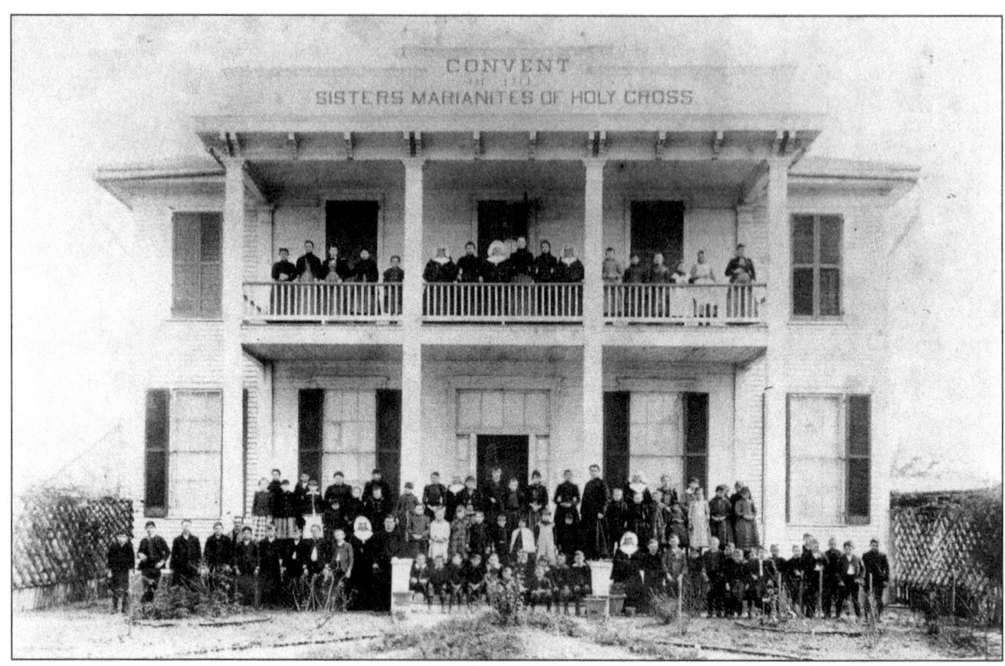

The Congregation of the Marianite Sisters of Holy Cross from Le Mans, France, founded many hospitals, orphanages, rest homes, and schools throughout Louisiana and the United States. Four Marianite sisters arrived in Lake Charles in 1882 to educate the city's schoolchildren at St. Charles Borromeo Academy. The sisters did not have a convent when they arrived, so they lived in a small two-room house (below), which they called Little Chateau, near the corner of Ryan and Pujo Streets. The new convent built in 1884 (above) was a white frame Victorian building with a veranda at both levels. At the time of its opening, it was the largest and most elegant building in Lake Charles. The immense structure stood until its destruction in the fire of 1910.

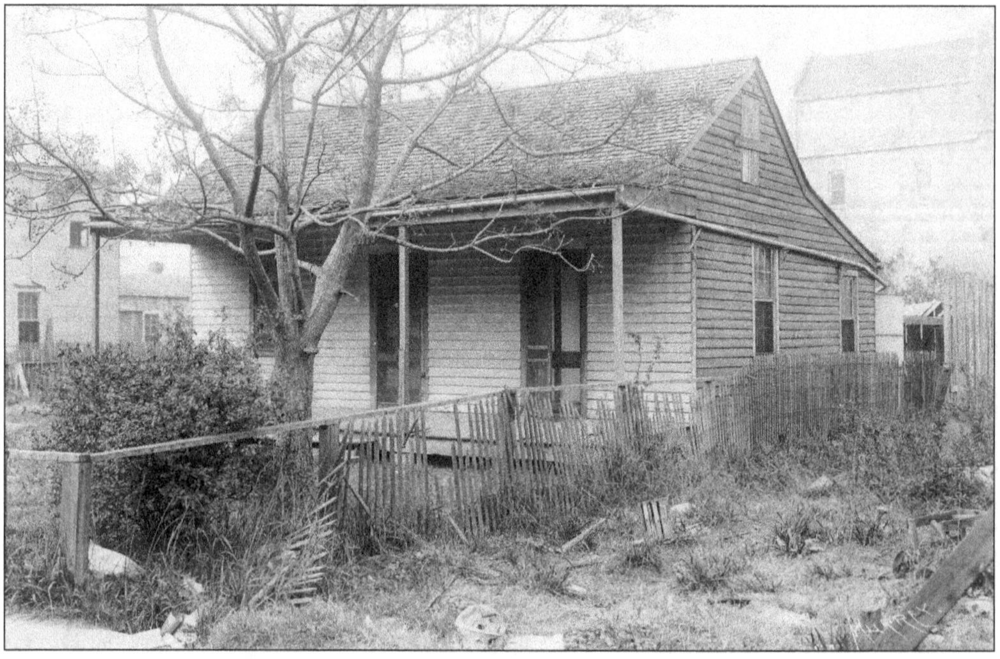

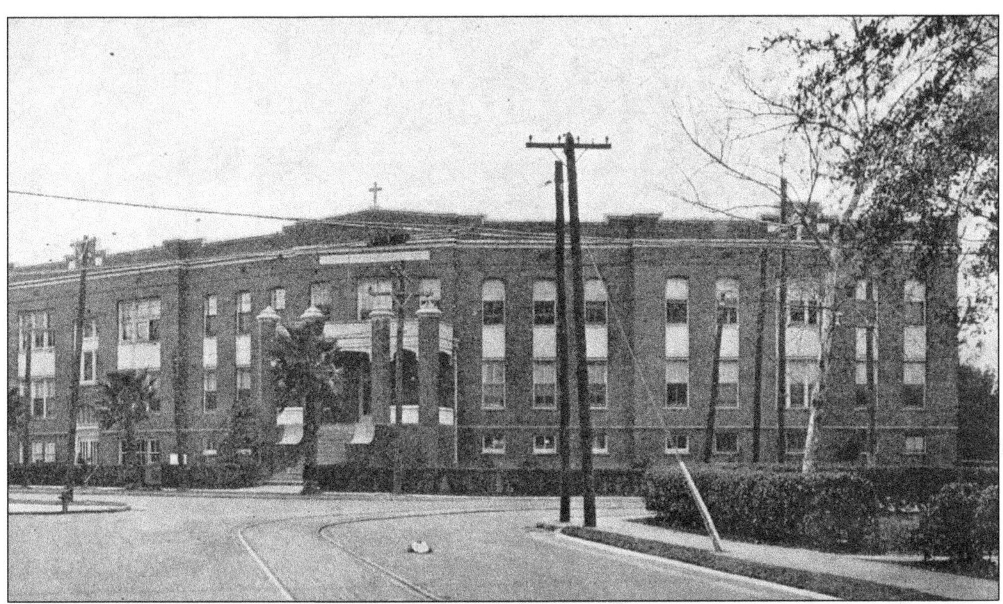

The original St. Charles Academy, a one-room building, was replaced in 1904 by a large Gothic structure that burned in the fire of 1910. The building pictured was constructed in 1914 and served as the home of St. Charles Academy until it merged with the boys' school (Landry) in 1970 and became St. Louis High. The building was demolished in 1974.

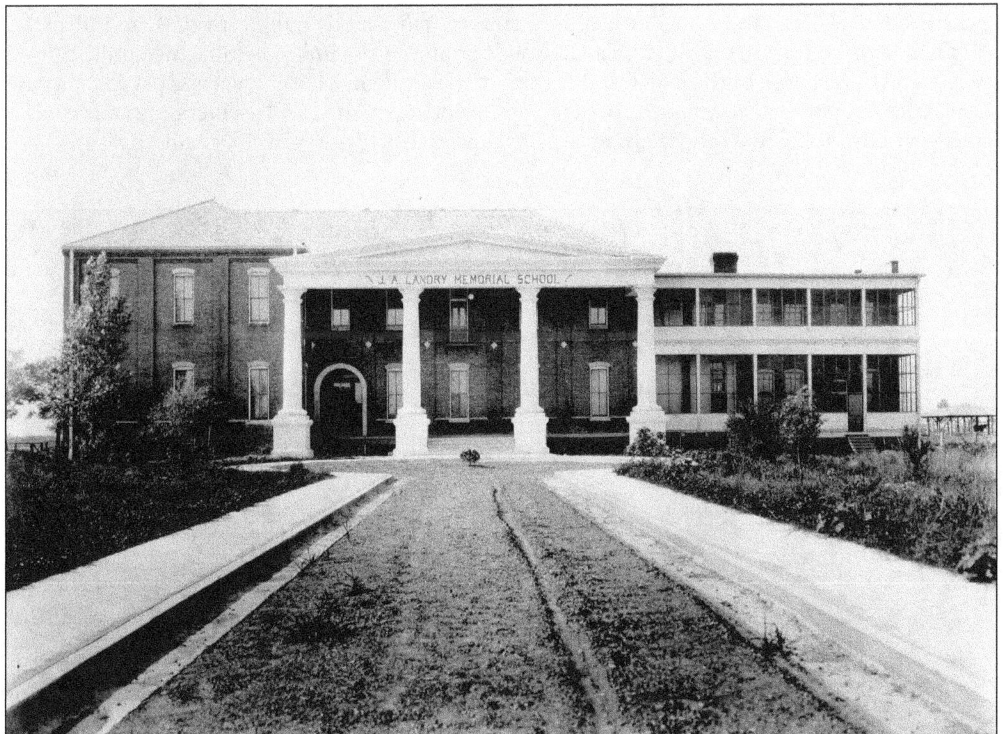

J.A. Landry Memorial School for boys opened in 1927. Run by the Christian Brothers until 1963, it accepted day students from Lake Charles and boarded students living out of the city. The screened porch of the dormitory is visible at right. The building was demolished in 1969.

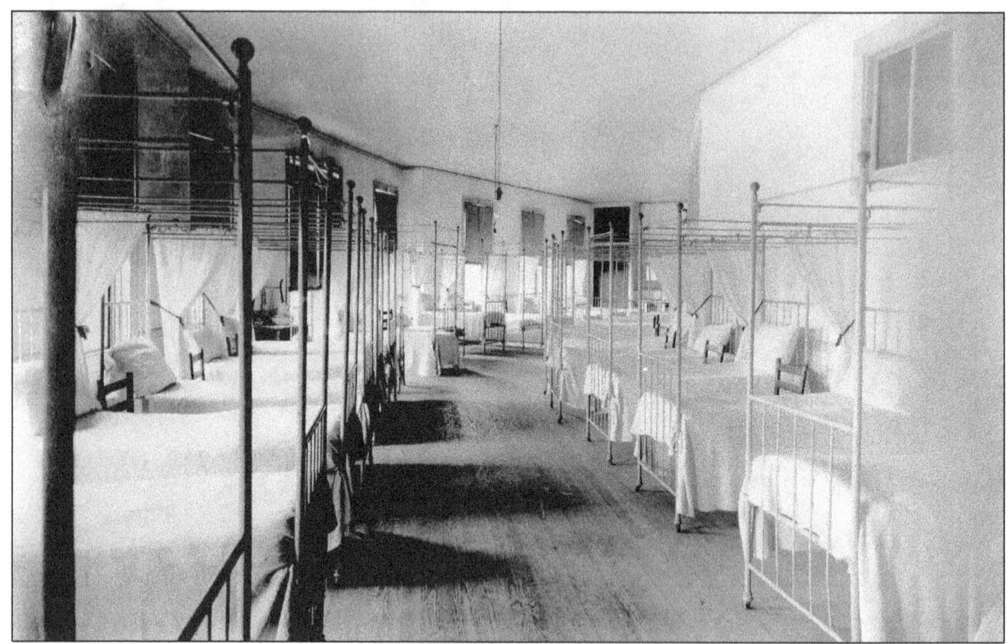

St. Charles Academy housed 50 female students who shared one large dormitory on the third level of the building. The brick building was fireproof, steam-heated, and electrically lighted. The building contained five classrooms, three music rooms, an art room, a study hall, restrooms, an infirmary, a kitchen with a pantry, a chapel, and a large auditorium. In the image below, three unidentified students take chemistry in the lab. The dirt floor of the academy's lower level was paved for a new science department, music practice room, and a reception room. The basement also served as a temporary boys' parochial school after the hurricane of 1918 destroyed their building.

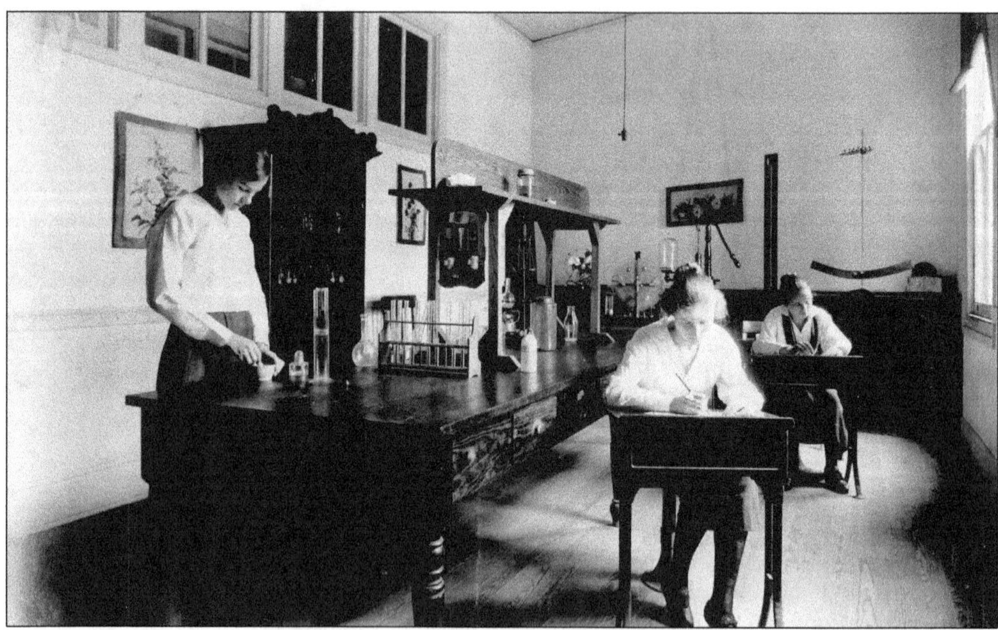

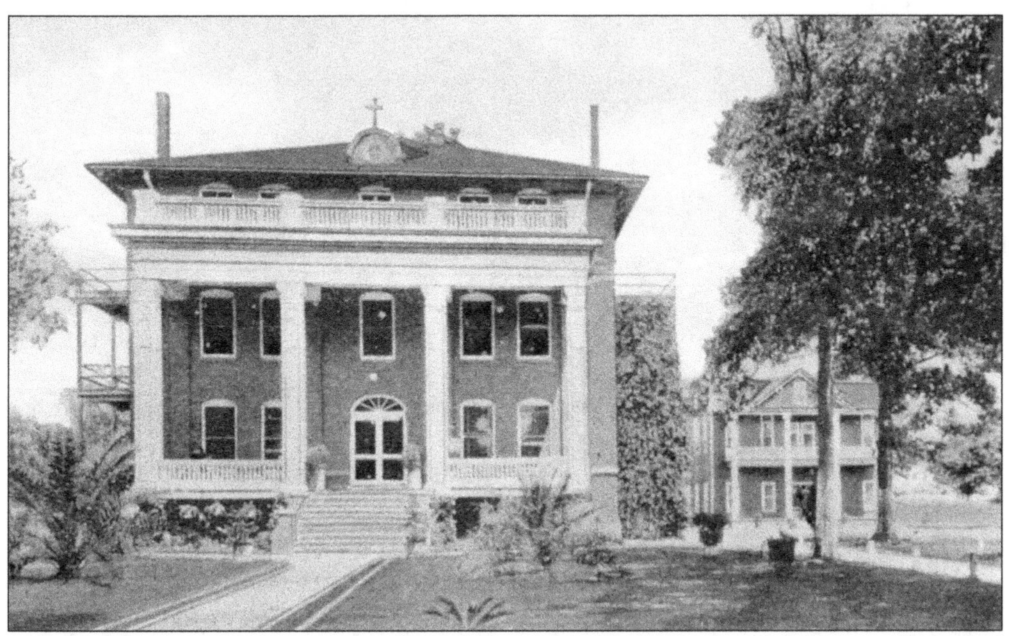

Numerous cases of yellow fever, epidemics of smallpox and diphtheria, and injuries sustained from the storm of 1904 prompted citizens of Lake Charles to raise money to build a hospital. The St. Patrick Sanitarium, later St. Patrick Hospital, was dedicated March 17, 1908, and was originally staffed with nurses from Sisters of Charity of the Incarnate Word. The third floor contained a chapel and living quarters for the nurses and eventually the students of St. Patrick nursing school, which opened in 1918. A new annex was added to the building in 1921, and it was expanded again in 1948.

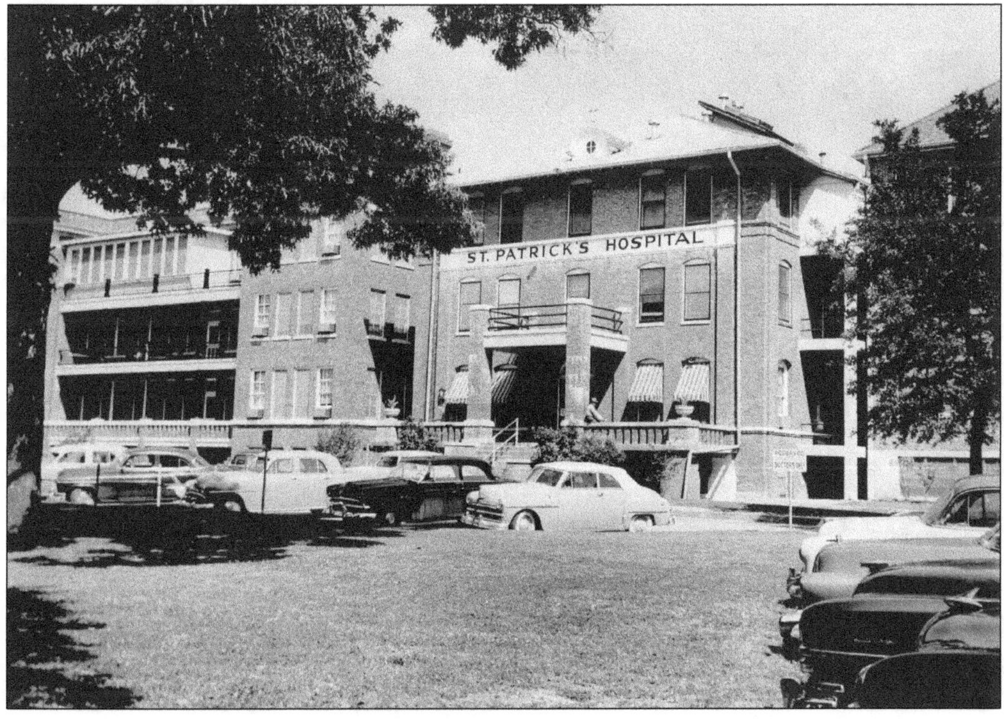

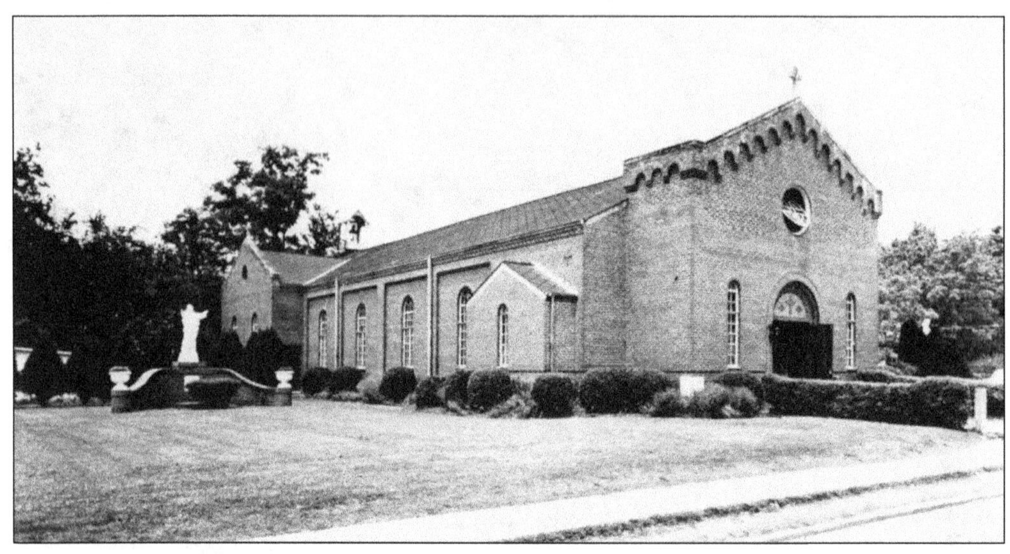

Sacred Heart, pictured above around 1990, is the first daughter parish of Immaculate Conception, and was created to serve the Catholics of North Lake Charles. Ordinarily, a parish is formed before a parish school; however, in the case of Sacred Heart, the school board organized in 1908 and the parish was established in 1919. When the school opened, it was the only private or parochial school open to blacks. The high school was added in 1923, but closed after segregation ended in 1967. Its students were encouraged to attend the new St. Louis High School. In 1989, Sacred Heart School was rededicated and renamed Blessed Katherine Drexel/Sacred Heart Elementary School. The 1970 photograph below shows Sacred Heart Elementary students in reading class.

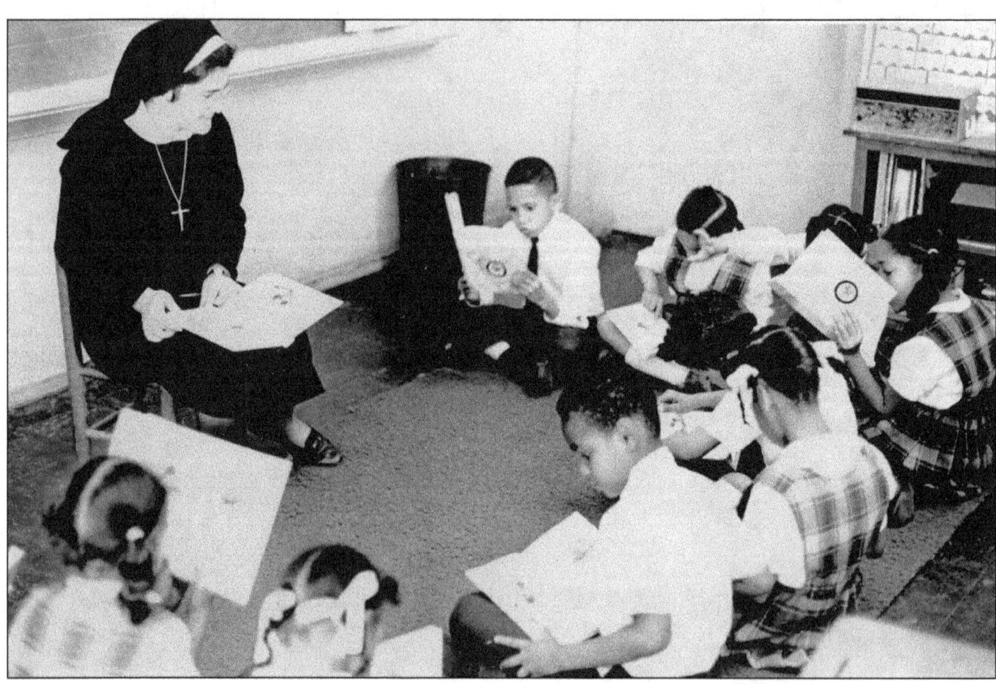

Most Rev. Harold R. Perry, SVD, became the first African American bishop in the United States in the 20th century. Born in Lake Charles to working-class Creole parents, he attended elementary school at Sacred Heart School near his home on Mill Street. He was ordained in 1944 at Bay St. Louis. Perry worked to establish social justice and the integration of Catholic institutions across the country, and in 1963, he became the first black clergyman to deliver the opening prayer in Congress. When he was consecrated in New Orleans in 1965, white protesters demonstrated outside St. Louis Cathedral with racist placards.

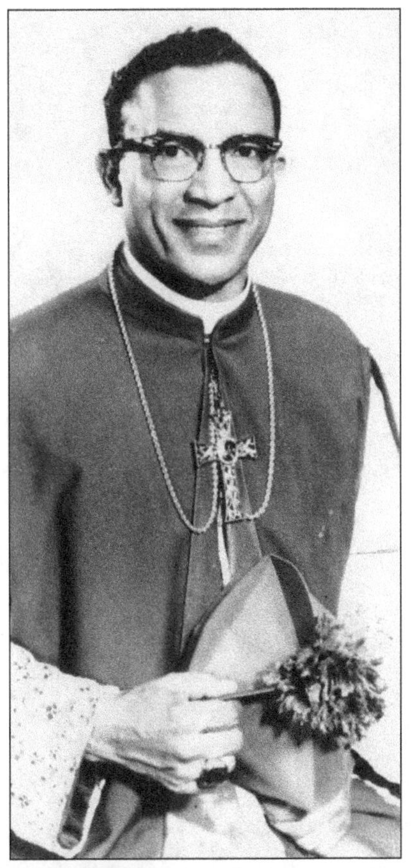

Rev. Victor. E. Washington was the pastor of New Sunlight Baptist Church for over 43 years, during which time the church expanded its property and membership. His accomplishments include the 1954 opening of the first licensed day care operated by a black church. He became the first black president of the Calcasieu Parish School Board and led a group of white and black clergy who smoothed the way for integration in Lake Charles in the 1950s and 1960s. Pictured here are Rev. J.L. Franklin, successor to Reverend Washington (left); Rev. Henry Lyons (center); and Reverend Washington. (Courtesy of Lawrence Morrow.)

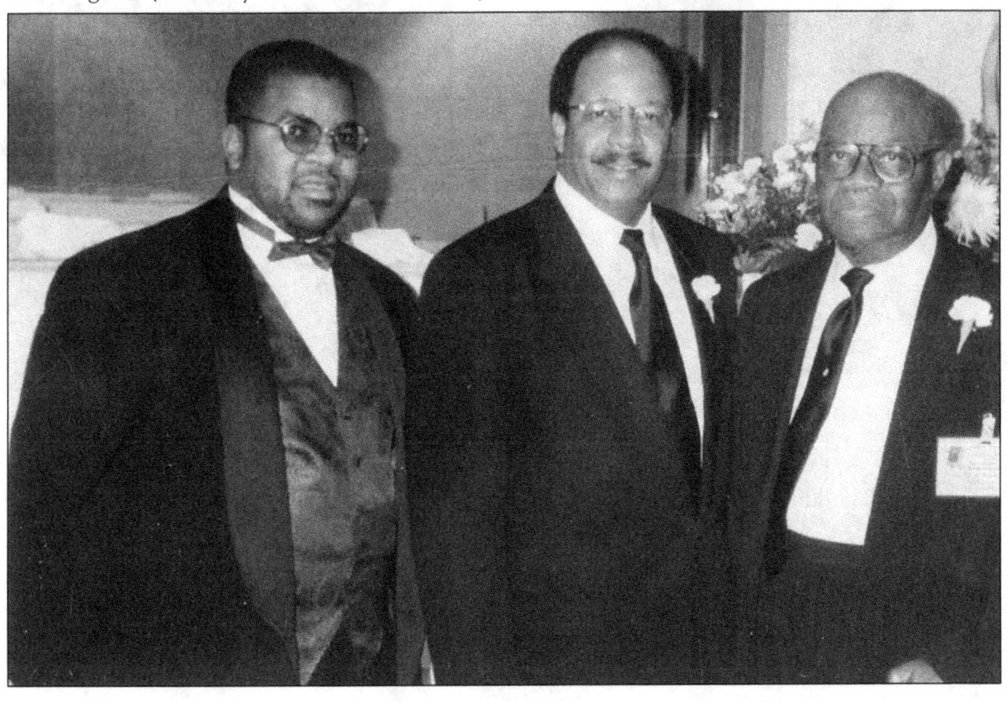

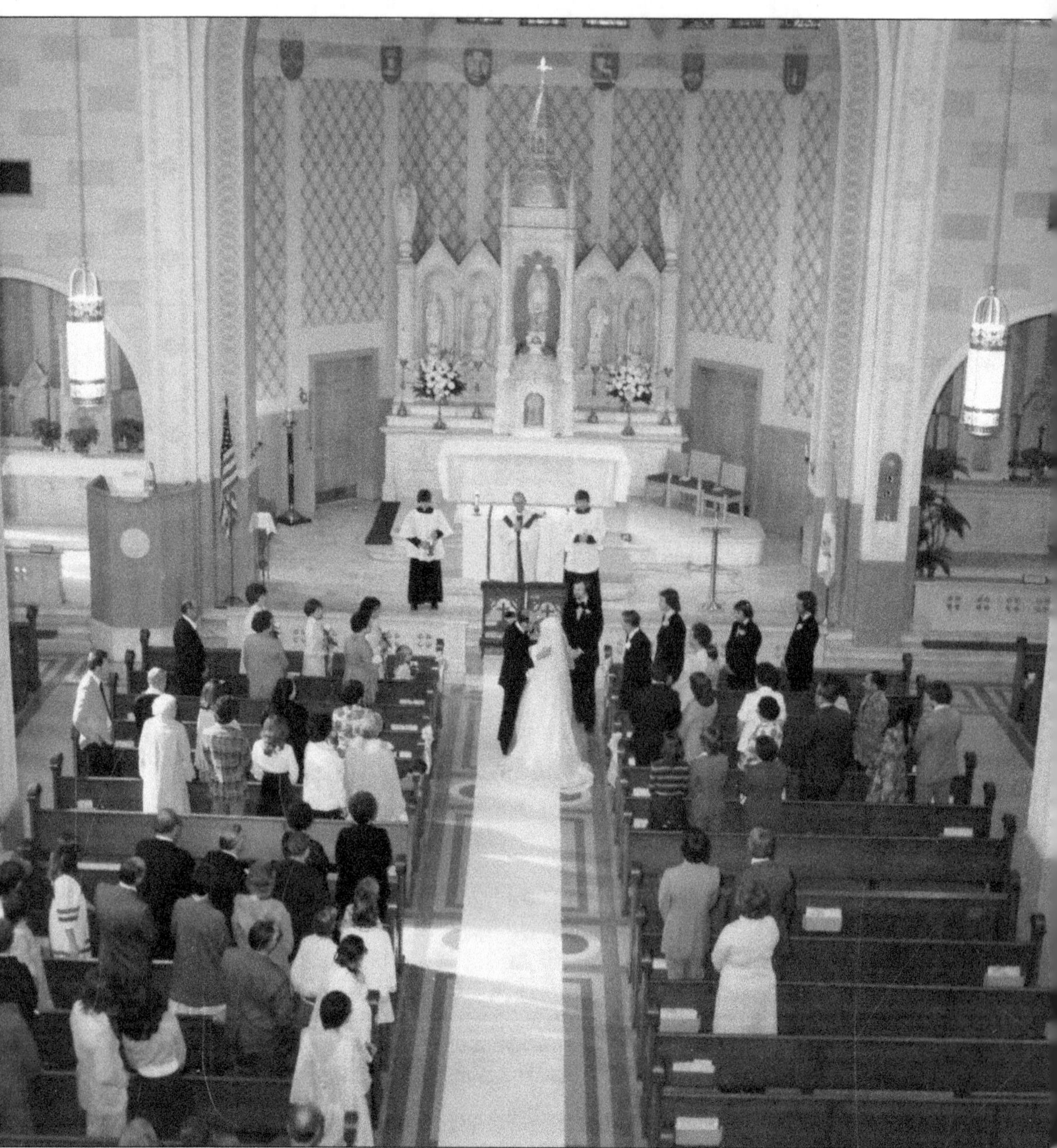

This photograph shows the interior of the Church of the Immaculate Conception, which features walls lined with stone blocks and a series of Viennese stained-glass windows, installed in 1939, that depict the story of Mary's life. The floor plan of the cathedral resembles the shape of a Greek cross. It is one of 16 buildings in Calcasieu Parish listed in the National Registry of Historic Places.

Four

AFTER THE FIRE

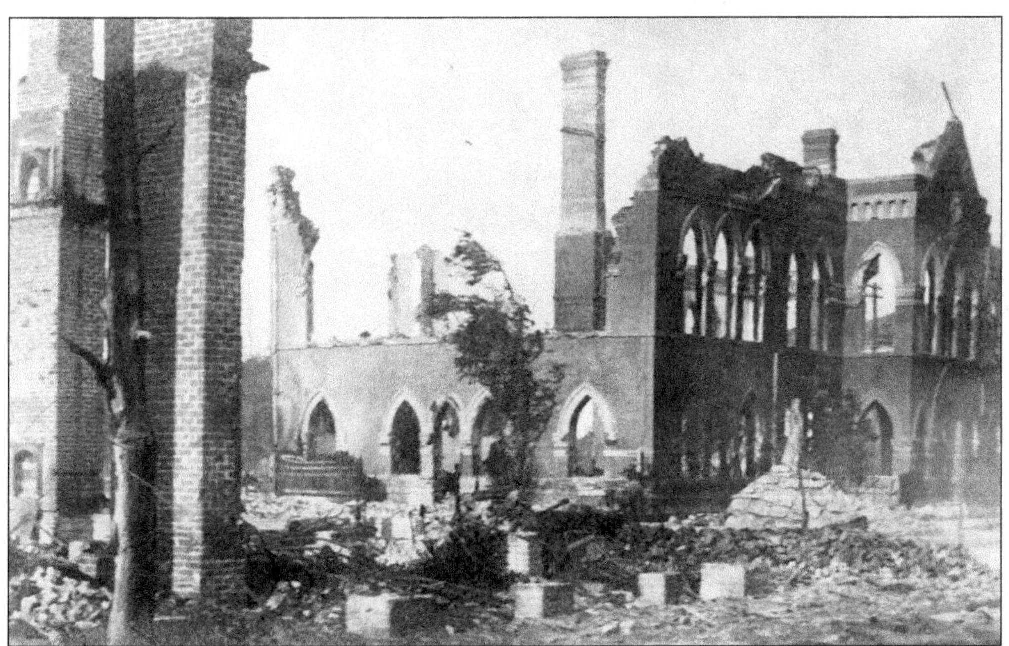

The "Great Fire" of April 1910 consumed 109 buildings in downtown Lake Charles, including the courthouse, city hall, and the Catholic church complex. This photograph shows the destruction of St. Charles Academy and the convent.

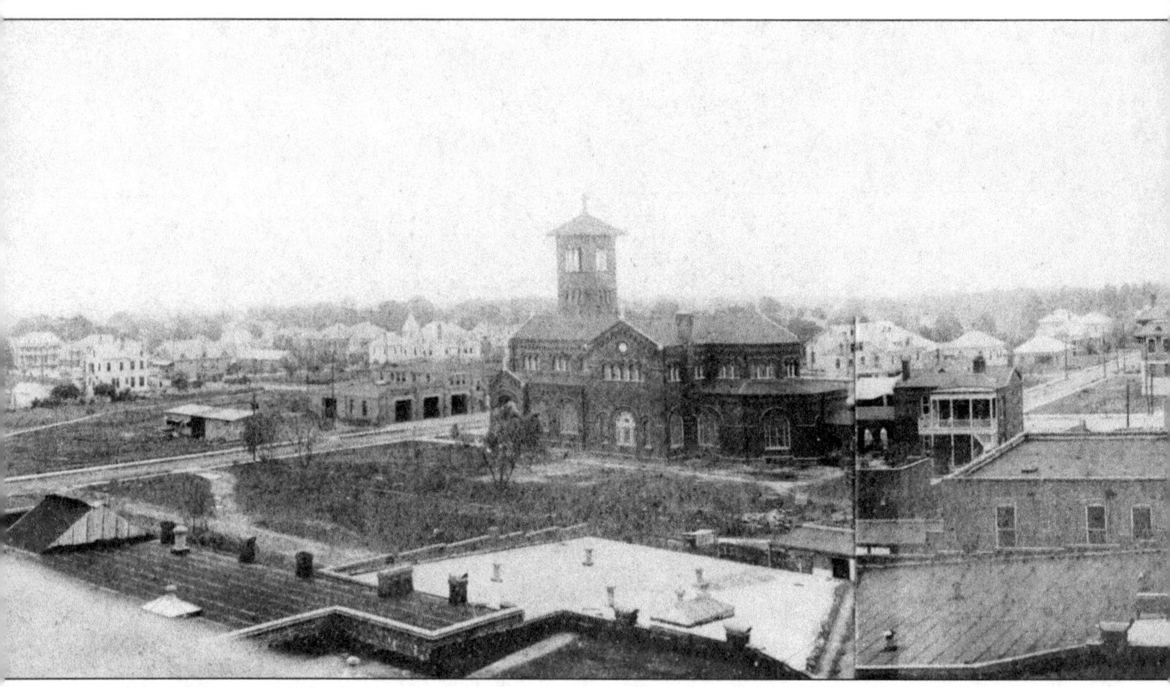

The devastating fire engendered a number of important reforms in the city. Charges of poor leadership and malfeasance in office led to an end to the old aldermanic system of governance and to the more progressive and businesslike "commission" form in 1912, better suited to a growing city. A new fire code for downtown structures required the use of stone and brick for public buildings and slate roofs on private structures. Many of the new masonry structures were designed by the

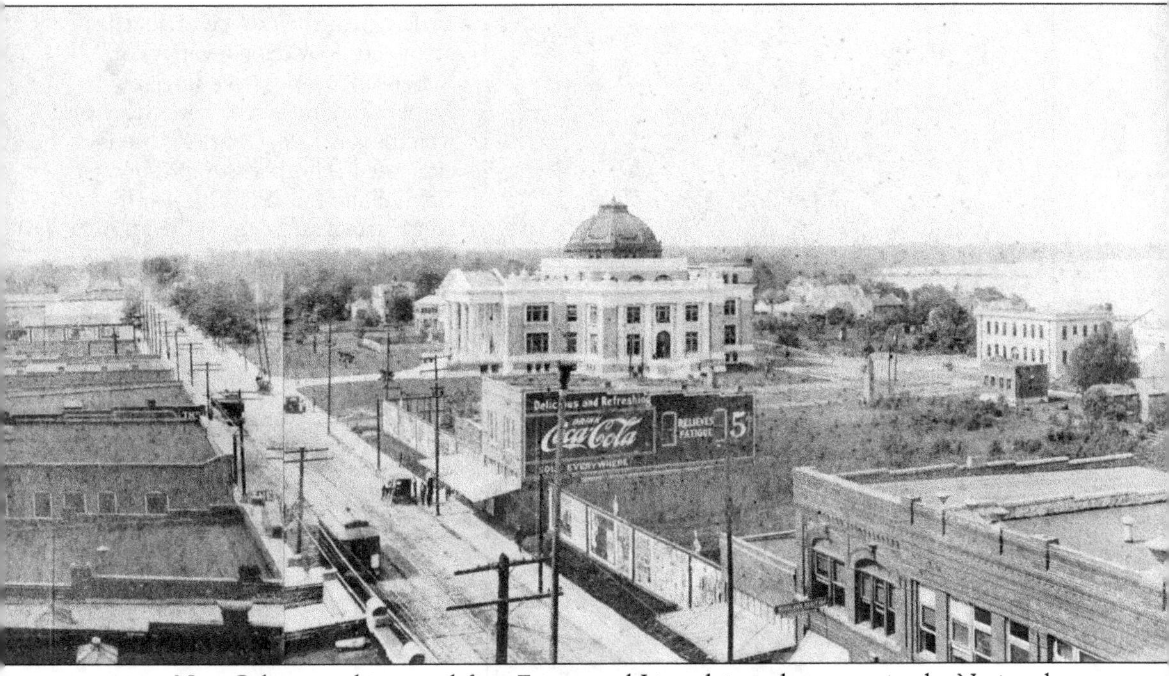

prestigious New Orleans architectural firm Favrot and Livaudais and are now in the National Register of Historic Places, including Immaculate Conception Church (which became a cathedral upon the creation of the Diocese of Lake Charles in 1979) at left, city hall in the center, and the courthouse at right. (Courtesy of Mayo Land and Title Company)

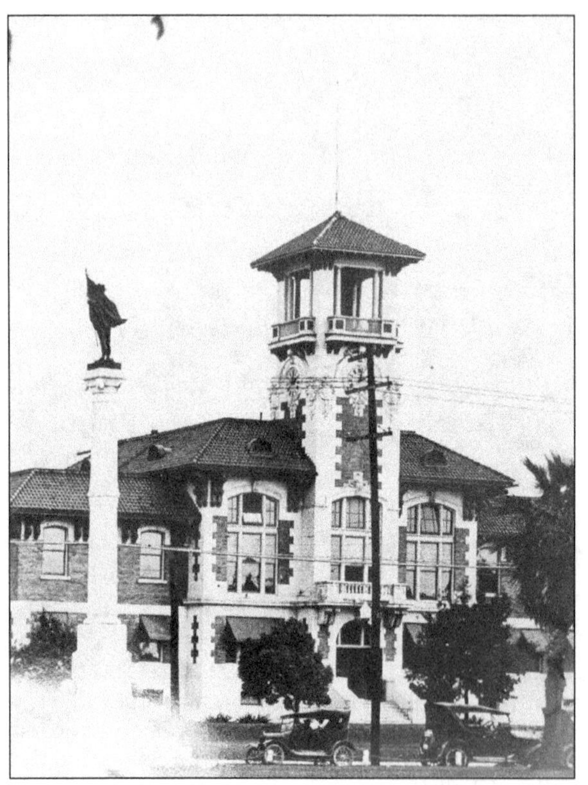

In designing the new city hall, the architects drew upon a variety of Renaissance styles from England, France, and Italy—the countries from which many Lake Charles citizens emigrated. This photograph shows city hall around 1911, the year it was constructed. After city hall moved to the Pioneer Building in the 1970s, this building was used as a city court. Under Mayor Randy Roach (2000–), it became an arts and cultural center.

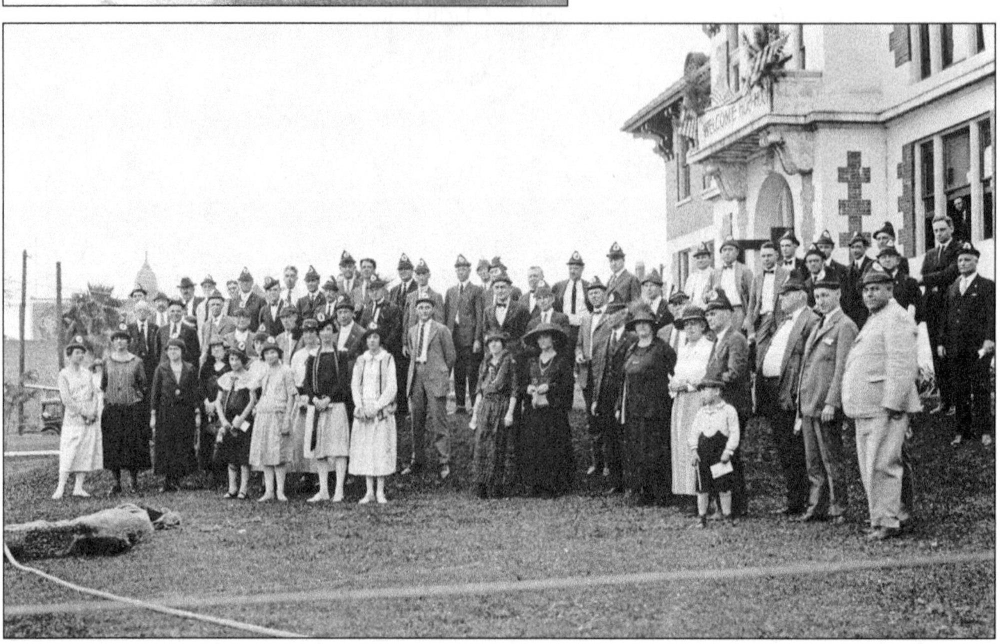

This image of the Concatenated Order of Hoo-Hoo, an organization concerned with the lumber industry and reforestation, depicts a gathering of members from Louisiana and Texas. One new inductee (or "kitten"), in the second row, second from left, was Lake Charles mayor J.A. Trotti, who issued a proclamation declaring April 28, 1923, as "Hoo-Hoo Day." (Courtesy of Jeanne Owens of Vintage Arts; photograph by David H. Levingston.)

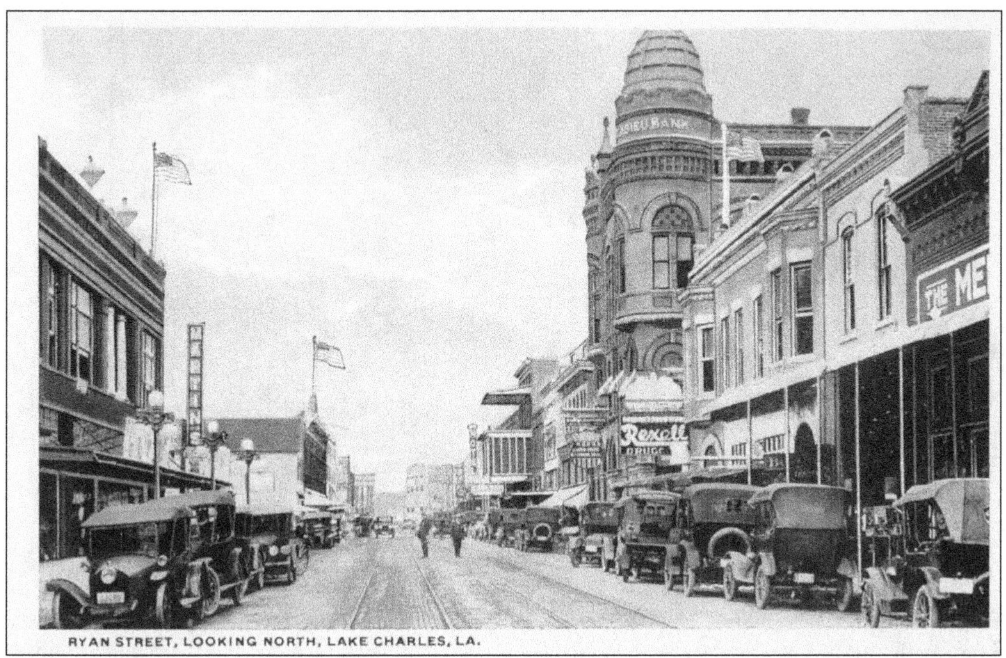

This c. 1920 postcard, looking north on Ryan Street, shows the trolley tracks down the middle and the brick and stone buildings that were built after the Great Fire. The tower at right is the Calcasieu National Bank.

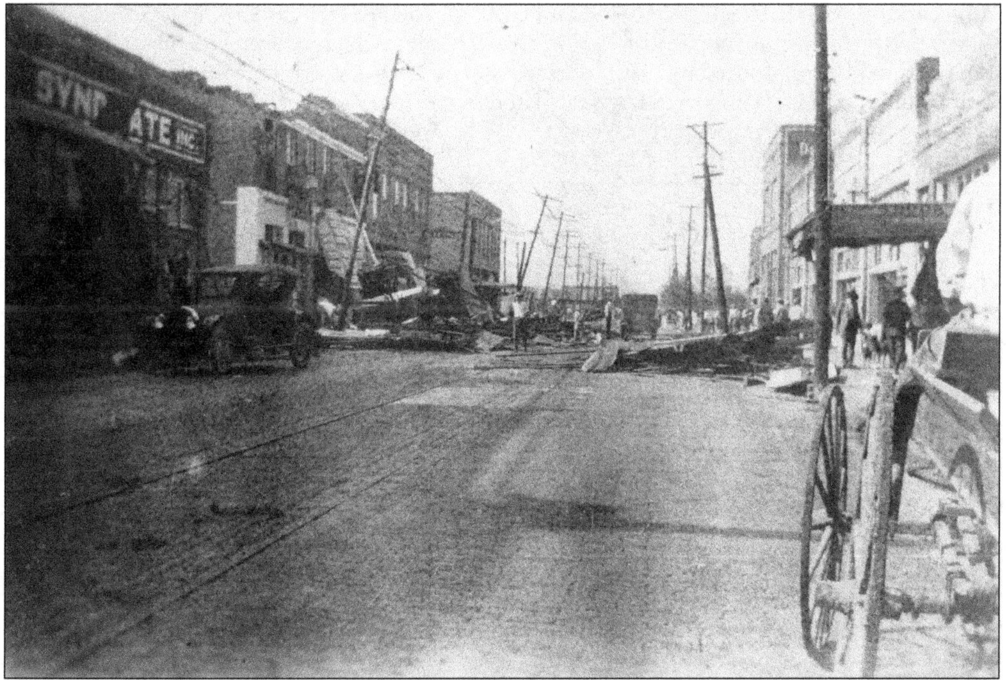

This photograph, taken two days after the August 6, 1918 hurricane, looks east on Broad Street. The storm ruined homes, damaged crops, and caused millions of dollars of damage in the milling district in North Lake Charles. After the most severe period of the storm, a fire erupted in one of the mills and spread throughout the district, destroying seven mills.

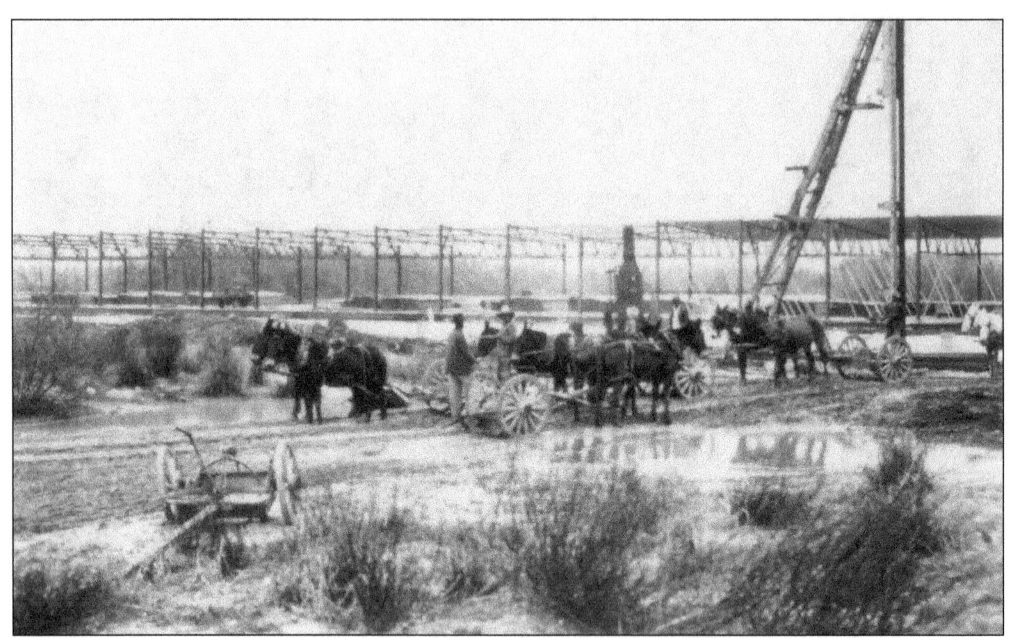

The hurricane of 1918 devastated the city the same year as the infamous influenza epidemic. Many left the area, never to return. As the timber industry faded, many timber towns in Louisiana virtually disappeared. To avoid a similar fate, Lake Charles business leaders decided to bring in business by improving the waterways. The community voted in bonds to deepen the small Intracoastal Canal, between the Sabine and the Calcasieu Rivers, into a ship channel, and to build a port, which is under construction in the 1920 photograph above. The first ocean-going ship (pictured below) docked in 1926. In 1938, Congress authorized the 34-mile direct channel to the Gulf, which was completed five years later and attracted the petrochemical industry that surrounds the waterways today. (Both courtesy of Jeanne Owens of Vintage Arts; photographs by David H. Levingston.)

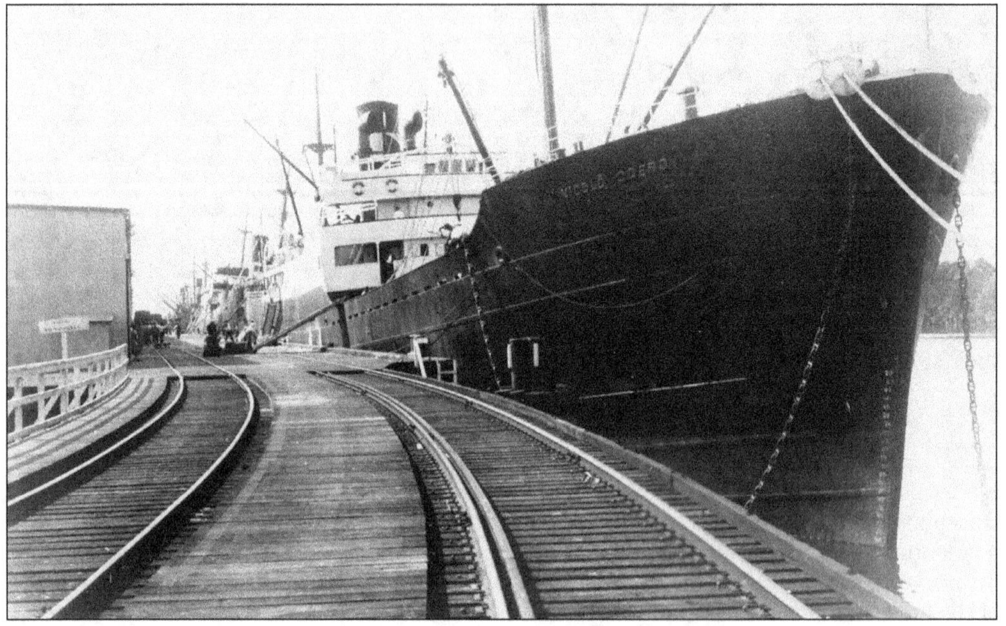

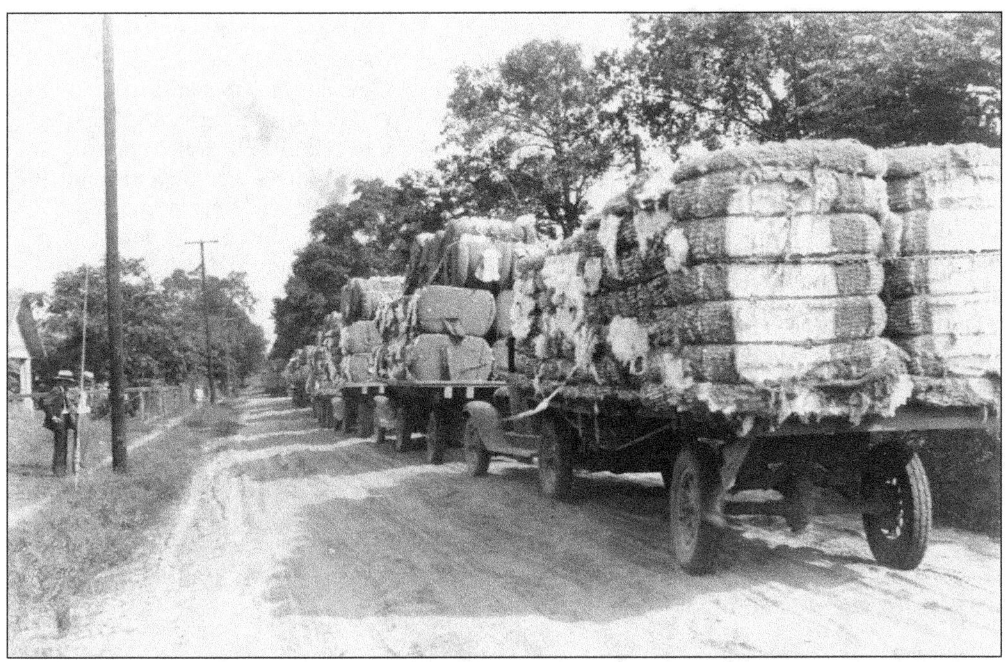

To advertise its shipping capacity, the port boasted in 1927 on its fourth birthday that it would ship 10,000 bales of cotton. However, more cotton showed up than could be handled; here, trucks line up to deliver bales of cotton to the port. (Courtesy of Jeanne Owens of Vintage Arts; photograph by David H. Levingston.)

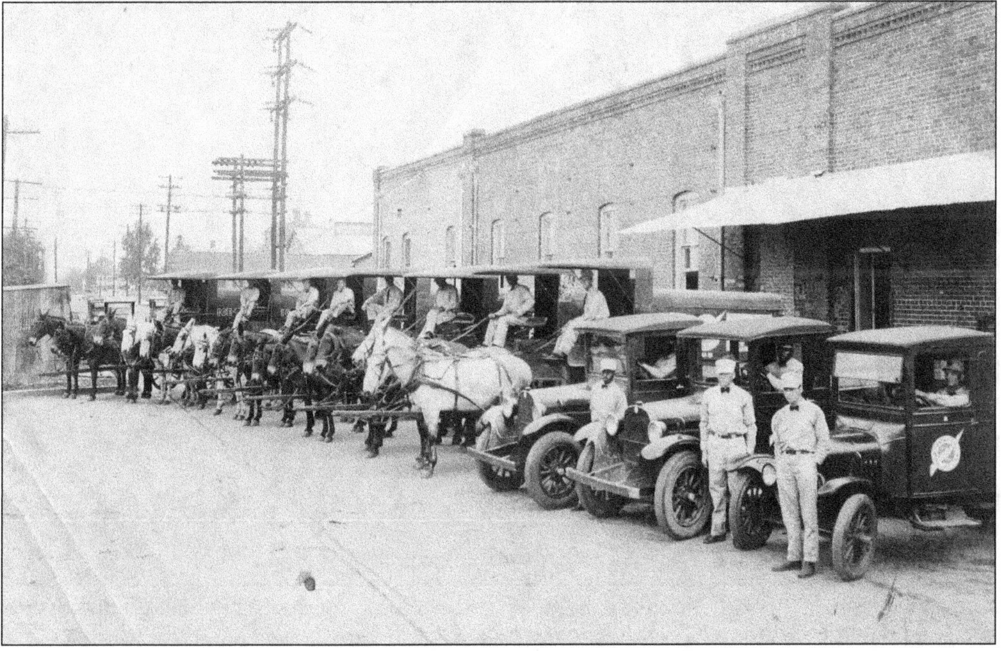

This 1929 photograph shows the employees and vehicle fleet of Gulf States Utility Company in front of the downtown power station. In addition to furnishing electricity and water to Lake Charles homes, Gulf States ran an ice delivery service. During the early 20th century, consumers could purchase refrigerators and other appliances at the company's showroom.

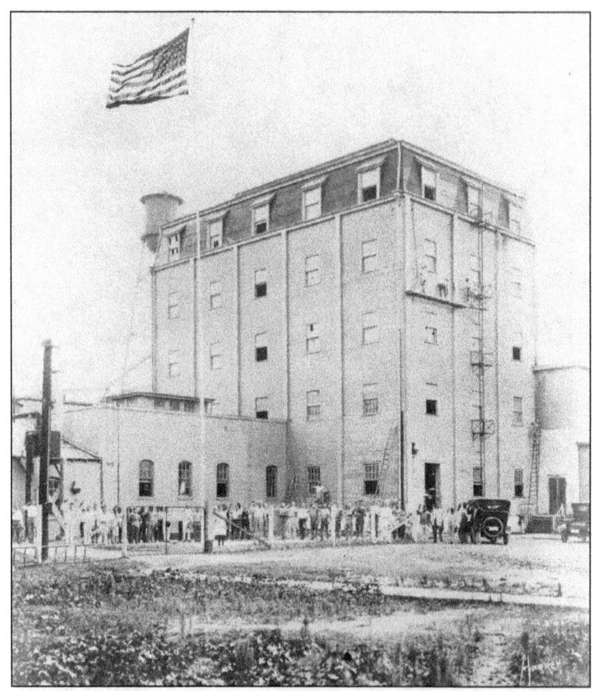

This is the original building of the Lake Charles Rice Milling Company, located at the north end of Kirkman Street, in 1920. Created in 1892, it became the world's largest complete rice mill and pioneered improvements in milling techniques. A devastating fire destroyed the mill in 1924, but the rice industry was so important to Lake Charles that it was quickly rebuilt. Another fire struck in 1984, causing the facilities to close permanently.

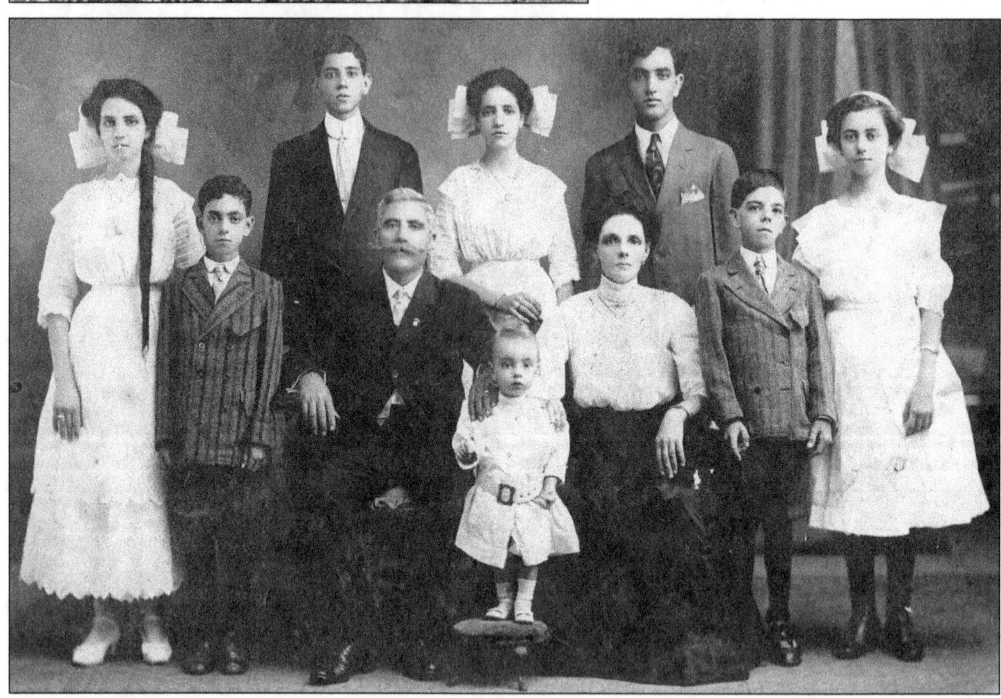

Many immigrants from Catholic areas of Europe found a home in southwest Louisiana. The DiCarlo family, pictured here around 1925, like many Italian immigrants, opened one of the area's first Italian restaurants in 1946, although it served American food. It closed in 1976. Parents Antonio and Angelina DiCarlo, born in Italy, are seated with baby Evelina between them. Standing are, from left to right, Lena, Louis, Jovanni, Luccia, Castrenzi, Antonio, and Caterina. (Courtesy of Emma DiCarlo-Vincent.)

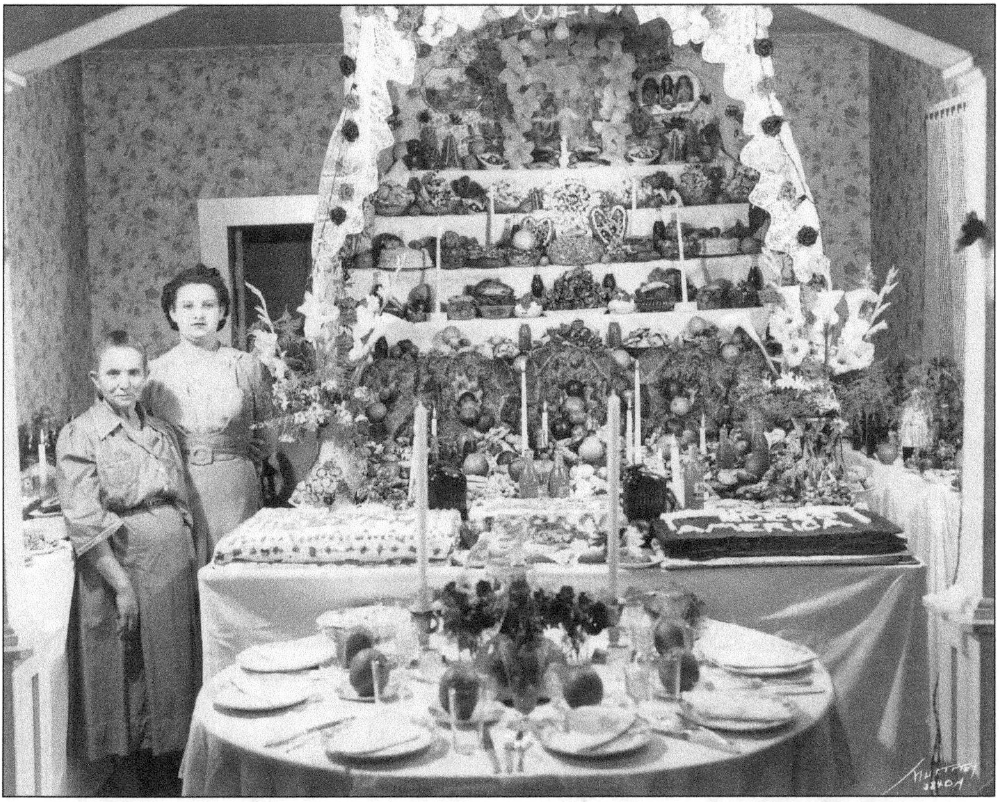

Keeping traditions alive, Italians like the Glorioso, pictured here in 1940, celebrated with a St. Joseph's altar in their home on Shattuck Street. These altars took weeks to prepare, and the food would be shared with fellow church members. The area of town on and around Belden Street included a variety of ethnicities—Lebanese, Italians, Irish, and French being the dominant ones—who preserved their traditions in organizations like the Italian-American Hall and Cedars of Lebanon club. At right, an Italian shoemaker stands outside his Lawrence Street shop in 1941.

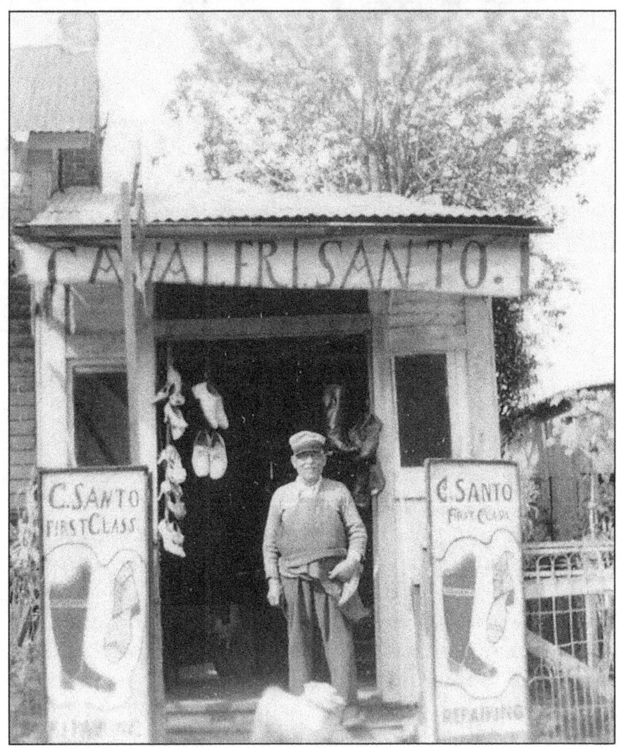

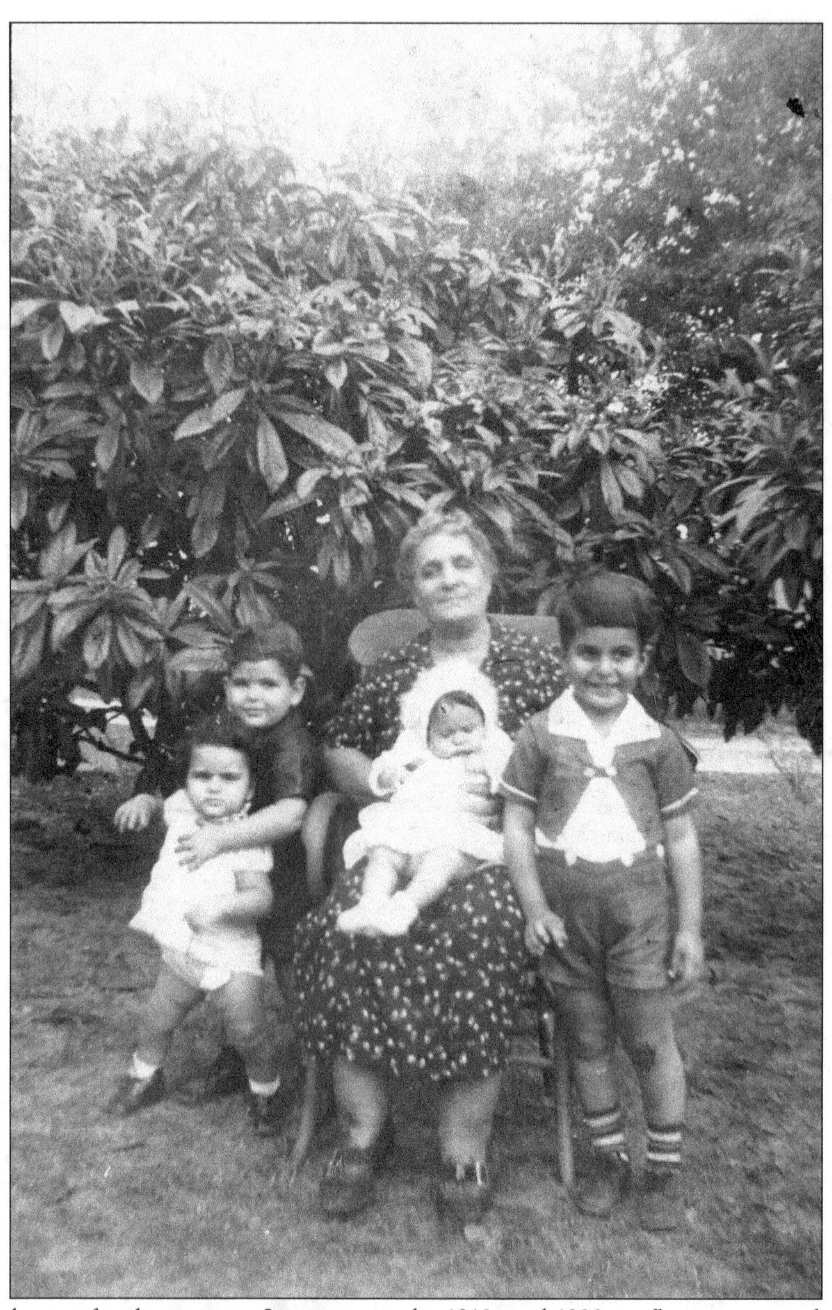

Many Lebanese families came to Louisiana in the 1910s and 1920s to flee poverty and political oppression from the Turks. Because Lebanon was previously a French protectorate, they were Christian and some spoke French, making the move to south Louisiana a relatively easy transition for them. At age 18, Philip Ieyoub came to the United States, where he met and married Virginia Khoury, whose parents had emigrated from Lebanon. In this c. 1940 image, several of their children pose with their grandmother at her home on Lake Shore Drive. Pictured are, from left to right, Ernestine and Kalil Ieyoub, Zareife Khoury (holding an unidentified cousin), and Daniel Ieyoub. Other Lebanese family names in the Lake Charles area include Abraham, George, Stoma, Saloom, and Debakey. (Courtesy of Daniel Ieyoub.)

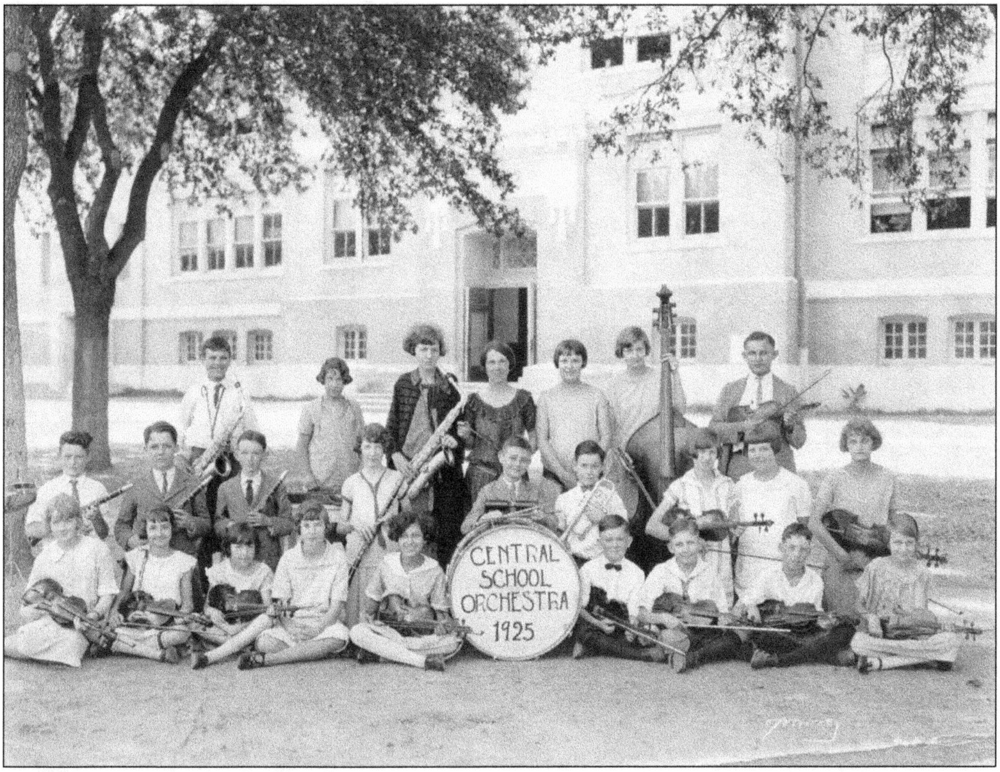

In the wake of the Great Fire, four brick schoolhouses—one for each of the four wards—were designed by the New Orleans architectural firm of Favrot and Livaudais. The largest of the four was Central School, also called Third Ward School, which opened in 1913 and is the only one that still stands. As the population of the city moved south and enrollment declined, the school board leased it to the city to be used as an arts and humanities center. This 1925 photograph shows that music has been an important facet of education throughout the school's history.

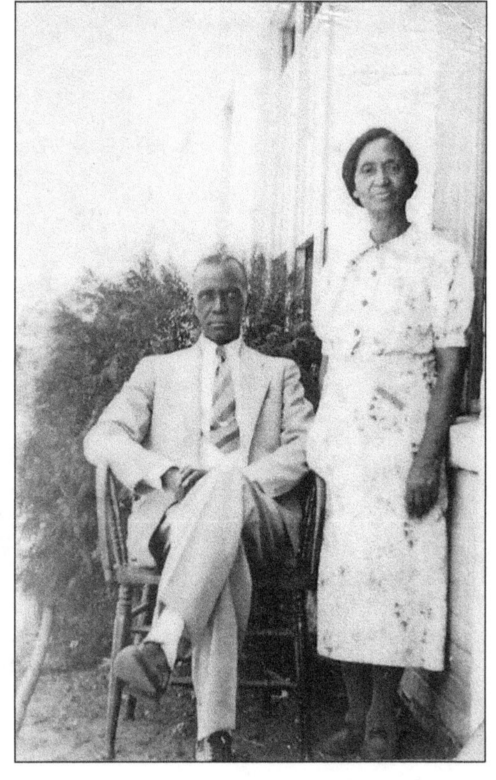

William Oscar "W.O." Boston was an African American teacher and principal at the First Ward Colored School. He completed 50 years of teaching in 1938 and is pictured with his wife, Mary, who taught school for 31 years. First Ward and Second Ward each had "colored" schools. When the buildings were destroyed in the hurricane of 1918, the African American community raised money to replace the two structures themselves.

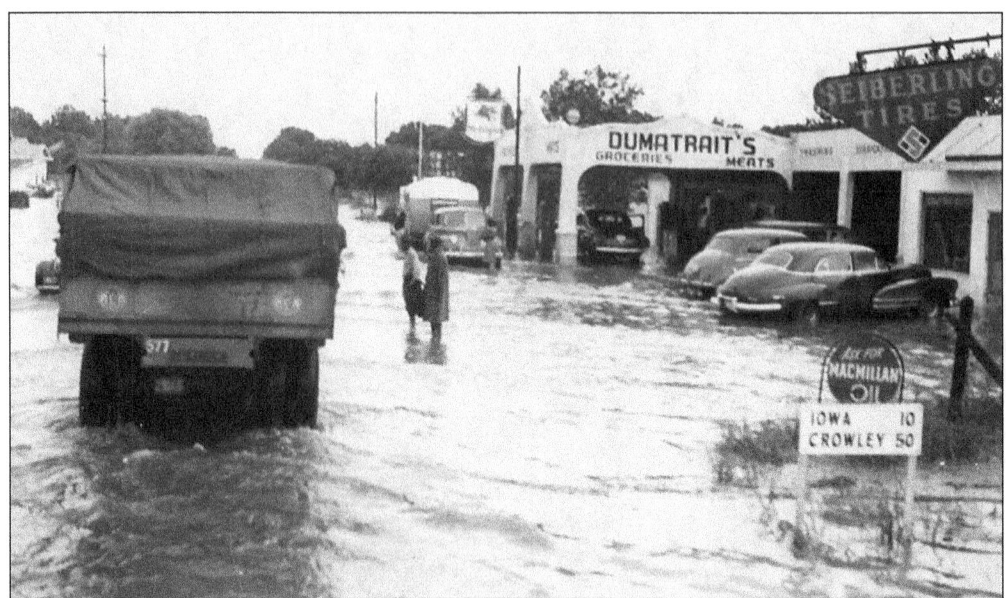

Heavy rains may cause flooding in the streets of Lake Charles, and this 1947 photograph depicts the aftermath of a particularly enormous thunderstorm. In four and a half hours, the storm left nearly 10 inches of water in Lake Charles, topping all of the bayous and coulees; the city's flood damages totaled over $250,000.

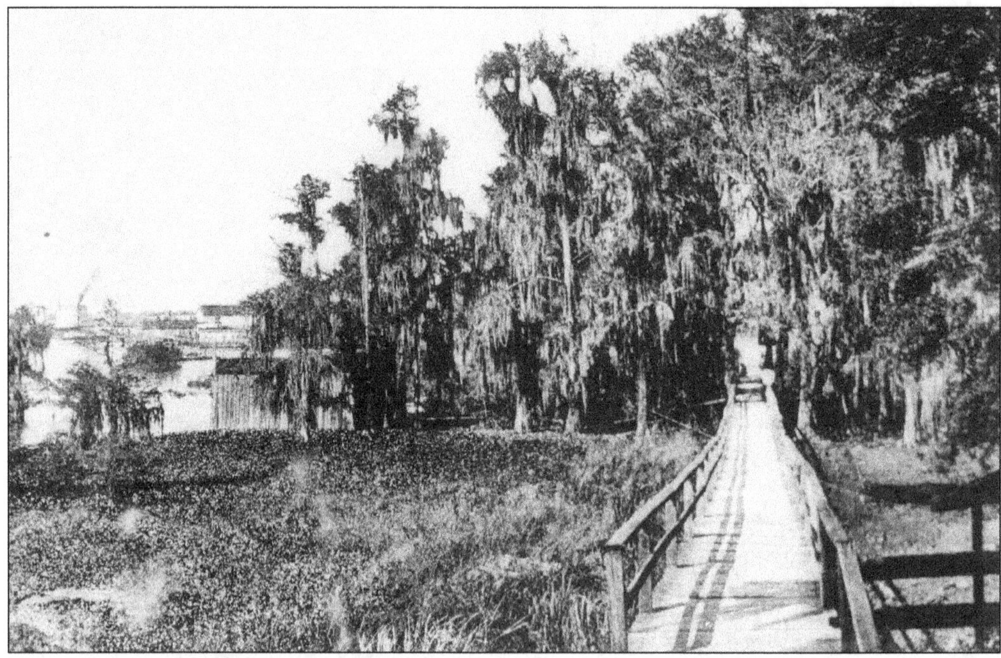

This wooden footbridge crossed the Pithon Coulee off Shell Beach Road and was a popular retreat for young couples. Initials of lovers and other amorous expressions were carved into the wooden railings of the bridge and on surrounding trees. People often crossed the bridge on their way to Walnut Grove, which was cleared decades later to make way for the Port of Lake Charles. The bridge was eventually replaced with a concrete structure. The Pithon Coulee pump house is located at this spot now.

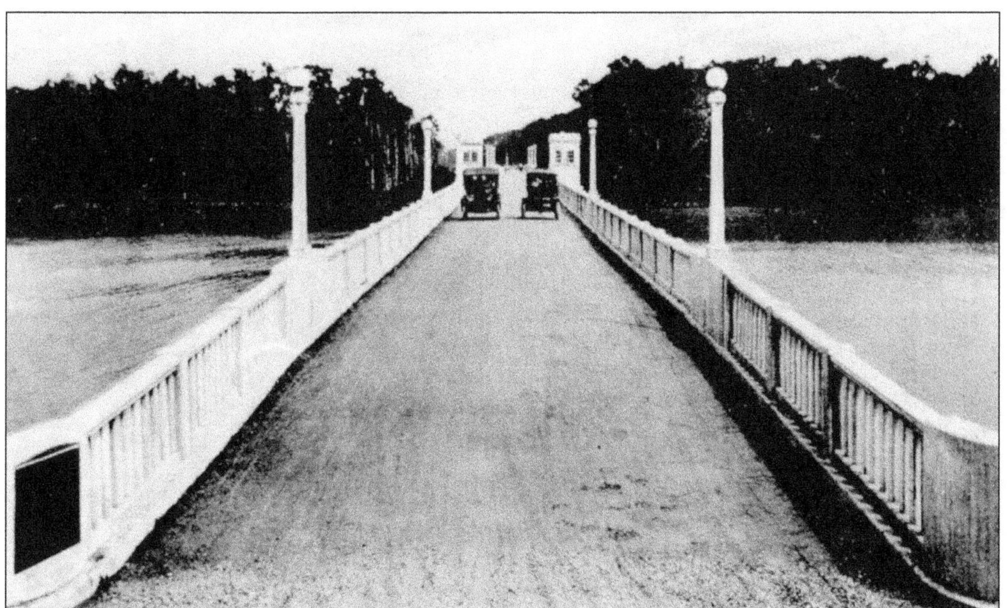

This 1929 photograph shows the original Highway 90 bridge that spanned the Calcasieu River. The bridge began at the end of Shell Beach Drive, near the current Port of Lake Charles, and led to Willow Drive, south of Westlake. Remnants of the bridge can still be seen near the Bridge Point Yacht Club in Westlake.

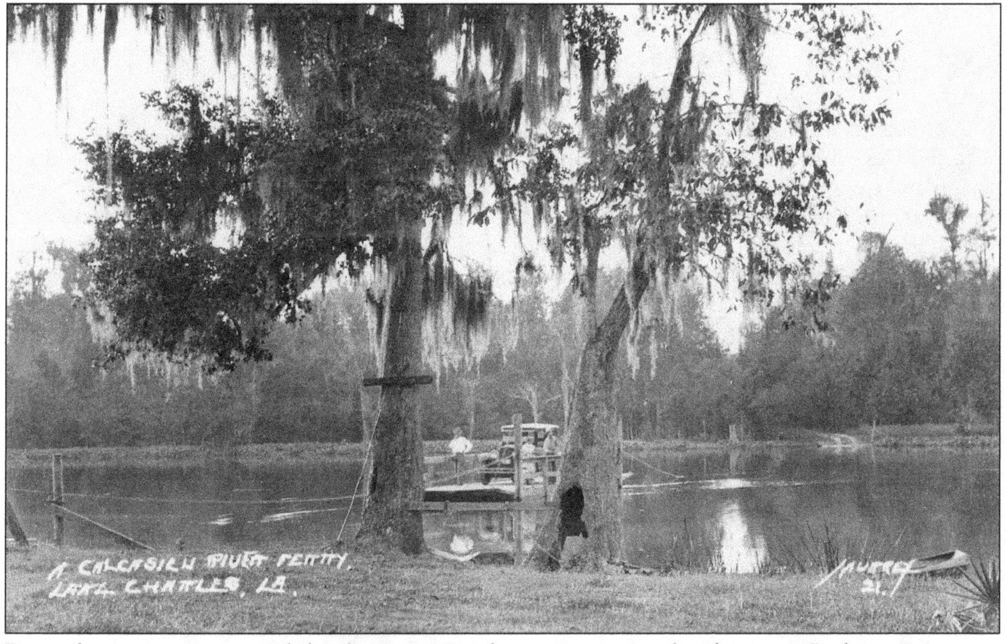

River ferries were some of the first means of transportation for the area. Perkins Ferry was established in 1817, and this 1920 photograph shows a car crossing the Calcasieu River on the ferry. The cypress trees with Spanish moss were common along the riverbanks.

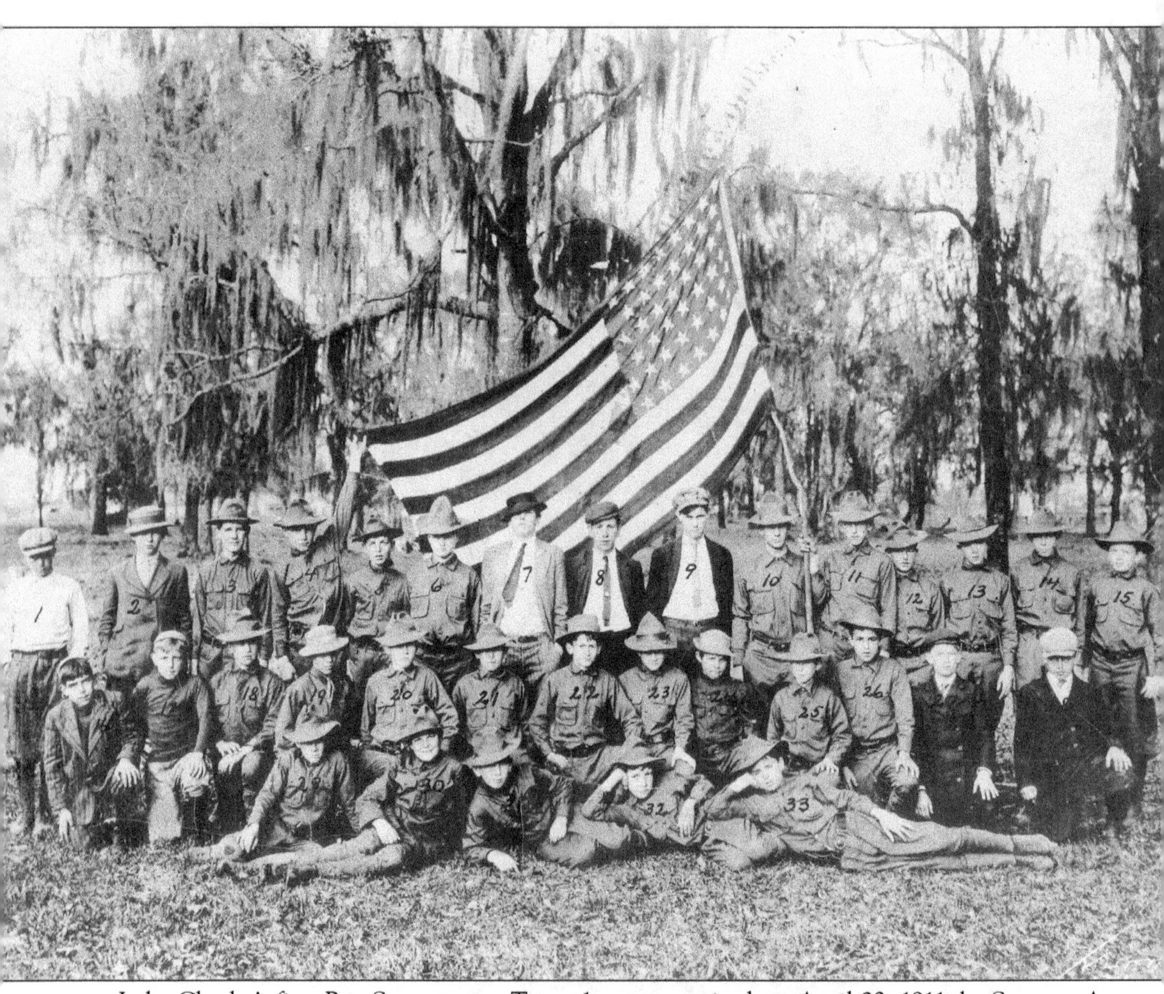

Lake Charles's first Boy Scout troop, Troop 1, was organized on April 23, 1911, by Seaman A. Knapp and the northern Methodist church (later Simpson Methodist). The original Boy Scout camp was on 27 acres near Prien Lake. One of the oldest Boy Scout troops west of the Mississippi River, Troop 1 celebrated its 100th anniversary in 2011. Pictured here in 1912 are: 1. Clarence Lalanne, 2. William Stewart, 3. Francis Lawler, 4. Henry (Harry) G. Chalkley, 5. Allie Jackson, 6. H. Moss Watkins, 7. Rudolph Lake, 8. Sim Shattuck, 9. Elmer Gunn, 10. Scoutmaster Seaman A. Mayo, 11. Martin Ryan, 12. Alfred E. Roberts, 13. Lisle Peters, 14. Joe Gaunt, 15. Earl McCain, 16. Lamar Cunningham, 17. Rudolph E. Krause, 18. Ralph W. Peyton, 19. Sherdie Jones, 20. Carol Hiscock, 21. John W. Cox, 22. Curtis Hickman, 23. Henry Goodman, 24. John Tuttle, 25. Eugene Wilcox, 26. Sam Kushner, 27. George Haar, 28. Ed Bluestein, 29. Dudley Pipes, 30. Frank Edwards, 31. Sol Cohn, 32. Claude Morris, and 33. Carl Bendixon.

Five

Growth and Change in the 20th Century

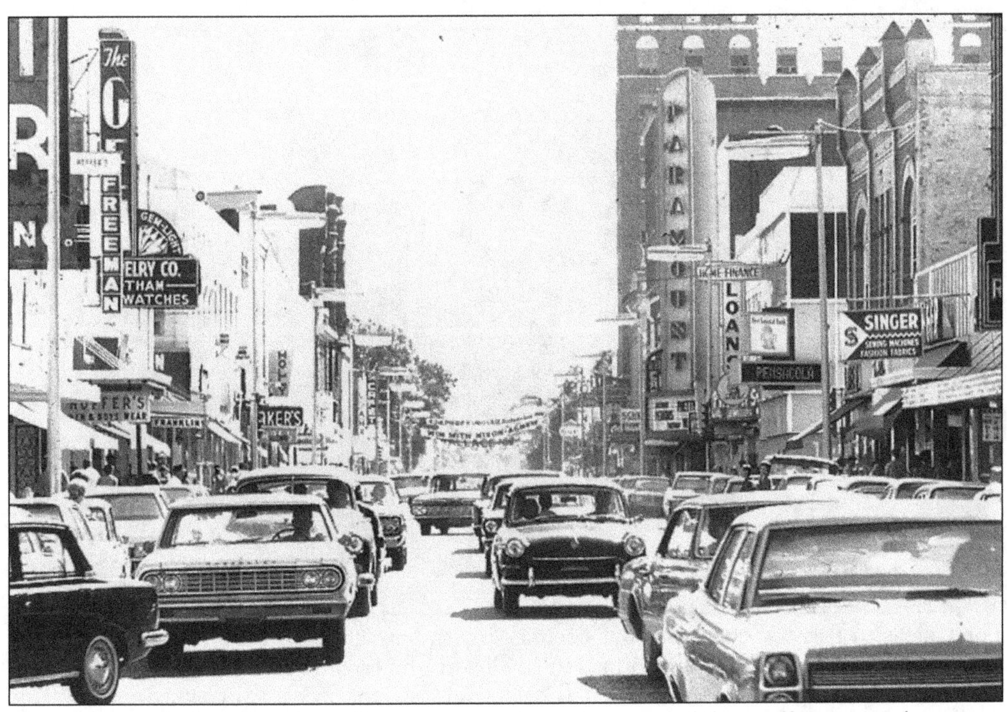

This photograph shows how Ryan Street was transformed as automobiles, traffic jams, and on-street parking replaced the streetcars and pedestrians shown in earlier images. Businesses include the Paramount Movie Theatre, Baker's Shoes, and Singer. The banner across Ryan Street reads "Win with Nixon & Agnew," indicating that the photograph was probably taken in 1968.

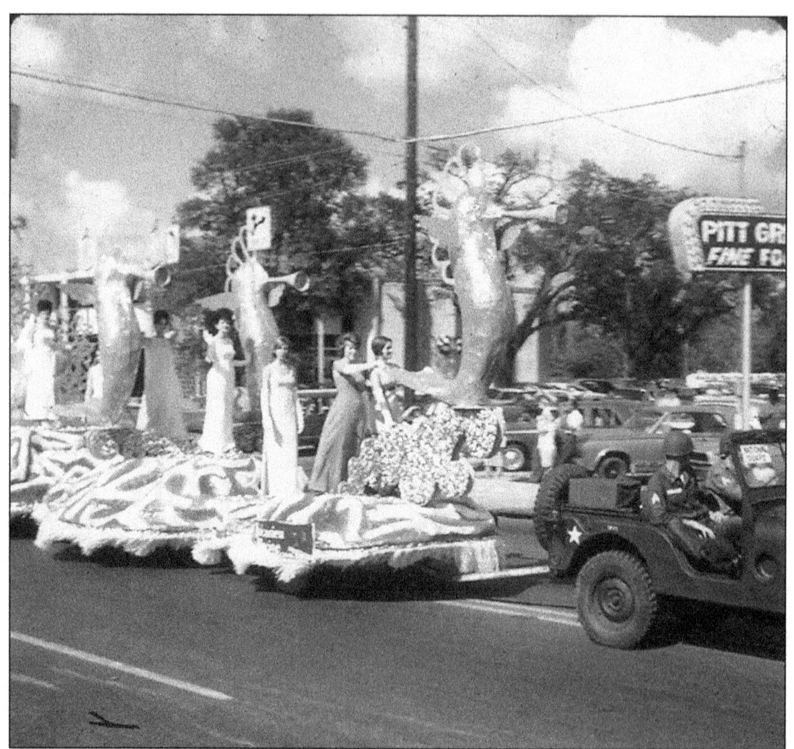

Lake Charles celebrated its 100th anniversary as an incorporated town with a huge parade that rolled down Ryan Street on April 23, 1967. The Rodeo Queen, the Rice Queen, Miss Lake Charles, and several others stand on one of many locally made floats. Festivities celebrating this milestone went on for more than a week.

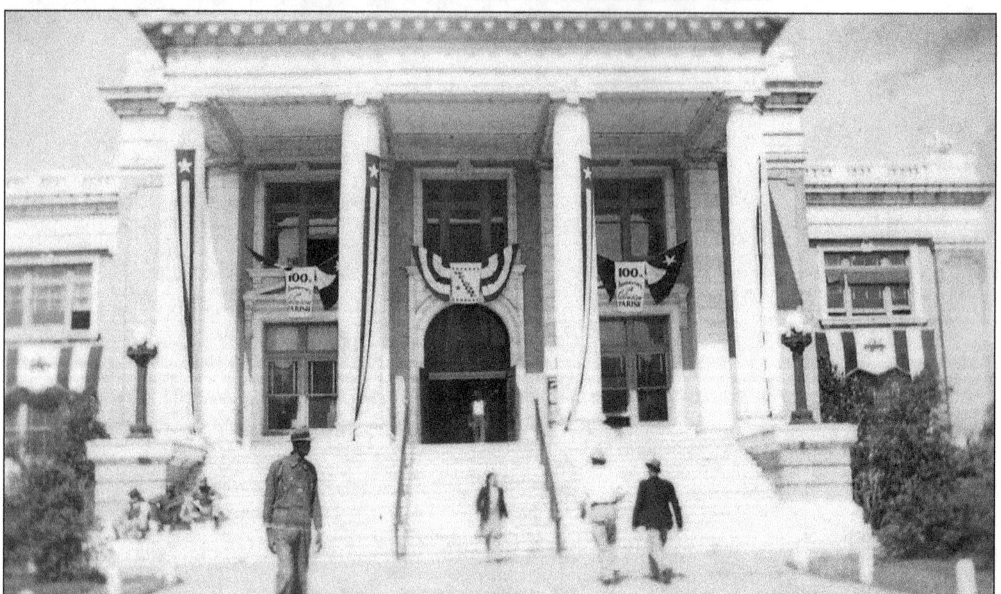

The Calcasieu Parish Courthouse was decorated with banners in 1940 to celebrate its 100th anniversary. Calcasieu Parish was formed in 1840, with the original parish seat being Marion, a town located in the path of the trail from Texas to New Orleans. Jacob Ryan owned a sawmill on the bank of Lake Charles between what is now Broad and Pujo Streets. He began the discussion of moving the parish seat to Lake Charles because he saw the economic potential of the growing settlement. He succeeded in 1852 in getting the approval of the state authorities, who said they didn't care where the seat of justice was placed if it did not involve any expense to the state.

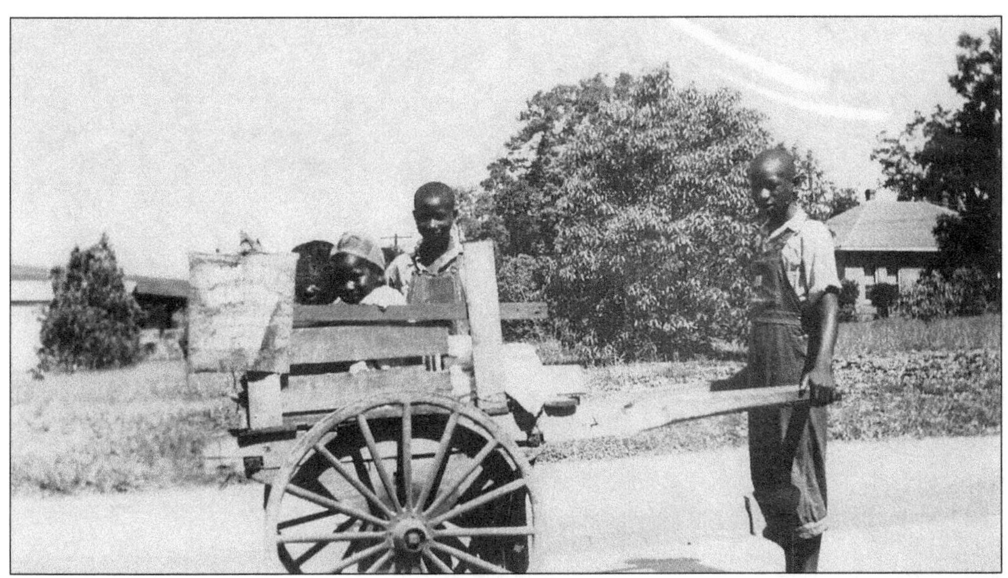

These boys are on their way to the new Calcasieu Parish Health Unit, located on Kirkman Street, in 1942. The health unit was established during World War II at the urging of the federal government, which provided matching funds. The Army was concerned about public health problems, such as outbreaks of epidemic diseases that might accompany the hundreds of thousands of soldiers moving into the area's bases. At the time, Lake Charles was the only large city in the state with no public health unit, and Calcasieu Parish was one of only three parishes west of the Mississippi without a unit.

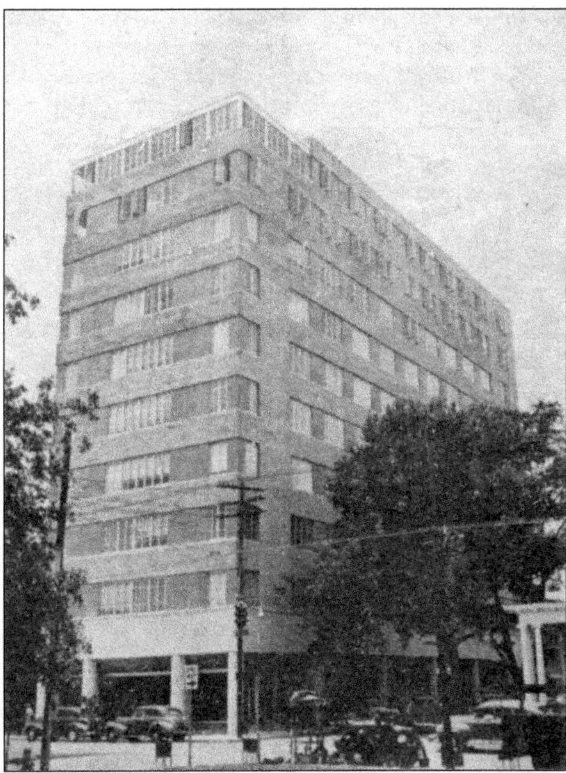

Now used as Lake Charles's city hall, the Pioneer Building was erected in 1949 on the site of the former Leveque home on the southwest corner of Pujo and Bilbo Streets. The 140-foot-high office building included such architectural marvels as two Otis elevators, an air-conditioning system, and all-aluminum folding windows (replaced with more energy efficient windows in 2011). In 2006, the Calcasieu Parish Historical Preservation Society presented the building with a Landmark Award.

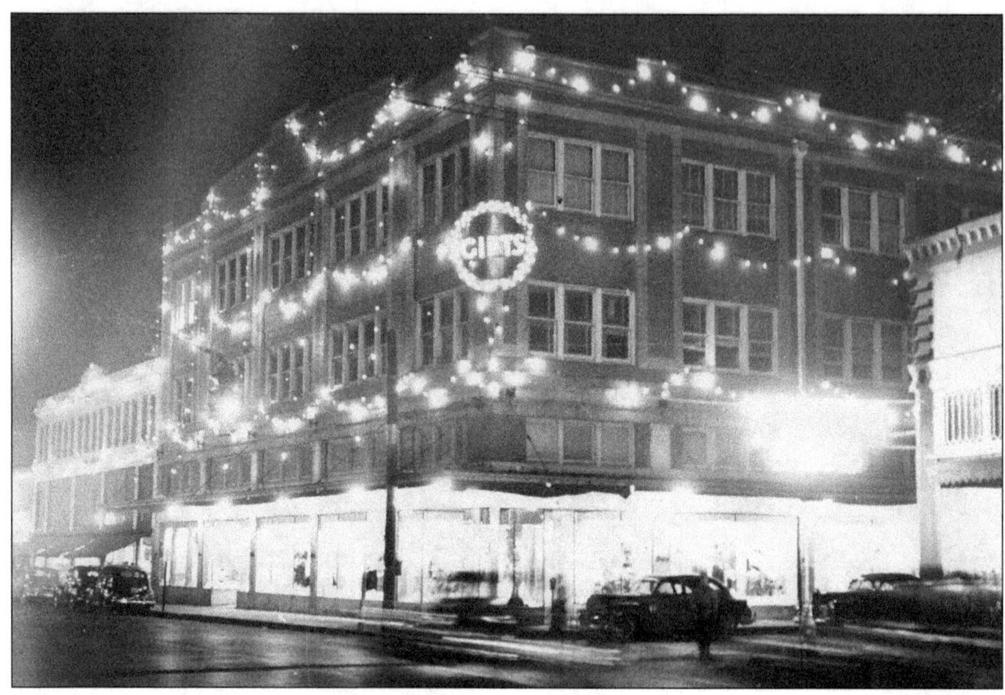

This 1949 photograph shows Muller's department store decorated at Christmastime. Located at the corner of Ryan and Division Streets for more than 104 years, the store opened at this location in 1890. Julie Marx Muller originally opened the store as a hat shop in 1882 after the death of her husband to help support herself and her two children. Primarily serving lumbermen and agricultural workers, Muller's was the largest department store between New Orleans and Houston. The escalator was the first in the city, and many shoppers came to the store just to ride it. In 2007, it reopened as loft apartments as part of the downtown revitalization efforts of Tom Shearman III.

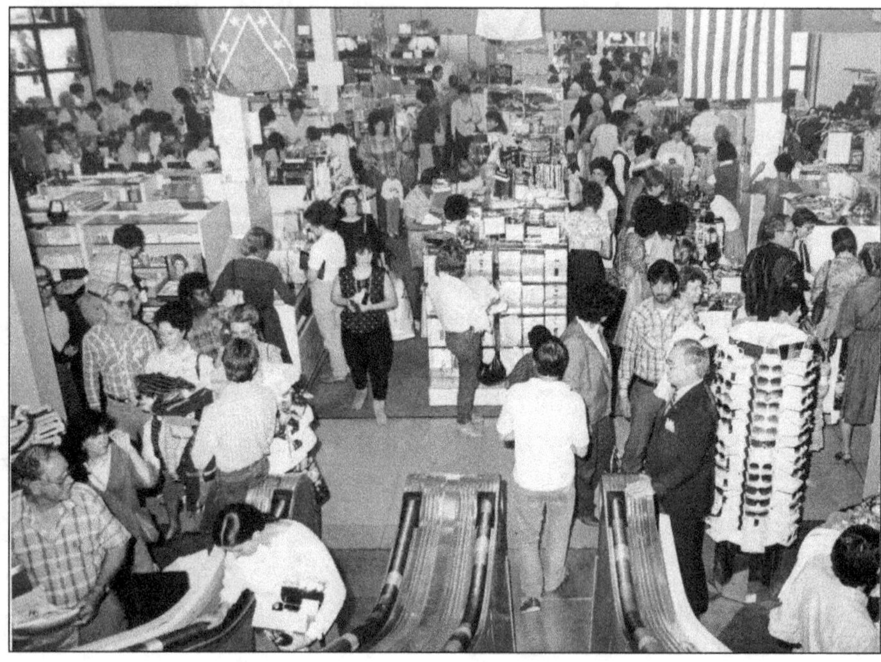

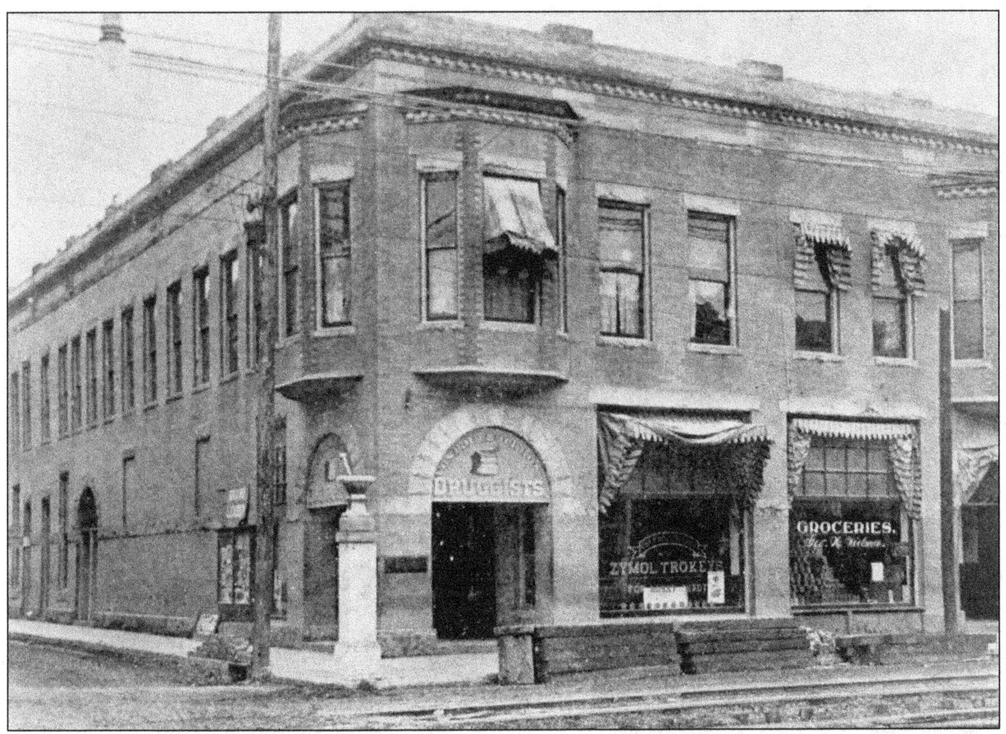

Since it was built in the late 1800s, this building at the corner of Ryan and Pujo Streets has been one of the most desirable business locations in the city. Erected by A.H. Moss, it contained the original Lake Charles Drug Store before Frank Von Phul and S.W. Gordon, druggists, purchased the store in 1899. In 1914, Gordon bought Von Phul's share of the business. The building survived the Great Fire of 1910 and currently houses Pujo Street Cafe.

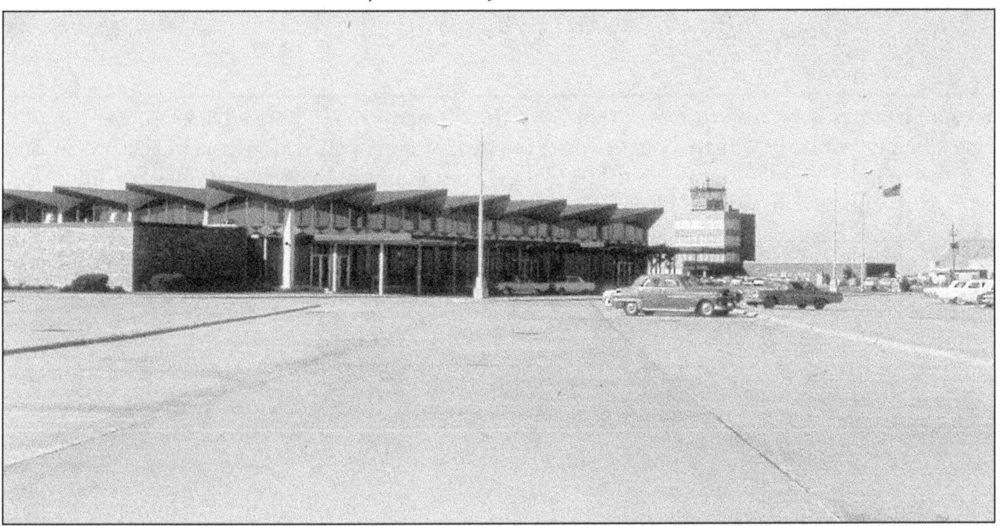

Lake Charles Regional Airport began operations in 1961 with commercial air service, provided by Continental and American Airlines, to more than 180,000 residents of Southwest Louisiana. The original facility (pictured) was destroyed during Hurricane Rita in 2005. A new $2.7 million airport opened in 2009, with funding provided by FEMA. The airport also includes a 300-acre industrial park that leases space to businesses and individuals.

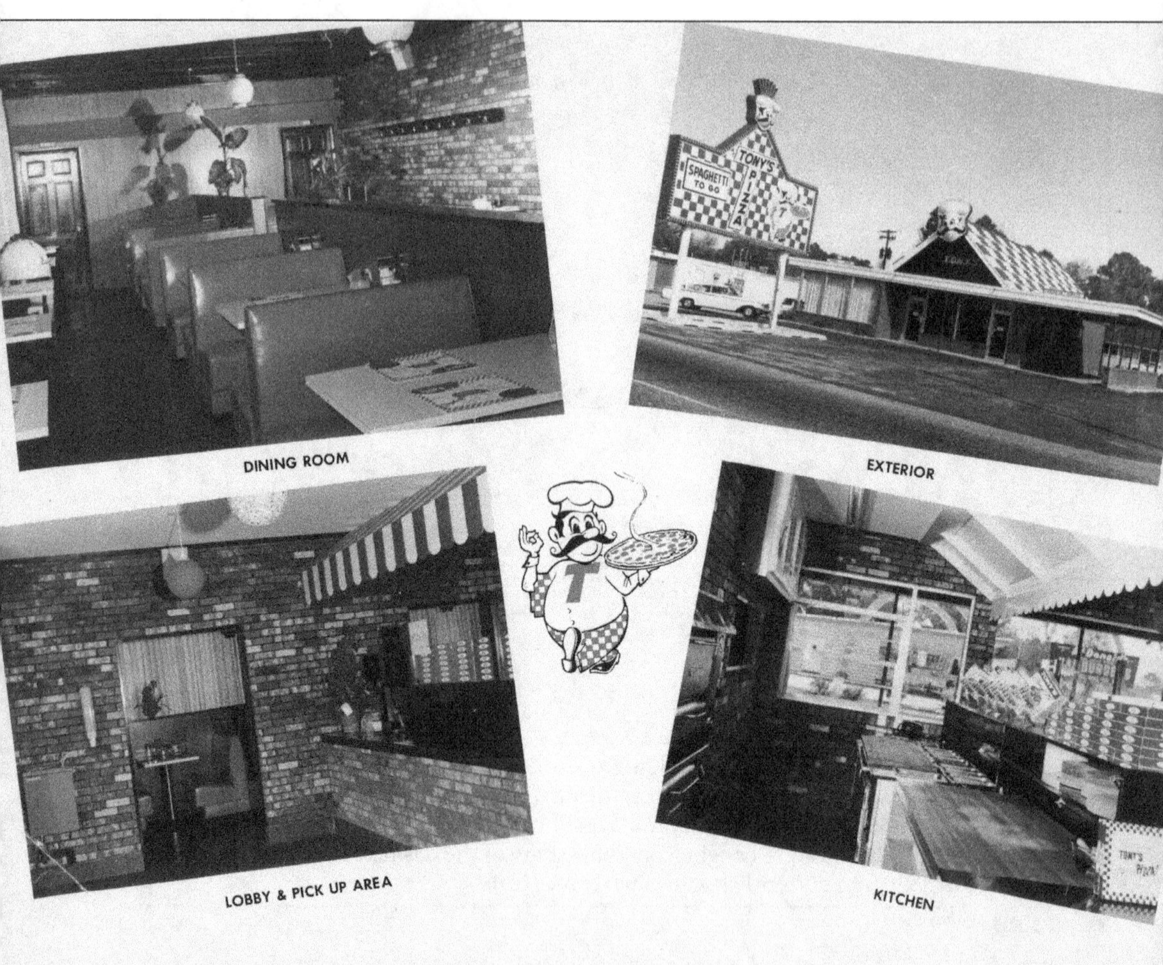

Tony's Pizza has been a fixture on Prien Lake Road since 1968. Charles Dickson, the son of a Greek immigrant businessman, bought Tony's one year after it opened. Tony's was Dickson's second business in Lake Charles; he operated The Galley, a restaurant in Recreation Lanes Bowling Alley on First Avenue, from 1957 to 1968. These photographs show Tony's as it looked when Dickson purchased the business in 1969. (Courtesy of Charles Dickson.)

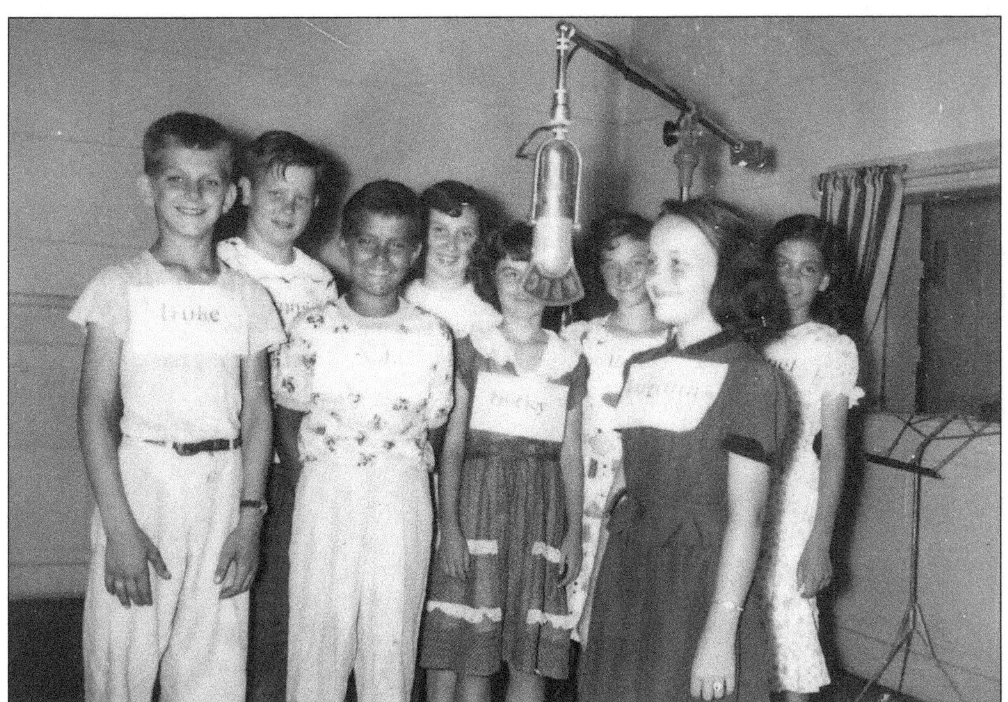

Calcasieu Broadcasting Company opened Lake Charles's first radio station, KPLC-AM, on April 26, 1935. The young station joined NBC as an affiliate on August 15, 1945, and expanded into television in the summer of 1954. The 1951 photograph above, of Lake Charles fifth graders from Second Ward School, shows the interior of a sound booth in the KPLC-AM studio. The photograph below shows an anchorman at the KPLC-TV news desk in the 1970s.

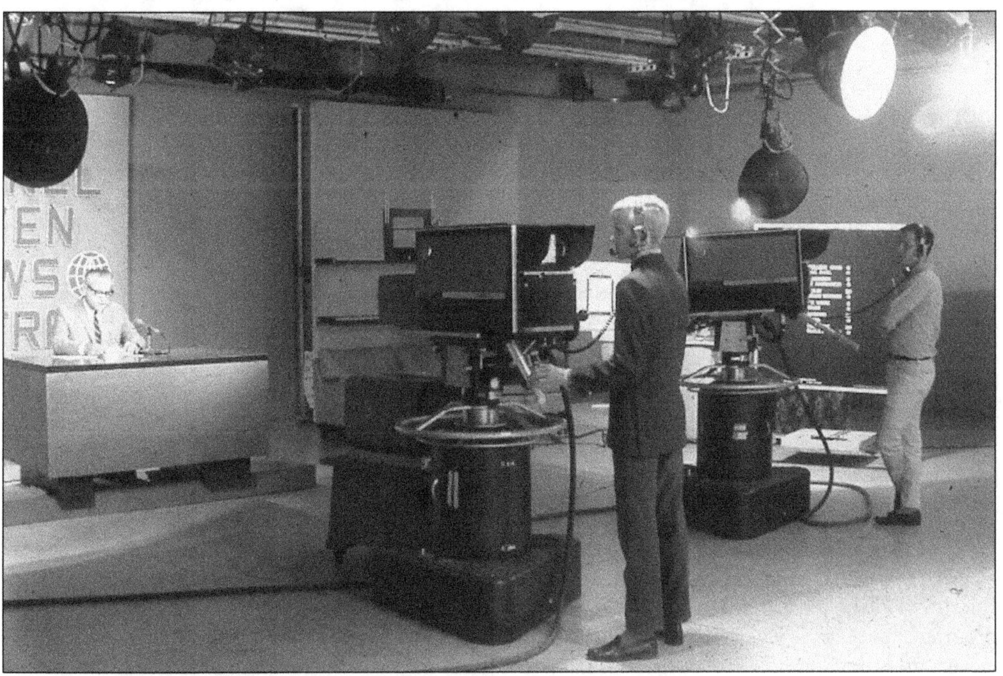

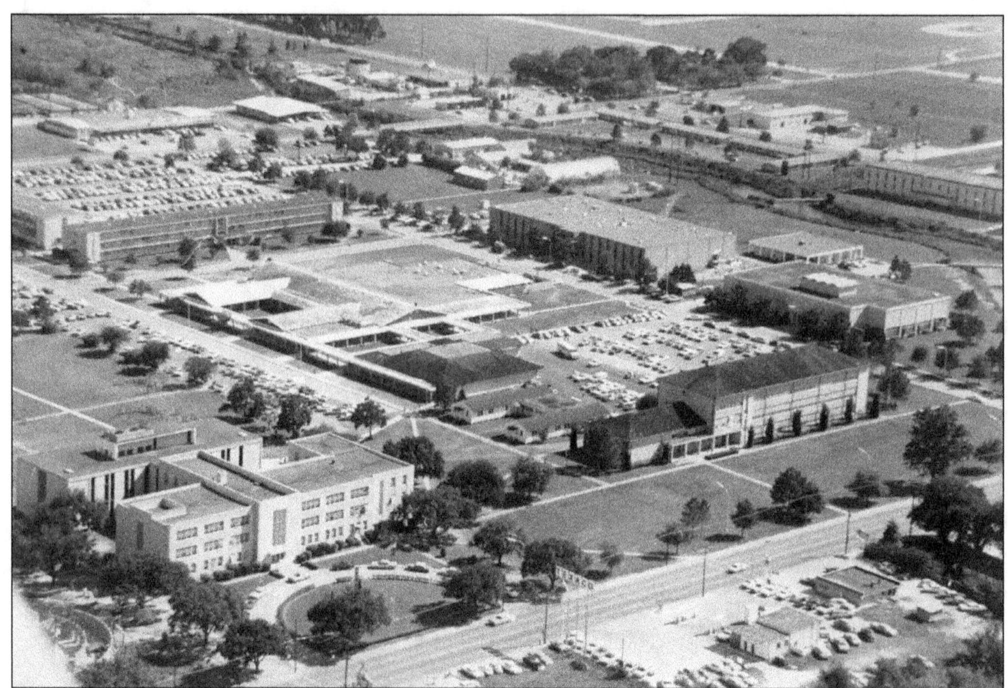

This 1960s aerial view of the McNeese campus shows the original Kaufman Hall building at lower left, with Frasch Hall (the science building) to the right. Kaufman Hall originally housed all of the school's administrative offices and classrooms. The building was named for Leopold Kaufman (see chapter one); his son, E.R. Kaufman, was one of the local citizens who supported the establishment of the college in the 1930s. Frazar Library, built in 1961, is visible at right, across the street from Frasch Hall.

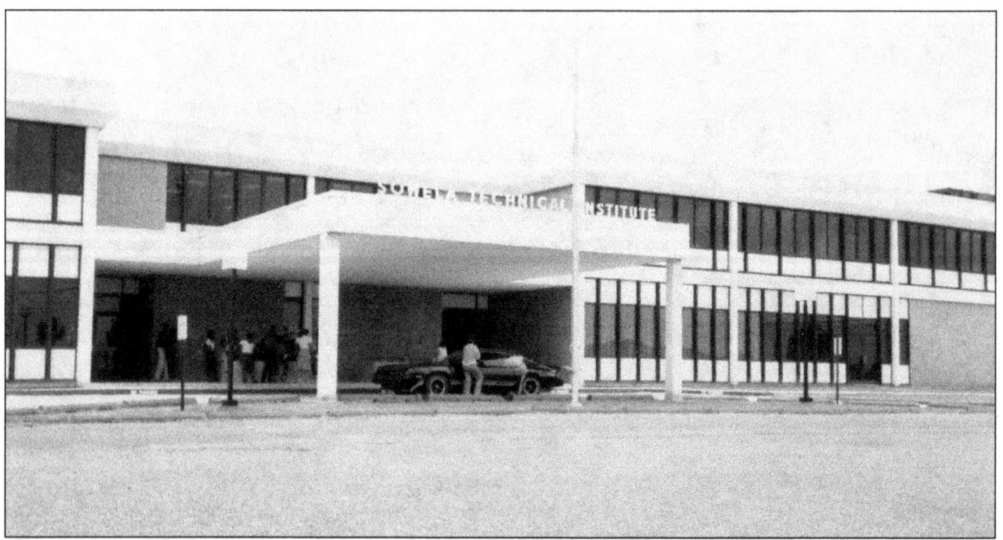

Established in 1938 as the Southwest Louisiana Trade School, this school changed its name to Sowela Technical Institute in 1962. Originally located on Broad Street, it moved to new facilities (pictured) at the old Chennault Air Force Base in 1977 in order to facilitate its aviation technology program. In 2003, it was renamed Sowela Technical Community College. Sowela is among the largest and most progressive post-secondary technical colleges in the state today.

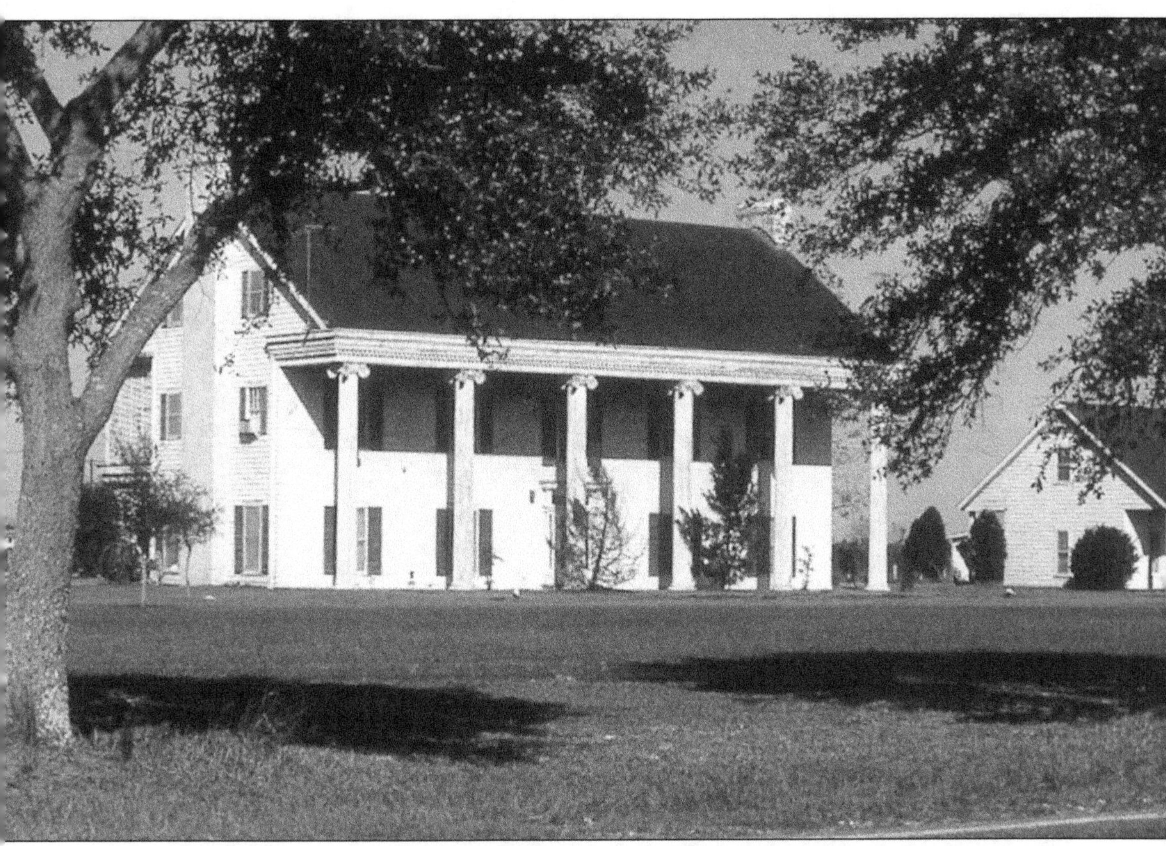

The Boys Village Home is pictured here in 1951. This building was the two-story Bel home erected by Dr. A.H. Moss in the 1880s and bought by Albert Bel in the 1890s. Boys Village was founded in 1947 by a group of local businessmen as a home for underprivileged boys. Located on US 90 East, the camp was comprised of cottages, an administration building, a chapel, a gymnasium, staff cabins, and other structures.

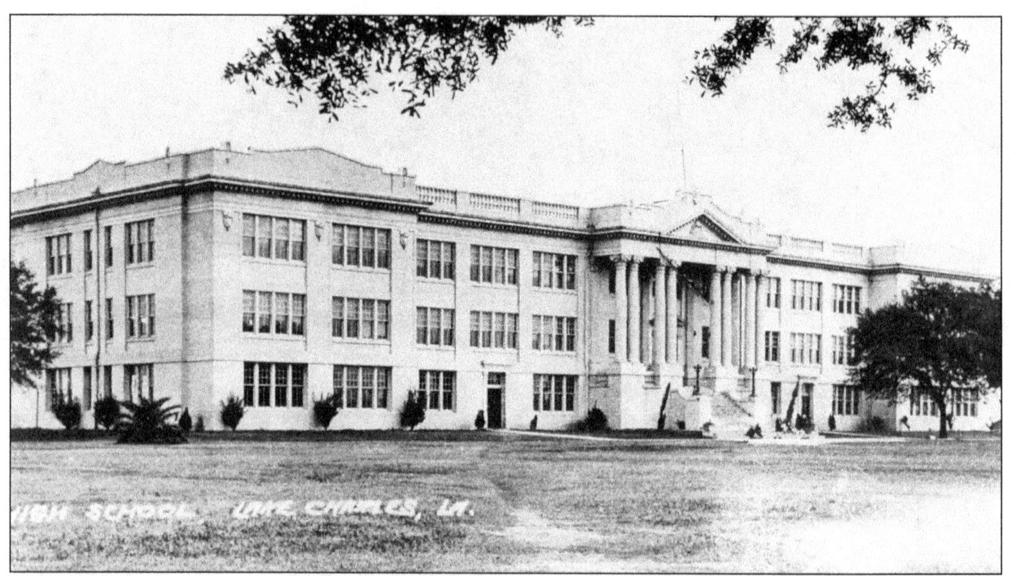

Lake Charles High School opened in 1890 as Lake Charles Central and High School. In 1893, city superintendent John McNeese divided it into two schools. The school was first annexed to a site at Central School in 1895; it was moved to Enterprise Boulevard in 1903 and remained there until 1983, when the school board merged Lake Charles High School and W.O. Boston High School to form Lake Charles–Boston High School. This photograph shows Lake Charles High School in 1930.

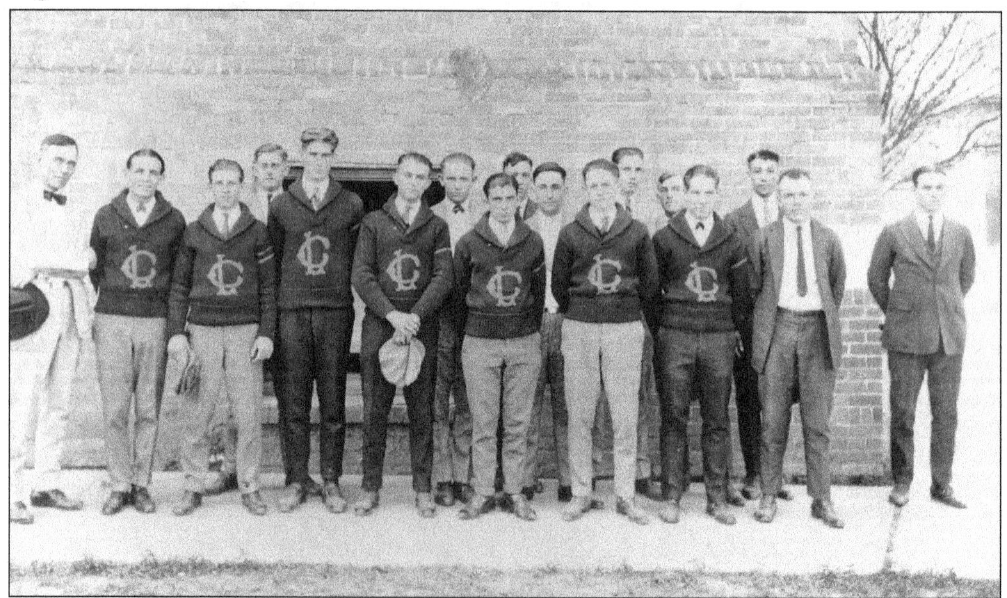

Lake Charles High School supported a variety of sports teams through the years, including football, basketball, baseball, golf, track, and boxing. The Wildcats particularly excelled in football, winning several championships. Pictured in this 1922 image are, from left to right, Principal Carson, Douglas Dunning, Pete Phillips, Frank Blackburn, Kirkland Ratcliff, Holly Hebert, Dale Lemon, Joe Terranova, Ab Nevils, Oliver Moss, Bill Fisher, Emile Winterhalter, Walter Reeves, Joe Fountain, Gyte Tritico, Coach Johnson, and William Shaddock. (Courtesy of Carolyn Woosley.)

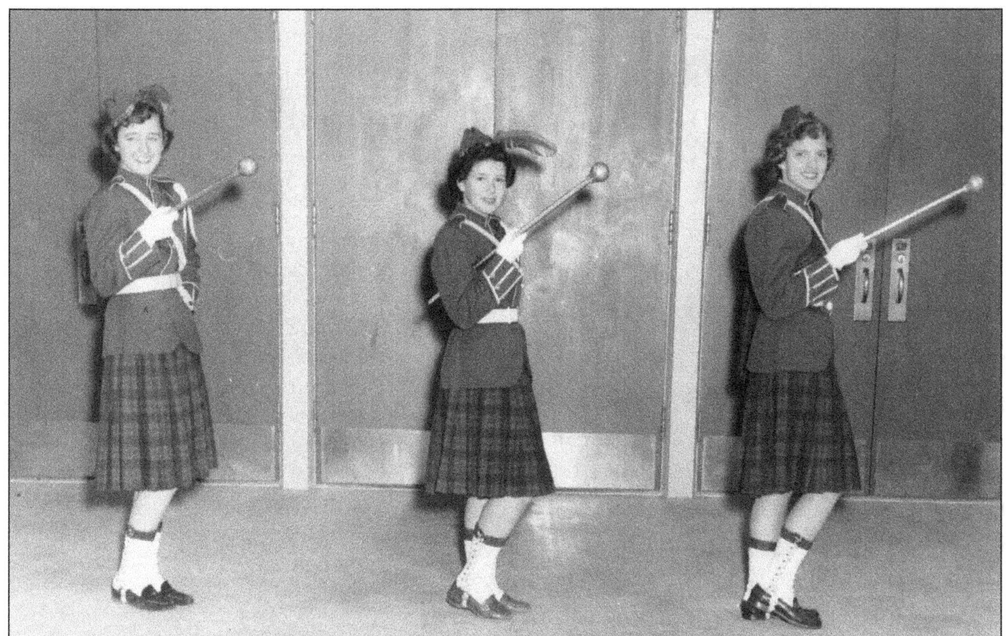

In 1939, Lake Charles High School organized a girls' precision drill team at the urging of principal G.W. Ford. Adopting a Scottish motif, they became the Kilties, an organization that lasted until 1983. In addition to marching at football games and in parades, the girls also performed community service. Under the longtime direction of legendary LCHS faculty members Iris Murphy and Lucille Leaton, the Kilties won many awards. Pictured here from left to right are colonels Patsy Boudreaux (Calhoun), Kay Krause (Blake), and Le Ann Horn (Greer), class of 1952.

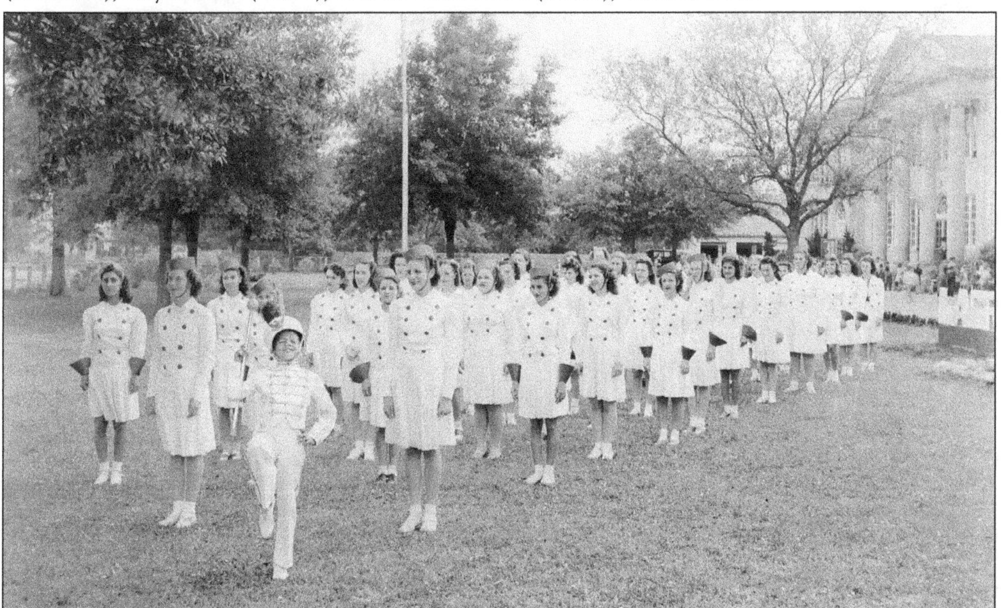

La Grange Royale Gatorettes pose for a yearbook photograph in front of the high school in 1942. In 1903, Mesant La Grange donated land for the school on South Street (now Ryan Street). Calcasieu Parish built a new high school in 1929, and it was destroyed by fire in 1931 because of a chemistry laboratory accident. The school was quickly rebuilt exactly as it was before the fire.

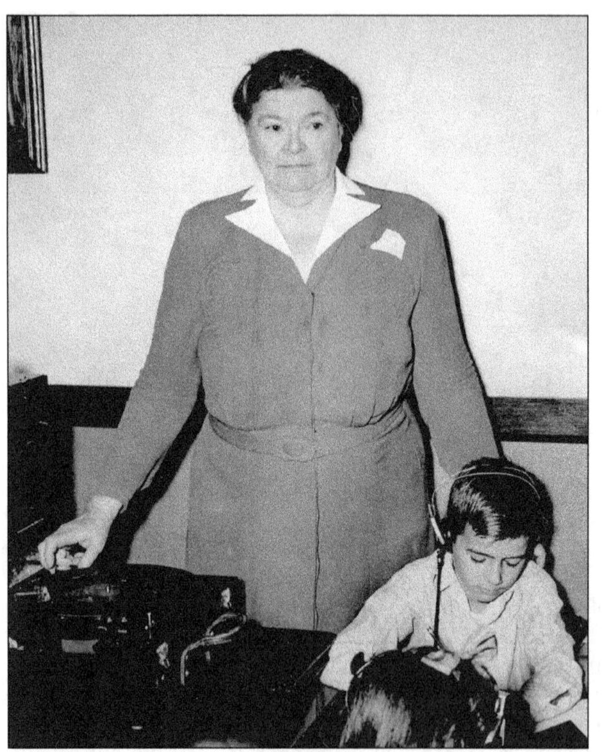

School nurse Maude Reid conducts hearing tests for a Central School student using an audiometer in 1938. In 1952, Reid ended her career as a school nurse and teacher of home nursing for Lake Charles City school system after 30 years of service. Reid left behind scrapbooks that document much of the history of Lake Charles, which are now housed in the Frazar Memorial Library archives. The Calcasieu Parish Public Library retains ownership of the Maude Reid Scrapbooks, which are under indefinite loan to the McNeese Archives and Special Collections in Frazar Memorial Library.

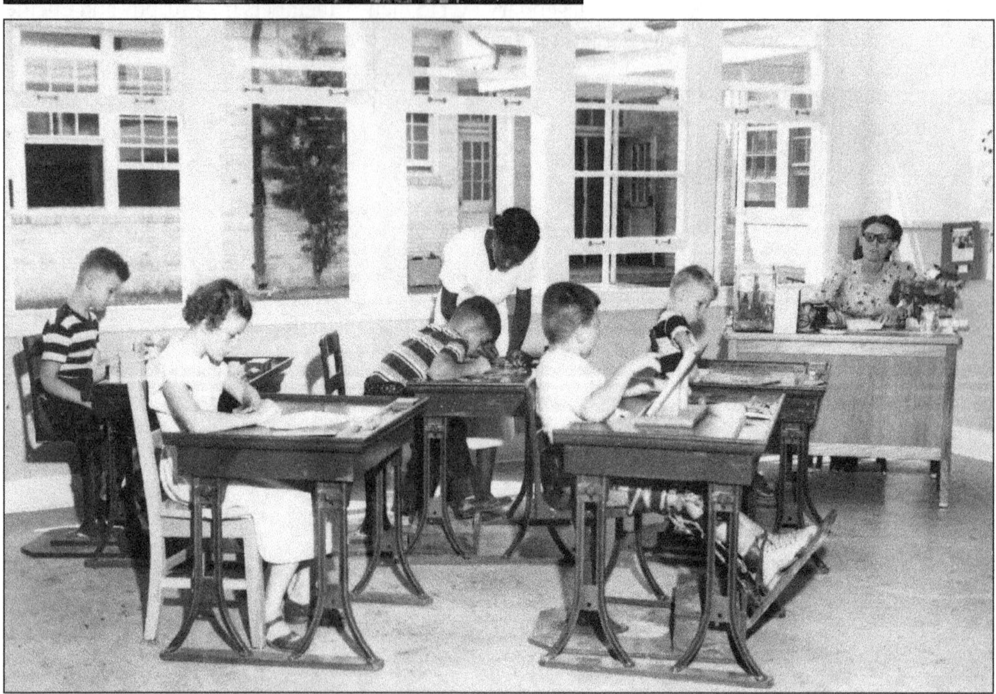

This 1951 photograph shows a Hamilton School class of differently-abled children. The pupils are, from left to right, Brantley Cagle, Suzanne Gregory, Skipper Dean, Franko Brame, and Bobby Duett. The assistant helping Dean is Winona Mouton, and the teacher at the desk is Beryl Long. Hamilton School opened in 1949 and reserved a place for students with special needs.

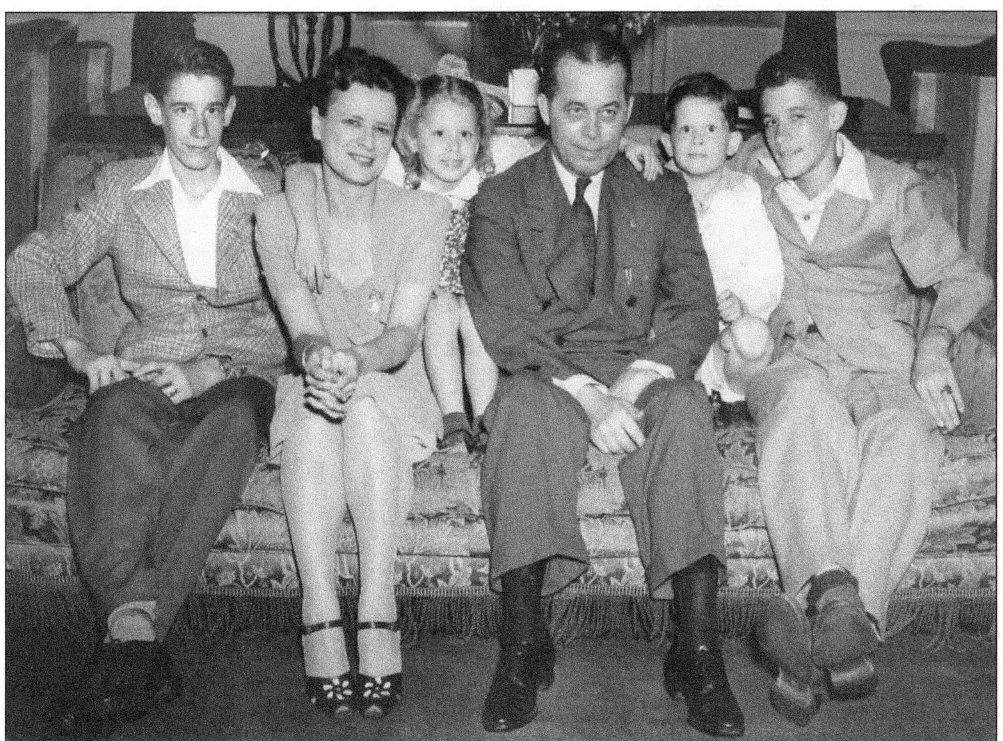

Sam H. Jones (1897-1978) was the only Louisiana governor from Lake Charles to serve a full term in office. (Alvin O. King served five months in 1932.) Born in DeRidder, he moved to Lake Charles to practice law. Elected as a reform governor in 1940, he presided during the years of World War II. He is pictured here in 1942 in the governor's mansion with his wife, Louise Gambrell Boyer Jones, and his children (from left to right) James G. "Jimmy" Boyer, Carolyn Jelks Jones, Robert G. Jones (who later served in the state legislature), and William Edwin "Bill" Boyer (mayor of Lake Charles from 1974 to 1981). (Courtesy of Robert G. Jones.)

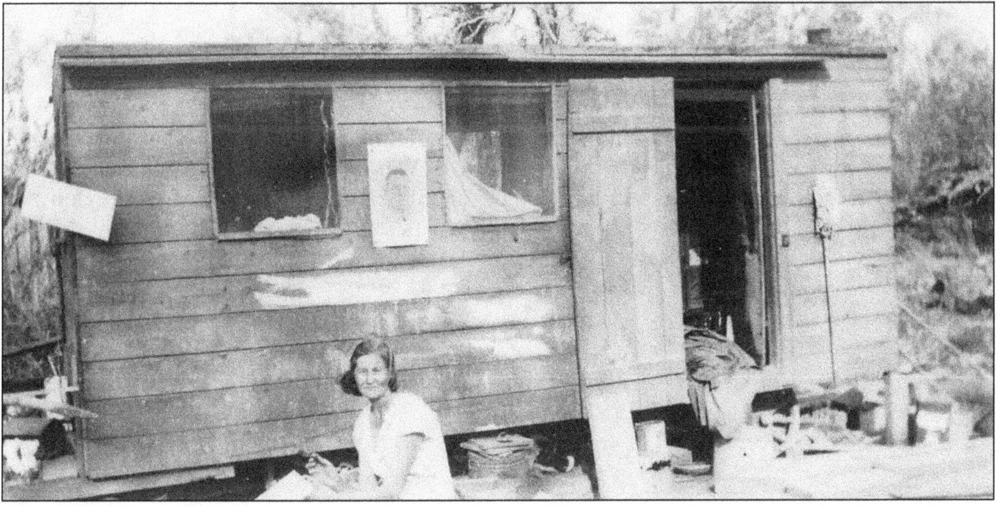

The land along the river and lake was home to many poor people in Lake Charles, including this unidentified woman posing in front of her one-room cabin. This 1935 photograph shows a campaign poster for Richard Leche on the front of the cabin. Leche, a protégé of Huey Long, was the first Louisiana governor to be sent to prison.

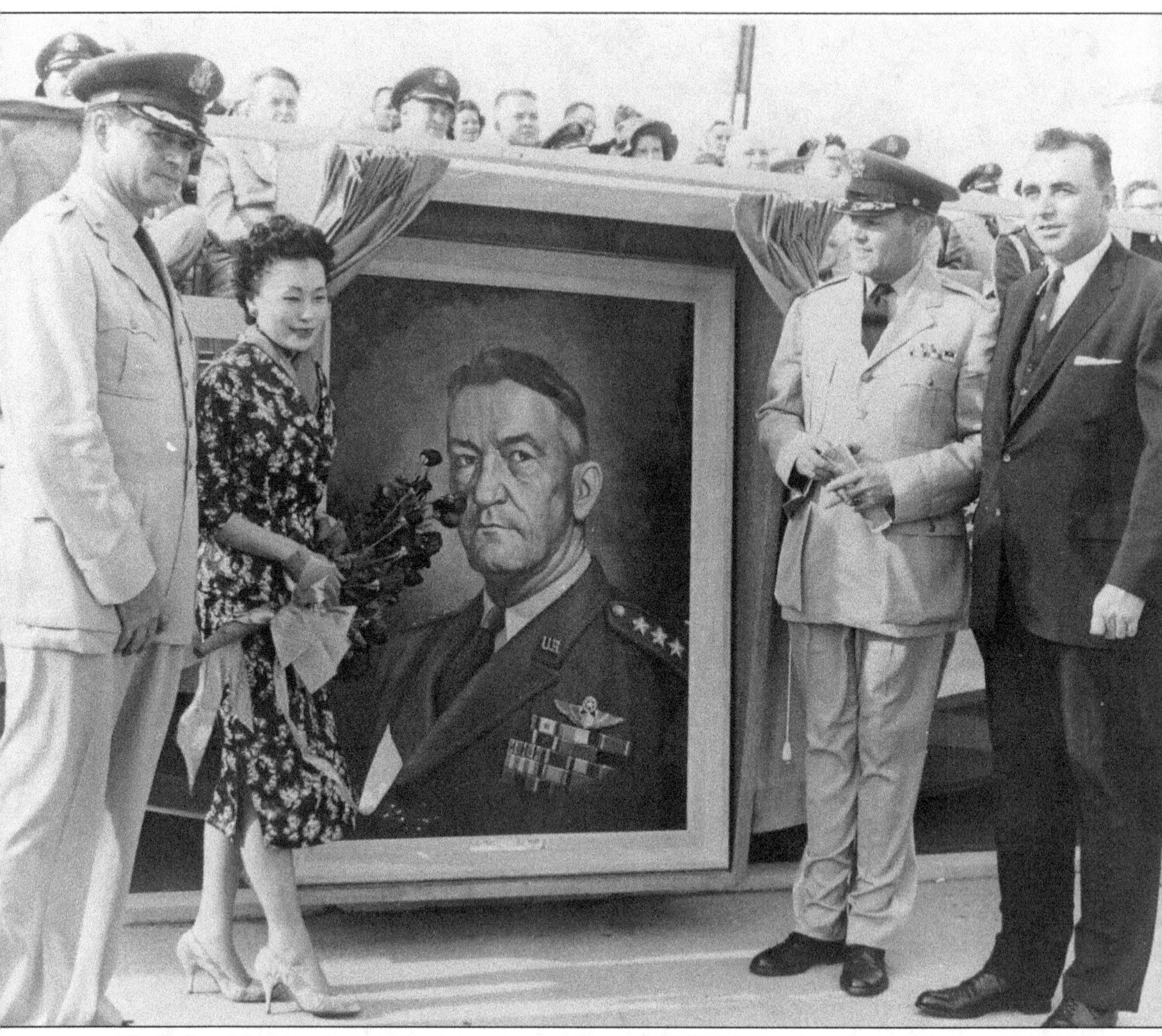

Claire Lee Chennault was a Louisiana native born in 1893. He was best known for organizing the Flying Tigers, a group of American military pilots who flew American-built planes for China in the 1930s. Eventually, Chennault became chief of US Army Air Forces in China. At this 1958 dedication ceremony for the renaming of the Lake Charles Air Force Base to Chennault Air Force Base, Anna Chennault stands beside the portrait of her husband. The men in uniform are Flying Tiger pilots. US Rep. T. Ashton Thompson is on the right.

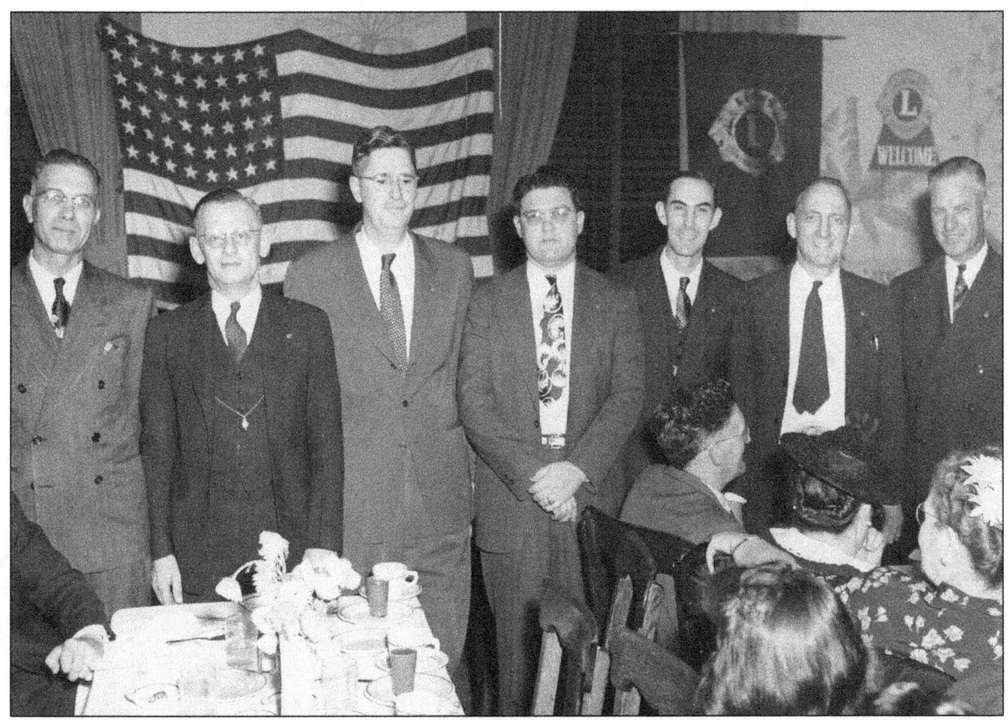

Lake Charles sported chapters of many national organizations that served a dual function of encouraging community service and providing networking opportunities for members. Before the Civil Rights Act of 1964, clubs were strictly segregated. The photograph above shows the Lions Club presidents from left to right (with the dates of their respective presidencies): J.E. Pace (1940), E.H. Paul (1941), architect Gus G. Quinn (1942), D.H.B. Hewett (1943), O.F. Maxfield (1944), George H. West (1945), and David B. Miller (1946). The Quota Club, pictured below, was organized in 1941 as a women's service organization.

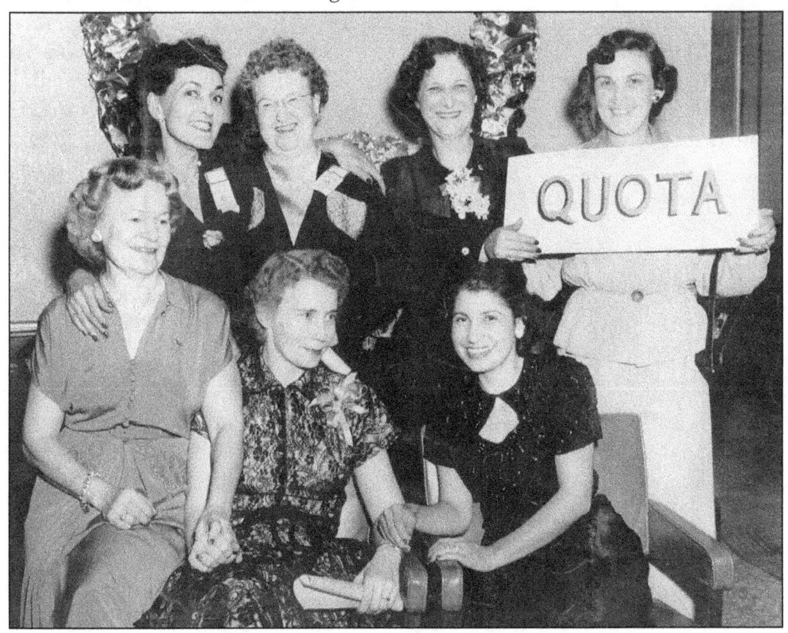

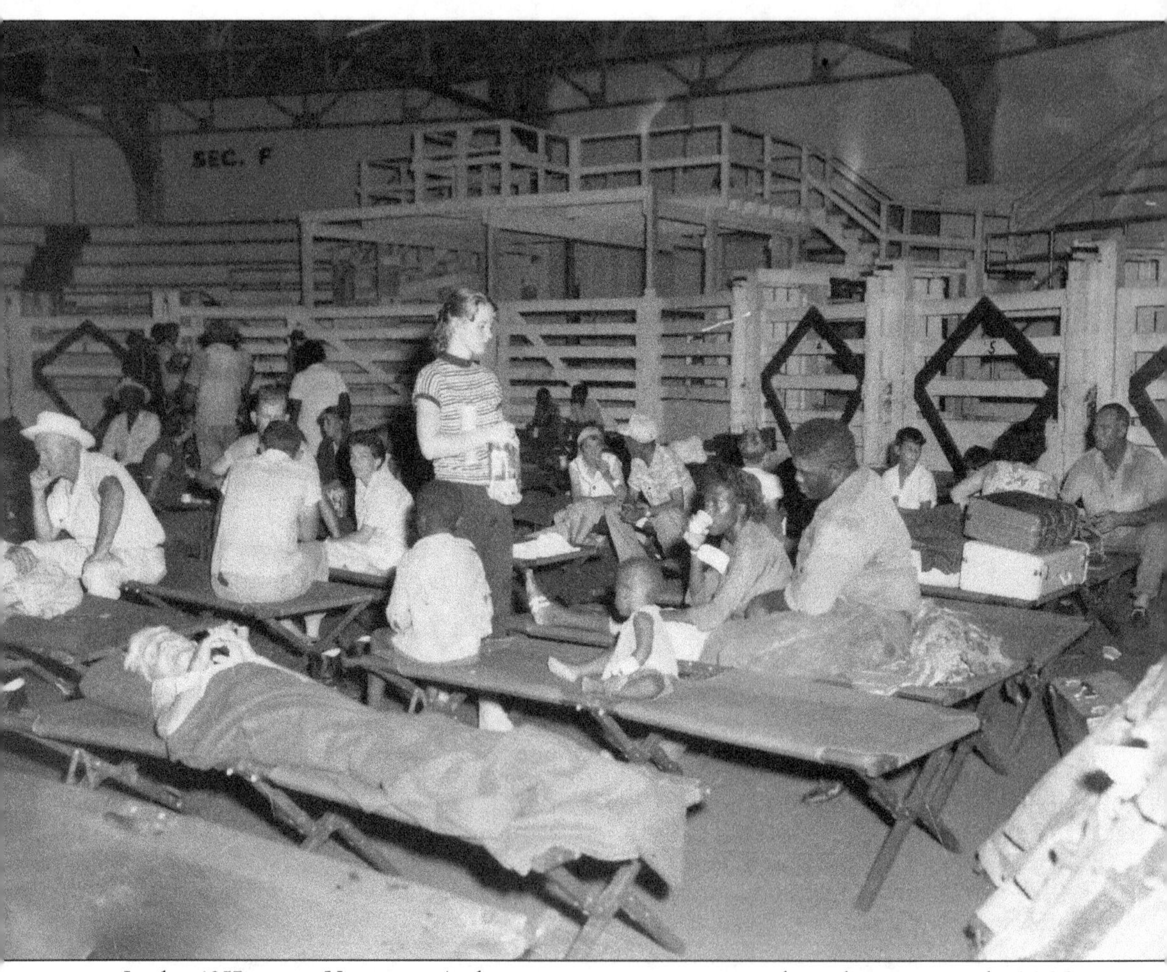

In this 1957 image, Hurricane Audrey survivors rest on cots in the rodeo arena on the McNeese campus. More than 500 people in Cameron Parish died in this storm, which had winds up to 160 miles per hour and waves up to 50 feet tall when it made landfall on the Cameron coast. Audrey was the first hurricane of the 1957 season and did approximately one billion dollars in damage.

Six

Fun and Festivities

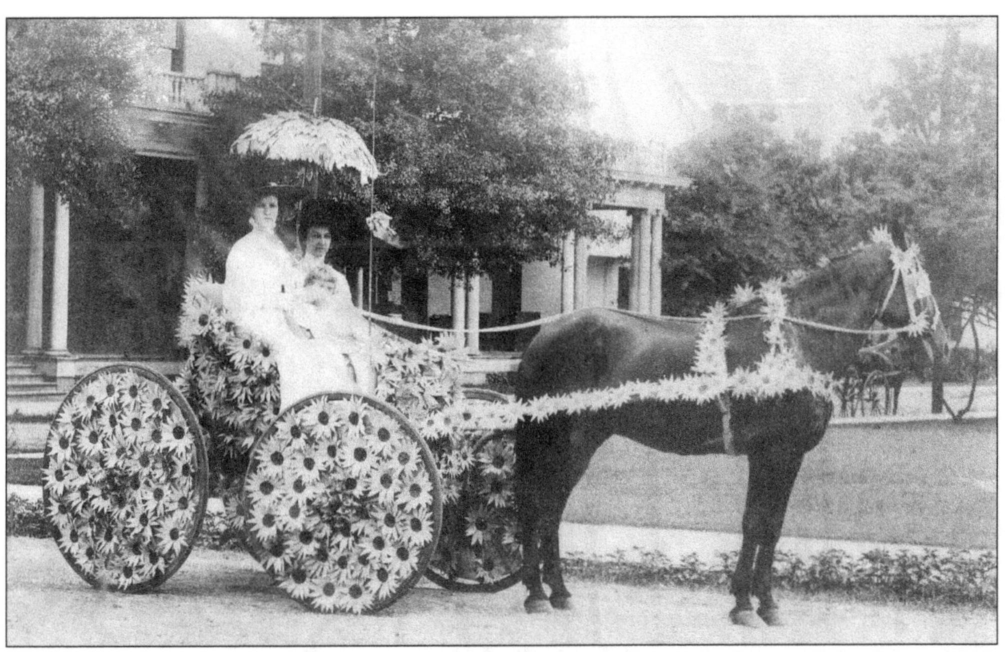

Rona Keener (left), pictured with Marie and Katherine Bel, was in charge of the July 4, 1907, parade in Lake Charles. She personally made the floral decorations on this buggy, which is in front of the original Carnegie Library on Pujo Street.

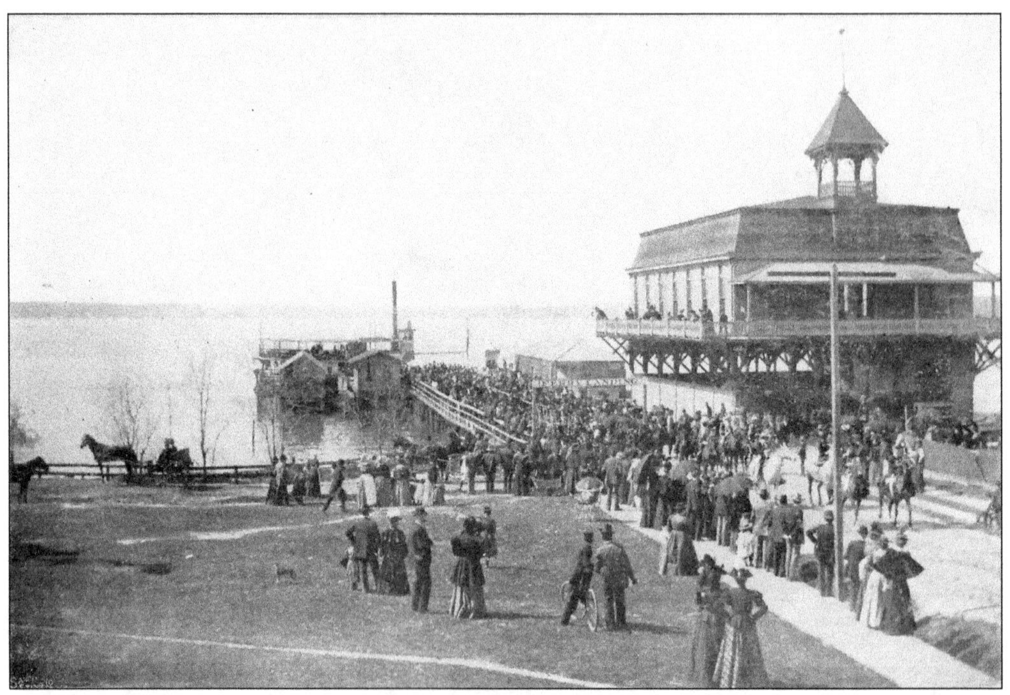

This photograph of an early Lake Charles Mardi Gras shows the king arriving with his retinue on his royal barge, the *Hazel*. The parade landed at the foot of Pujo Street, marched up Ryan, Lawrence, Kirkman, and down Kirby Streets, then went back to Ryan Street. The parade was led by the local band and followed by unnamed maskers. The building at right is the city market, erected in 1894.

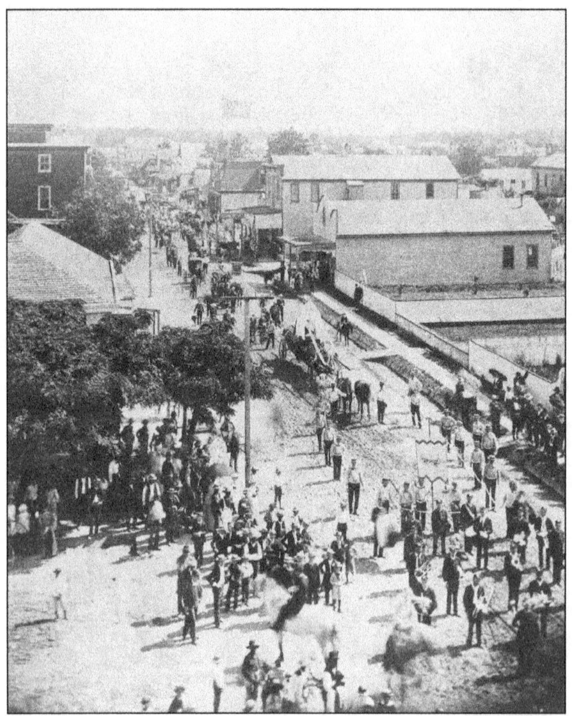

In the Grand Firemen's Parade, held on July 4, 1889, fire companies from as far away as Orange, Texas, came to show their decorated fire engines in Lake Charles. A feast and the crowning of the parade queen occurred that evening in the Williams Opera House, which is the building with the windows at left.

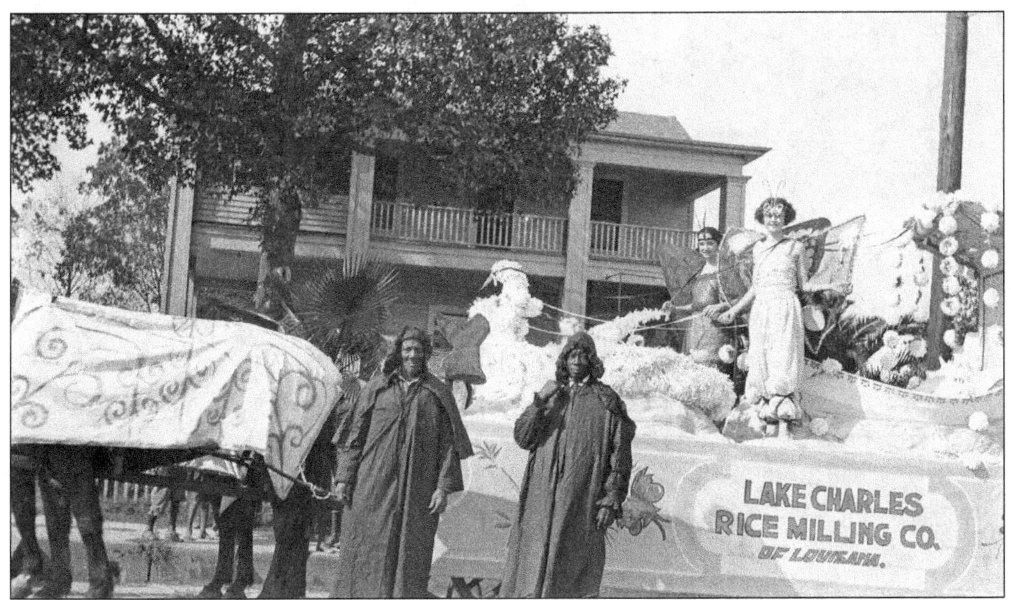

For a few years in the early 1920s, Lake Charles celebrated the Rice Day Carnival on the opening day of the Calcasieu Parish Fair. The carnival was promoted "in thankfulness of one of Louisiana's finest and most valued products" and featured parades with rice floats, athletic contests, band concerts, and a supper and dance at the Majestic Hotel. The Rice Day Carnival was short-lived, however, as the rice industry declined in the later part of the 1920s. Rice was no longer needed as a wartime staple, and overproduction and foreign competition caused prices to fall as living expenses rose. (Both courtesy of Jeanne Owens of Vintage Arts; photographs by David H. Levingston.)

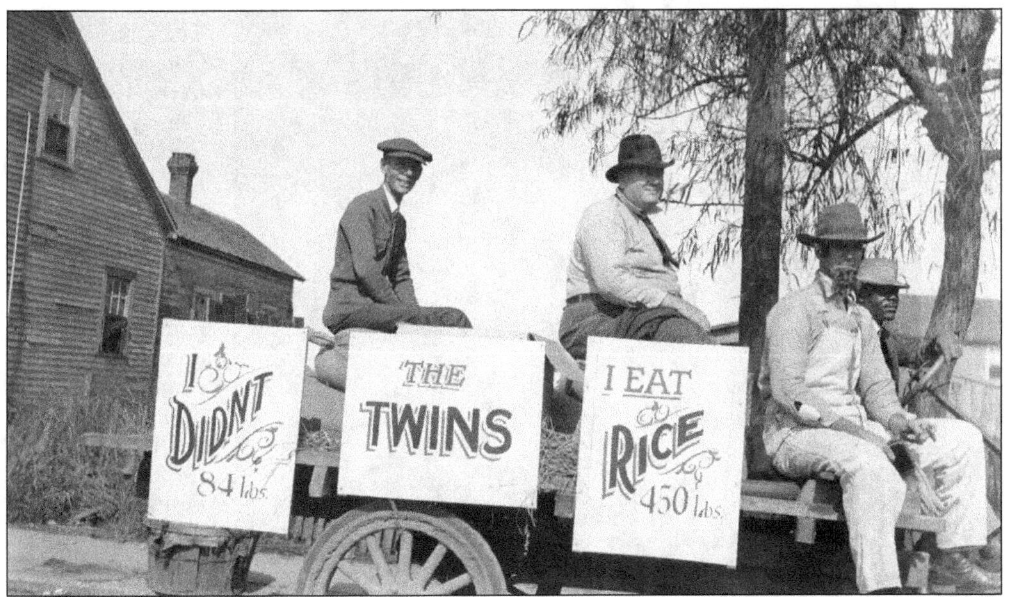

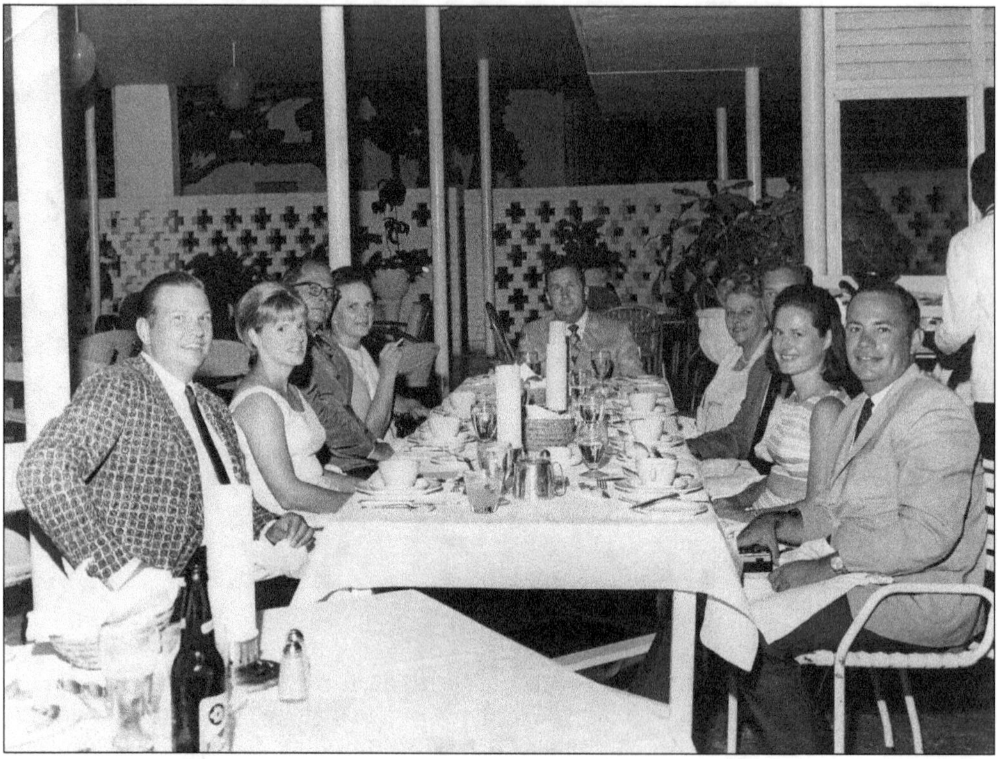

Many Lake Charles residents head south to the Gulf on days off to enjoy fishing, boating, or an island getaway. Enjoying a meal while on vacation with Lake Charles friends in Jamaica in 1968 are, from left to right, Billy Blake, Kay Blake, C.A. King, Louise Kay, William Smith, Daisy Bel Smith, James E. Taussig, Alice Taussig, and James "Jimmy" Hanchey. (Courtesy of Billy and Kay Krause Blake.)

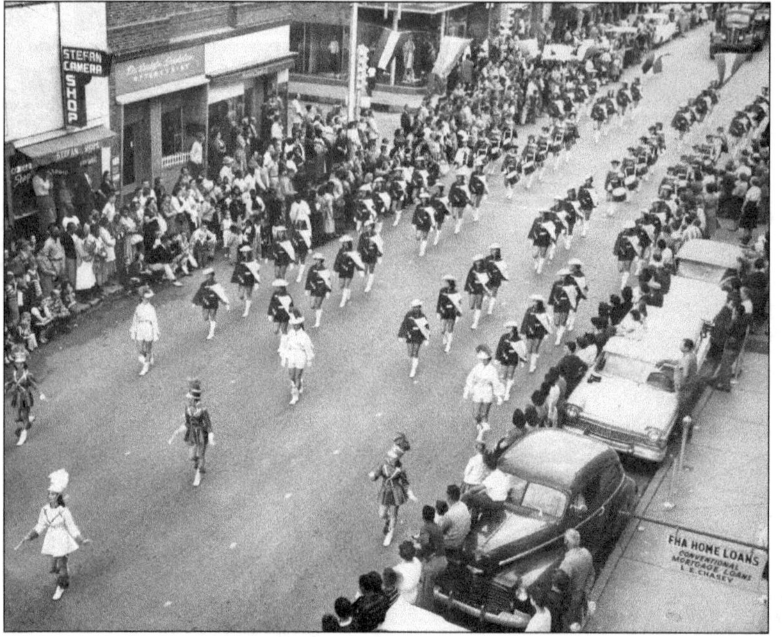

The LaGrange Gatorettes march in the 1958 Chennault Week Parade, which kicked off the week of festivities surrounding the dedication of Chennault Air Force Base. The unusually large parade took over two hours to wind its way through the business section of downtown on Ryan and Division Streets.

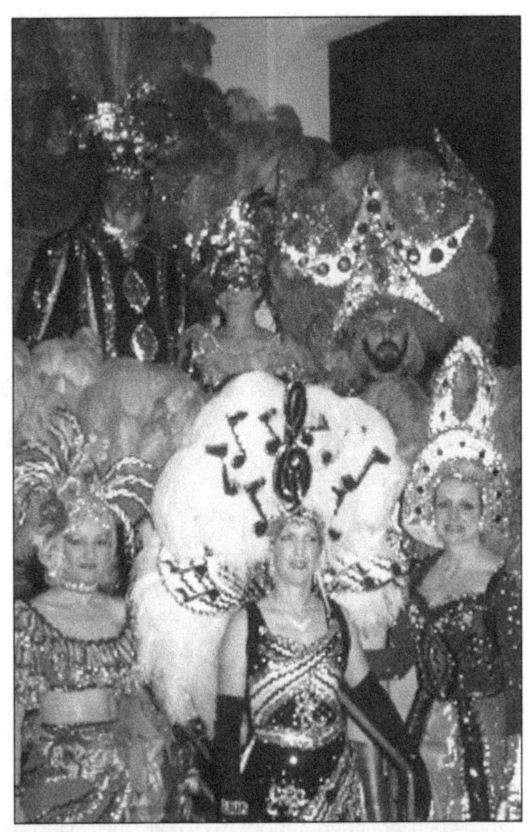

Lake Charles's Mardi Gras is second only to New Orleans in the number of krewes, now more than 50. It is proud of its family-friendly atmosphere. The public is invited to see the krewes parade in their lavish costumes, some weighing more than 60 pounds, at the annual Twelfth Night celebration at the Civic Centre on January 6. These members of the 1986 Mardi Gras royal court are dressed in regalia typical of the season.

Randy Feurst, representing the McNeese Banners Series, poses with the Black Heritage Festival Queens in 2003. From left to right: (first row) Youth Ambassador Morgan Jordan, Petite Miss Katelyn Pappion, Little Miss Jada Wilson, Deb Miss Alexxus Ceasar, and Teen Miss Tanaya Yidin; (second row) Jr. Miss Mercedes Lassien, Miss Ambassador Shantel King, Randy Feurst, and Miss Black Heritage Ashley Higgins. The Banners Series has collaborated with the Black Heritage Festival for years to bring high-quality artistic productions to the area, including *Porgy and Bess* and the Dance Theatre of Harlem.

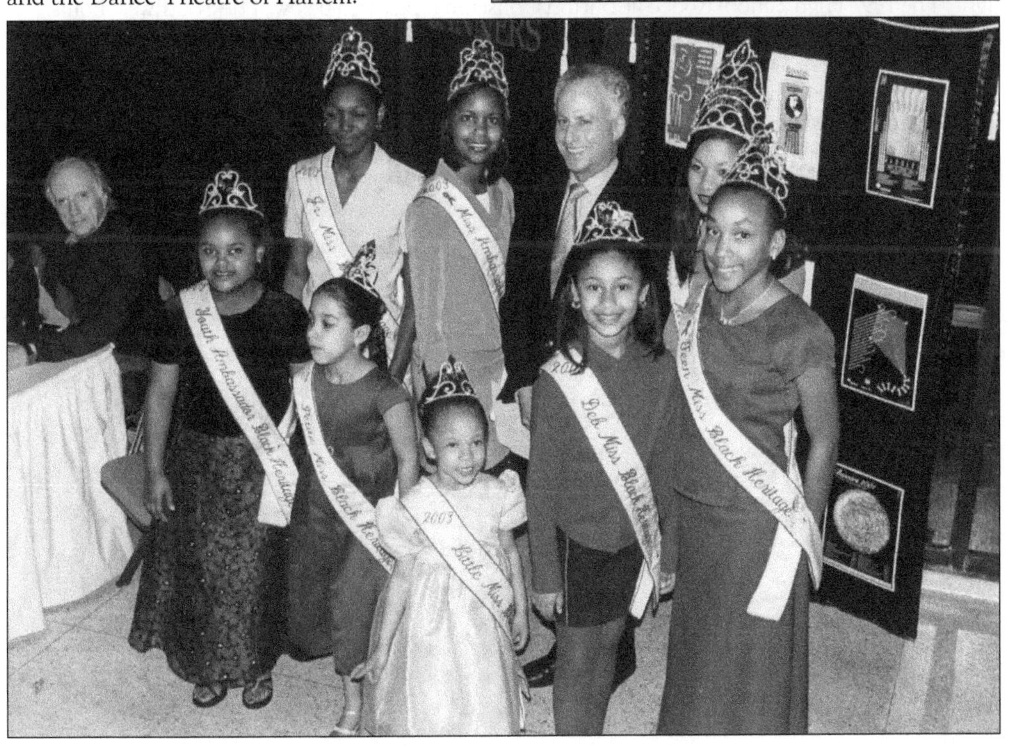

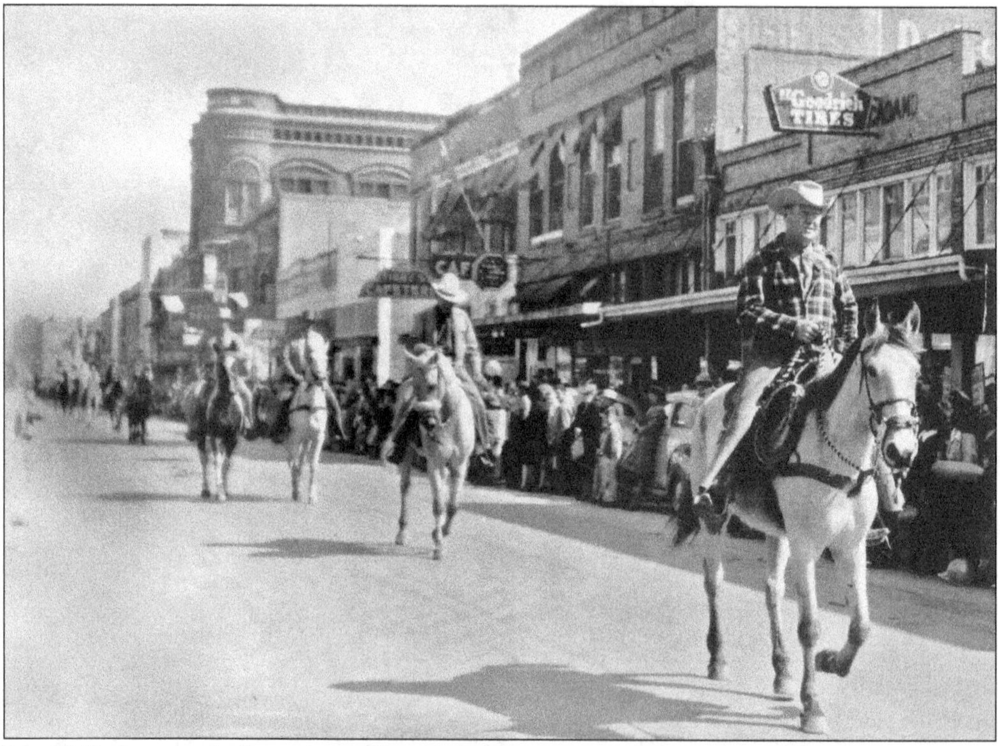

The 1948 photograph above shows Thomas D. Watson Sr. riding in the parade of the Southwest Louisiana Fat Stock Show and Rodeo. The east side of the 800 block of Ryan Street is visible at right. The 1992 High School Rodeo at Burton Coliseum is pictured below. The Southwest Louisiana rodeo began with the Southwest Louisiana Cattlemen's Association working in conjunction with the Calcasieu Parish Police Jury to open a junior college with an arena to host livestock shows and rodeos. Lake Charles Junior College (later McNeese State University) opened in 1939, and the cowboy was a prominent fixture on campus as rodeo was a major activity. The first McNeese basketball team formed in 1940, with the "cowboys" as their mascot. (Above, courtesy Thomas D. Watson Jr.)

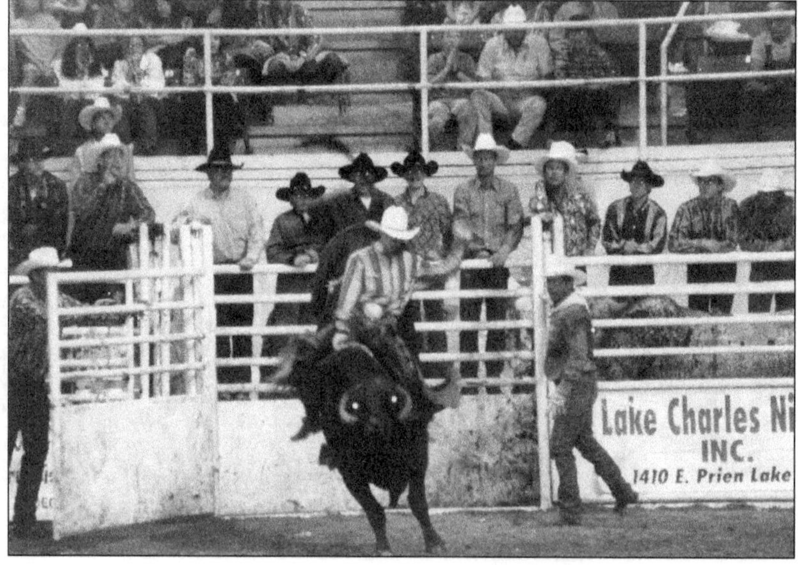

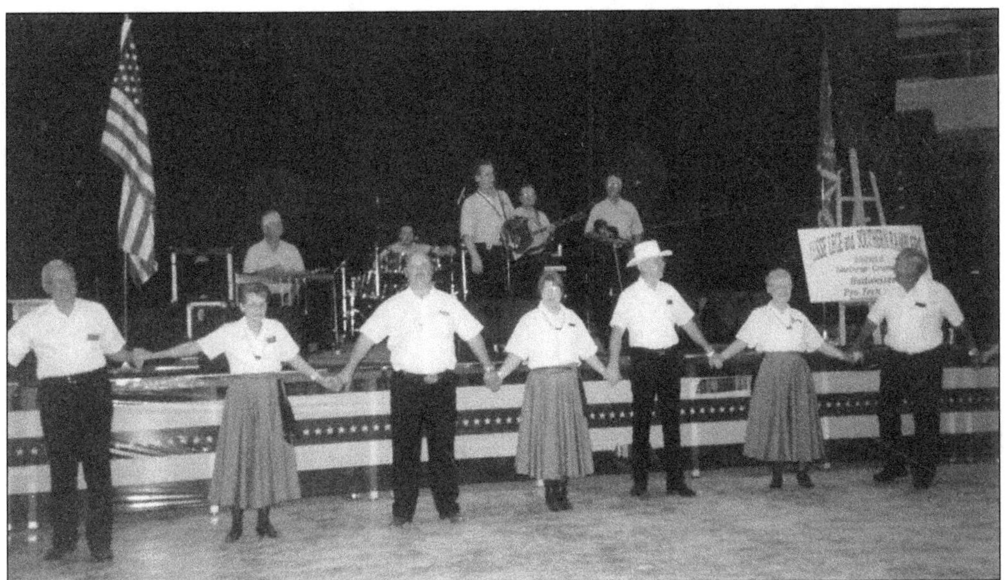

The annual Cajun French Music Association Festival celebrates and preserves the Cajun heritage of southern Louisiana. It draws big crowds to Burton Coliseum every year. This photograph of the 2002 festival shows CFMA dancers performing as Jesse Lege and the Southern Ramblers provide the live music. Members of the band include, from left to right, Orsy Vanicour, Morris Newman, Jesse Lege, Leetel Hanks, and Ray Guidry. The dancers are, from left to right, George and Anna Fruge, Ray Cart, Martha Gaspard, Larry and Marceline Miller, and Seeward Miller. (Courtesy of Cajun French Music Association.)

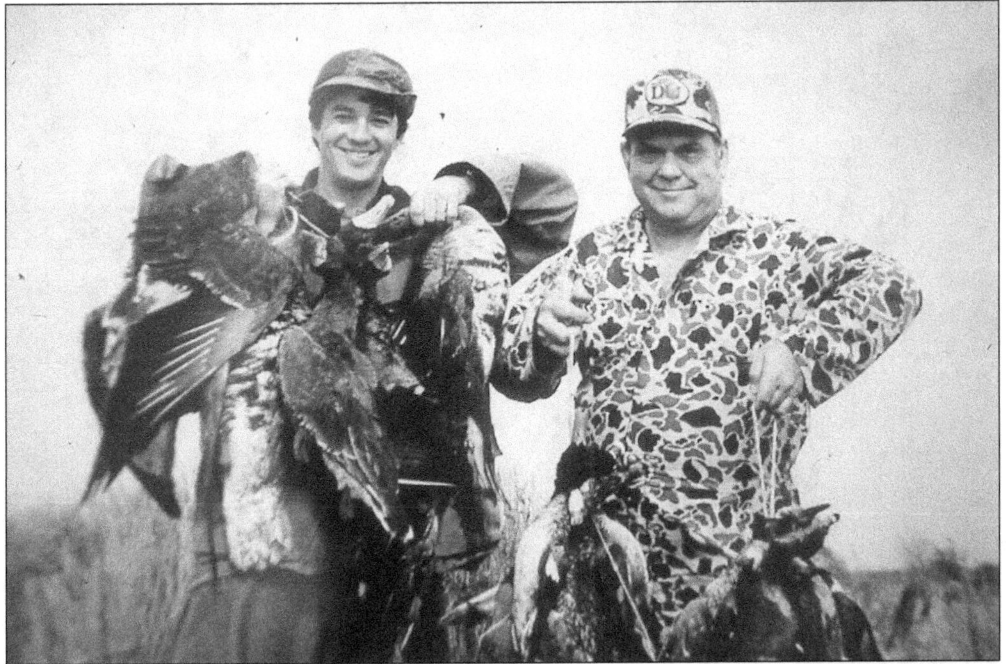

Louisiana has long been known as a sportsman's paradise. People come to the marshes of southwest Louisiana from all over the country to hunt waterfowl. Pictured here are two local hunters, well-known local photographer Victor Monsour (left) and Earl Barger.

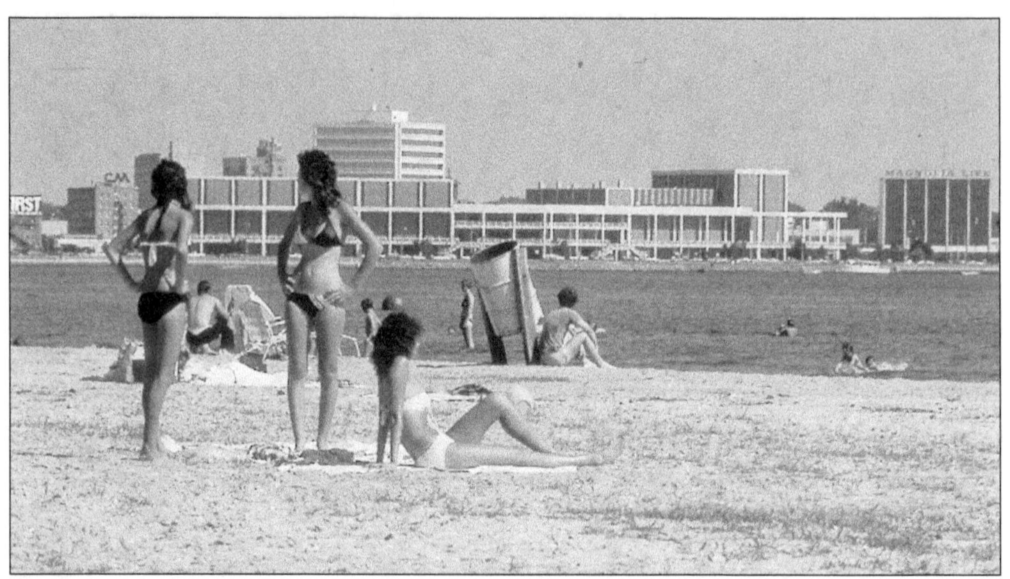

In early years, Lake Charles was primarily used for transportation and industry, but as other forms of transportation supplanted water, the lake became a site for recreation and a gathering place for community events. The North Beach underwent tax-funded improvements during the 1960s, which added picnic and concession areas, restroom facilities, and additional beachfront. Swimming, skiing, boating, and fishing are typical lake activities, while people enjoy sunbathing, jogging, volleyball, and picnicking on the shore.

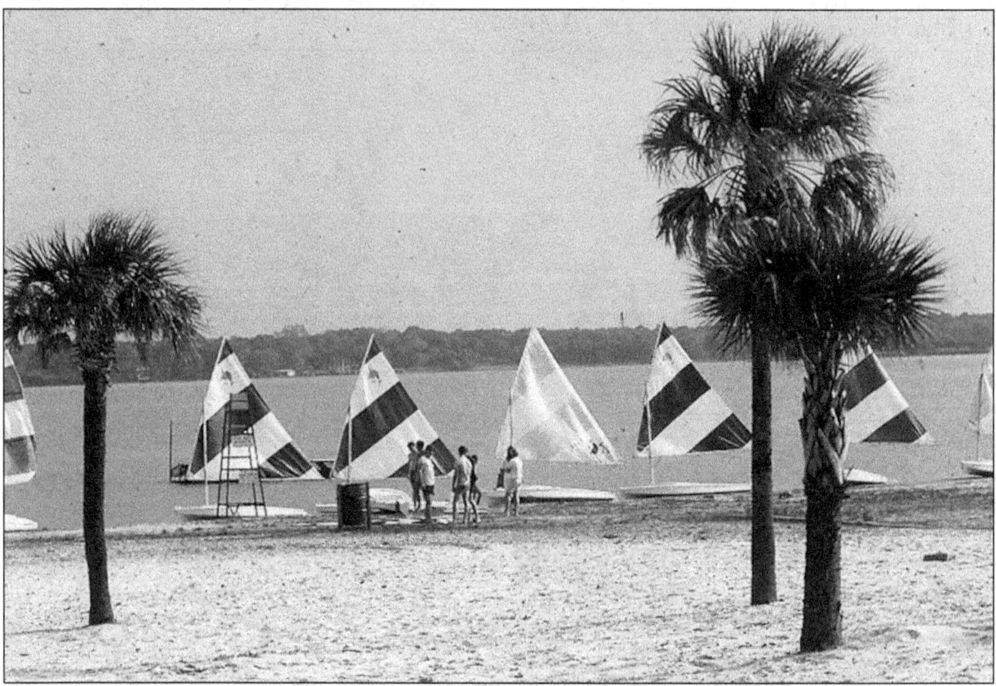

Cal Lakes Yacht Club moved to the west end of North Beach in 1967. The city shared some of the expenses of the land and a road to the club. After the move, the organization changed its name to the Lake Charles Yacht Club and built a clubhouse. These boats belong to the club and are often seen on the lake with other sailboats during Wednesday afternoon races.

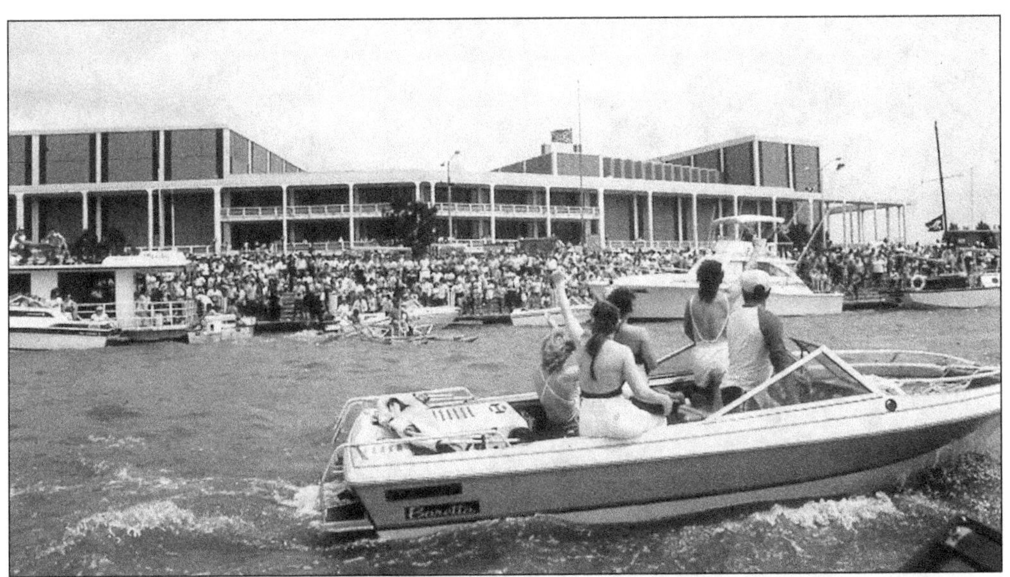

Contraband Days is a "pirate" festival held each May on the Lake Charles Civic Center grounds. Over 100,000 people attend Contraband Days on both land and water. The festival began in 1957 when a group of local businessmen, seeking to promote Lake Charles–area recreational and cultural activities and to attract tourists, decided to develop a pirate-themed festival. The idea came from the legend that the pirate Jean Lafitte and his band of buccaneers hid out along the waterways in Lake Charles while fleeing enemy ships. The legend held that the pirates' treasure (silver and gold) was hidden and buried by Lafitte in his favorite hideaway, Contraband Bayou. Above, boats and spectators crowd around the lakefront near the Civic Center, and below, Bryan Dorsey (left) and Charlie Bourne navigate the KLOU bathtub across the lake as part of the Contraband Days Bathtub Races around 1983.

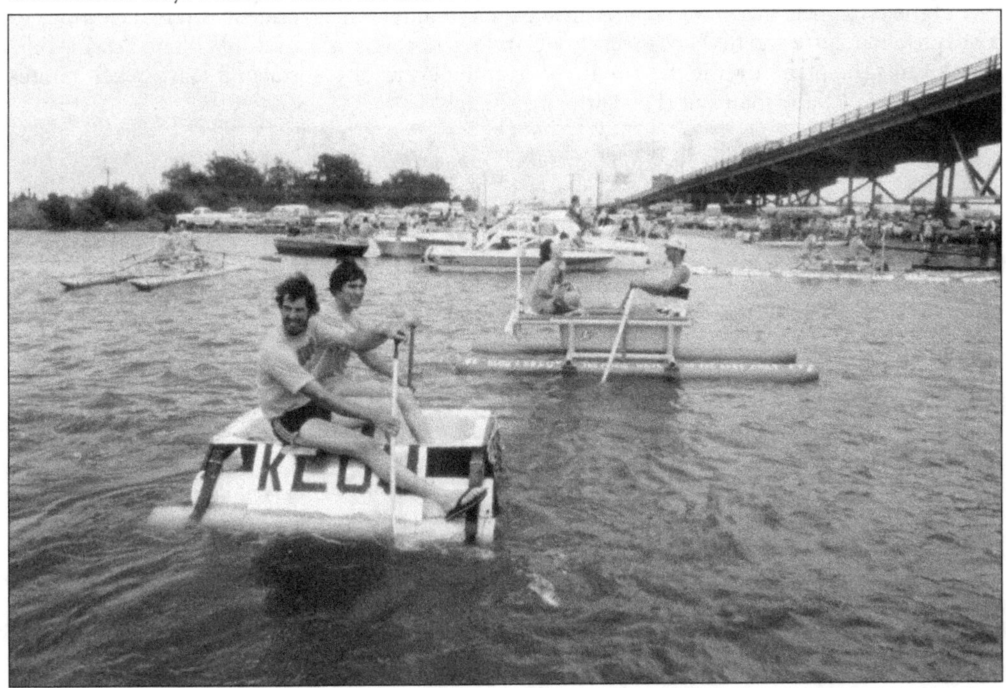

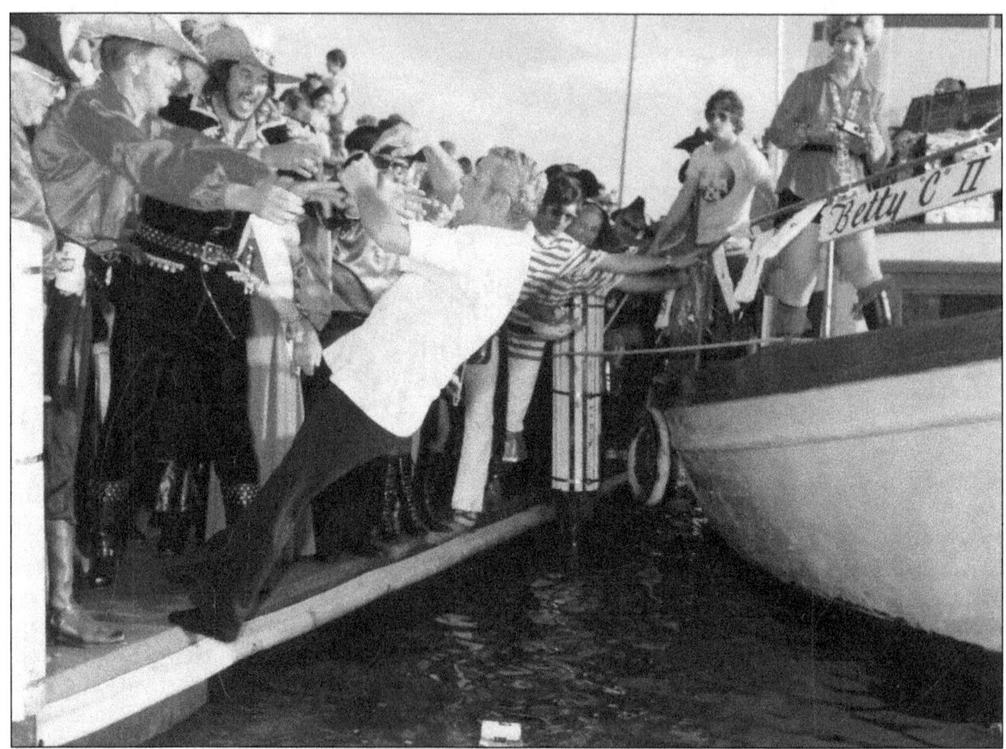

The first Contraband Days was held in June 1958 as a one-day event with a boat parade, water ski show, and boat races. A few years later, this group of men formed another organization called the Buccaneers of Lake Charles Inc., and added entertainment by dressing in pirate attire. A "Jean Lafitte" would be selected to lead the buccaneers to "capture the mayor and take over the city." Part of the buccaneer group would also dress in "city militia" attire, armed with real cannons to try to prevent Lafitte and his buccaneers from landing. In this image, Mayor William Edwin "Bill" Boyer walks the plank during the ritualized opening event of Contraband Days, when pirates take over the city and force out the legitimate officials.

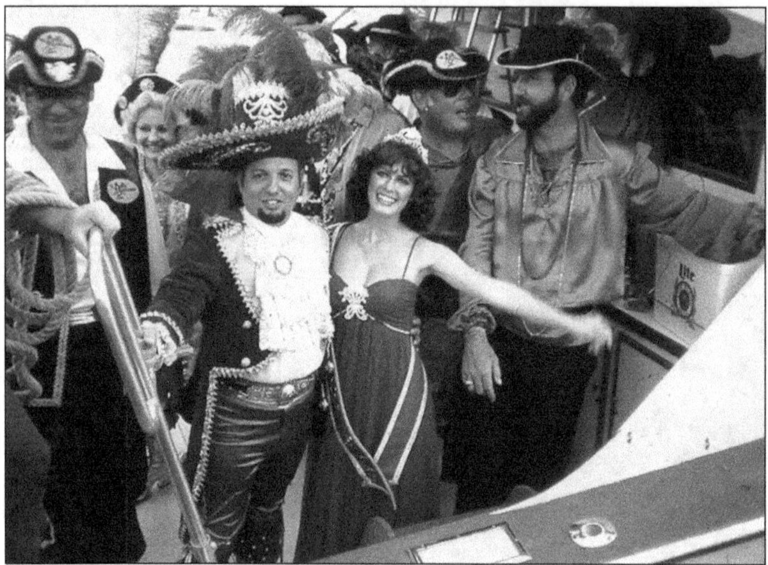

Jacquelyn Ewing (Jackie Morris Hood), Miss Contraband Days 1981, reigns over the festival along with Jean Lafitte, represented by Tony "Sonny" Hodges. Dolores Hodges is in the background. The Buccaneers of Lake Charles formed to organize and promote the festival.

Seven

Music and Arts

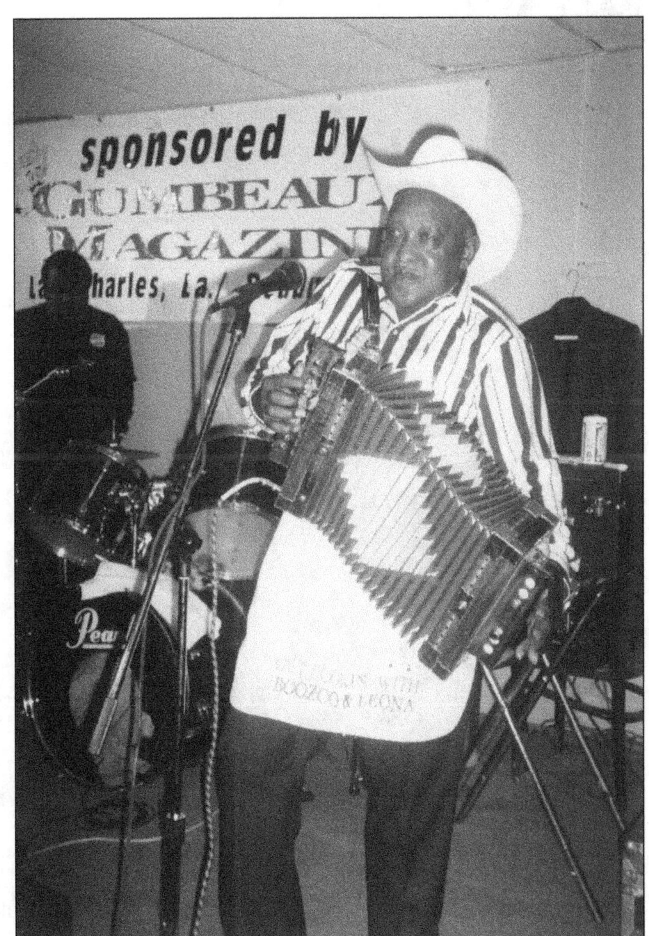

Zydeco legend Wilson "Boozoo" Chavis grew up in the Dog Hill neighborhood south of Lake Charles and learned to play the button accordion at age nine. His legacy lives on through the annual Boozoo Chavis Labor Day Festival, the Boozoo Chavis Memorial Highway, and the Dog Hill Stompers band, which includes several of Chavis's grandsons. (Courtesy of Lawrence Morrow.)

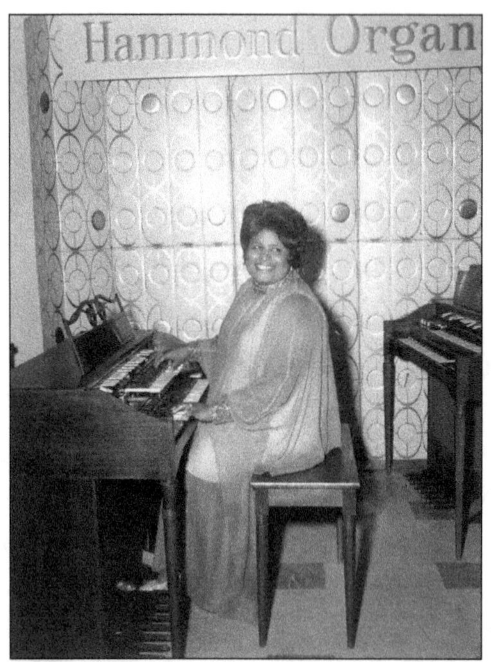

Nellie Lutcher was a jazz pianist, rhythm and blues singer, and songwriter. Born in 1912, Lutcher joined her father in Clarence Hart's Imperial Jazz Band at age 14. Lutcher moved to Los Angeles in 1935, where she landed a contract with Capitol Records. In 1950, Lutcher recorded "For You My Love" with Nat King Cole and later recorded a commemorative song for her hometown, "Lake Charles Boogie." A popular singer throughout Europe and America in the 1950s, Lutcher served as the first African American parade marshal in Contraband Days history in 1987.

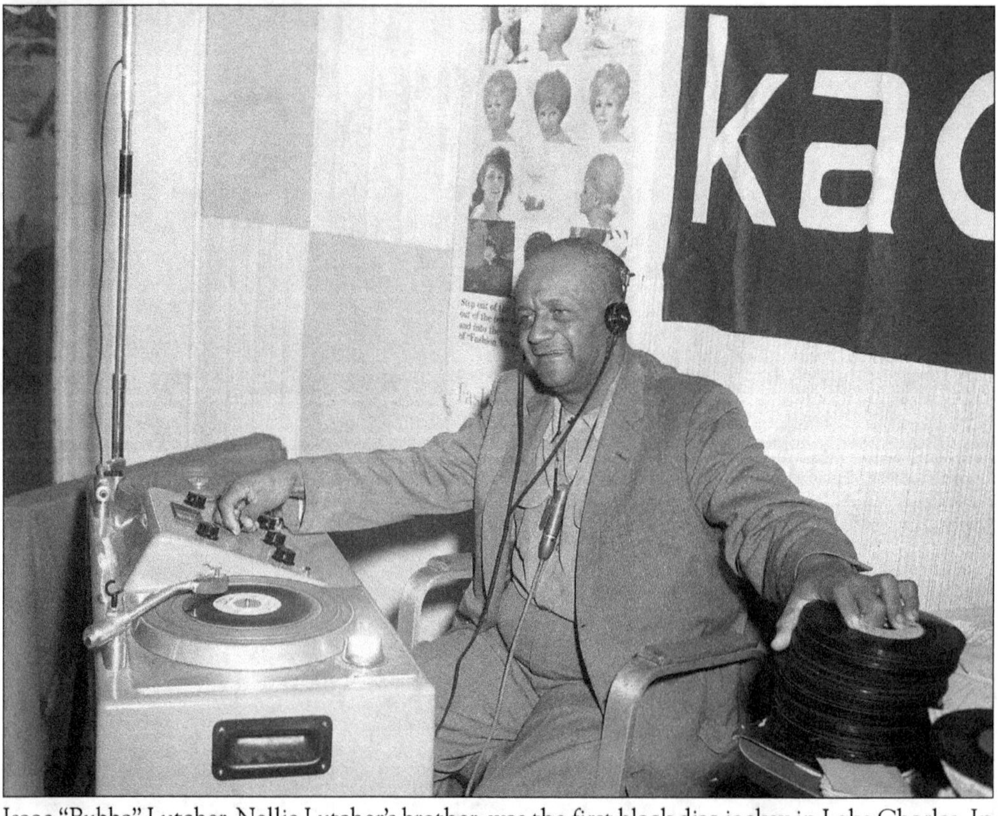

Isaac "Bubba" Lutcher, Nellie Lutcher's brother, was the first black disc jockey in Lake Charles. In the 1950s, he hosted a popular radio show called "Bubba's Cookie Shack" at KAOK radio. While a disc jockey, he sponsored benefits at Ball's Auditorium for the March of Dimes.

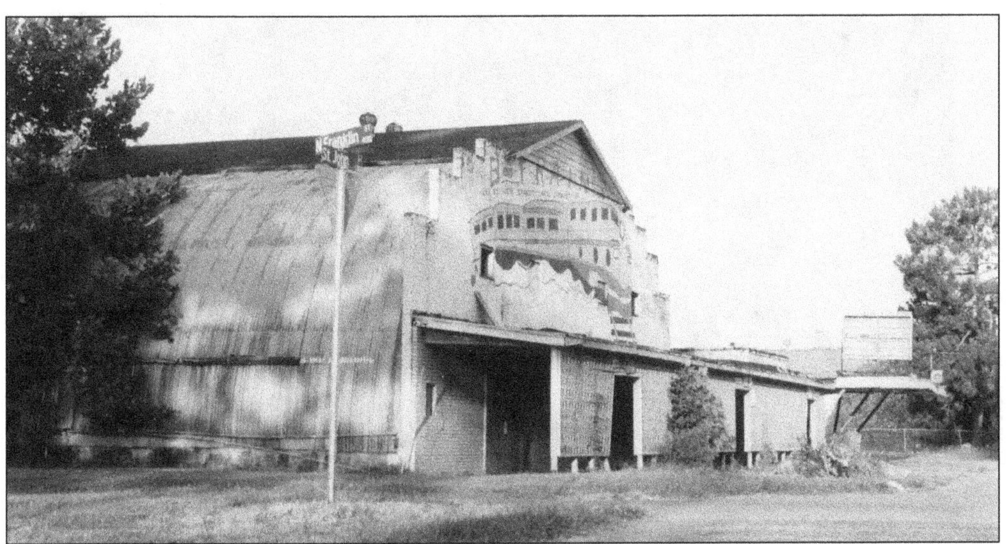

Originally erected by Reginald Ball Sr. as a trade school for black veterans returning from World War II, Ball converted the school into a "top-notch entertainment auditorium" in 1952. Located on the corner of St. John and North Franklin Streets in North Lake Charles, Ball's Auditorium hosted performers such as James Brown, Aretha Franklin, Ray Charles, and others. (Courtesy of Lawrence Morrow.)

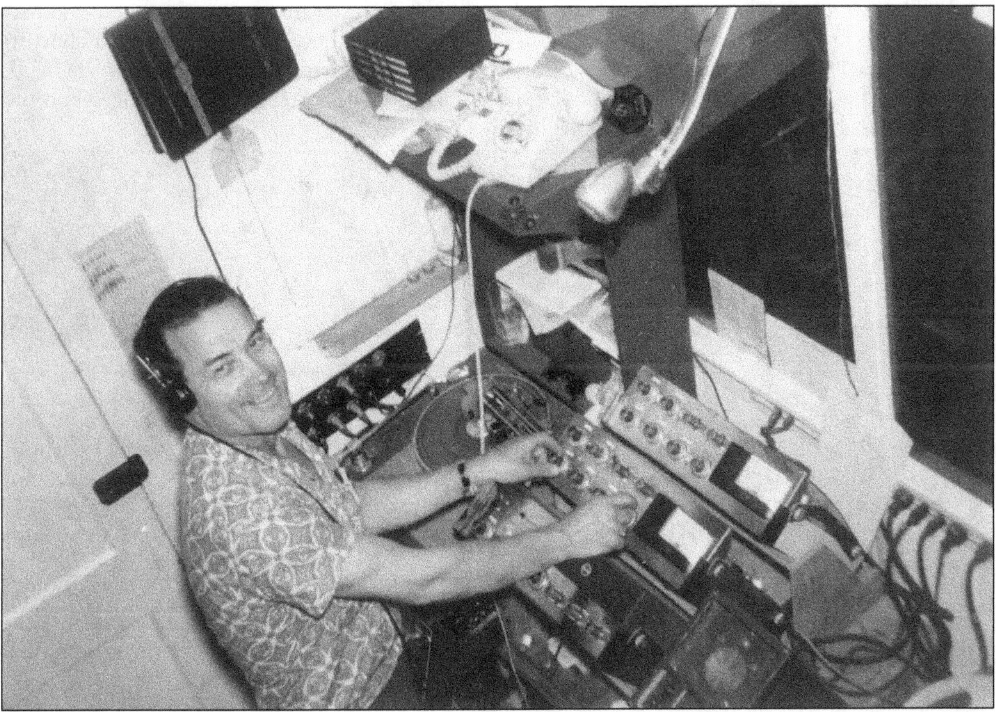

Eddie Shuler's Goldband Recording Corporation played a key role in documenting and shaping the music of Southwest Louisiana. Musical genres recorded by Schuler—including Cajun, blues, zydeco, boogie, gospel, country, rockabilly, swamp pop, and "watermelon rock"—reflect regional interests. This May 1960 photograph shows Eddie Shuler at the Goldband studio controls. (Courtesy of the Southern Folklife Collection at the University of North Carolina.)

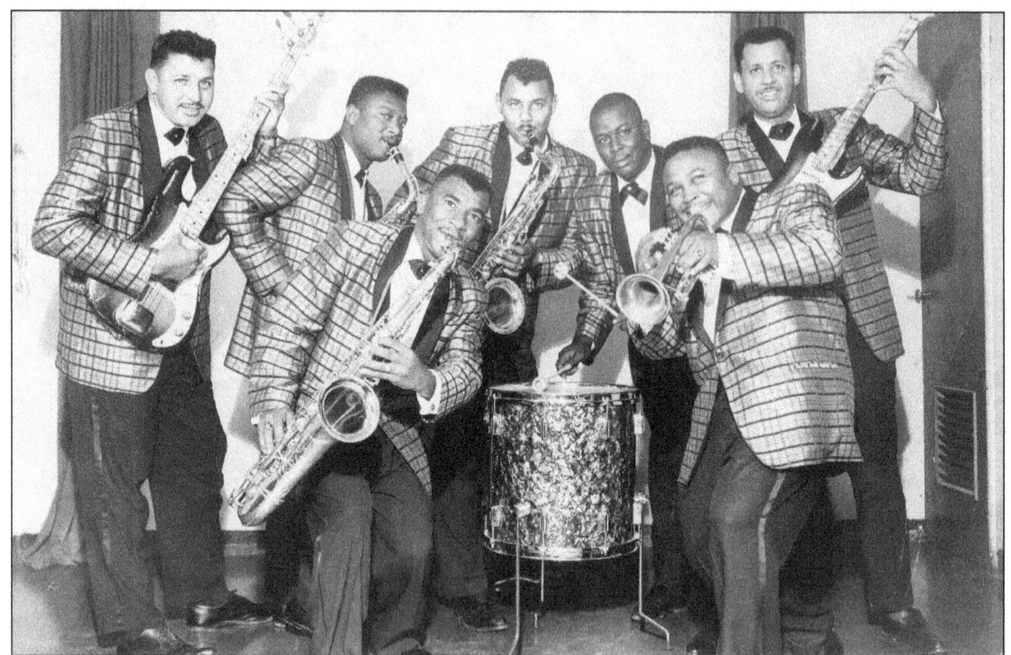

Cookie and the Cupcakes recorded several hit songs at the Goldband Recording Studio in the 1950s. They were considered the quintessential south Louisiana swamp pop band. Their number-one (in south Louisiana) hit record "Mathilda" climbed to number 47 on the Billboard chart in 1959. Bandleader Cookie (Hugh Thierry) is pictured here with band members Sidney Reynaud, Marshall Laday, Ernest Jacobs, Joe Landry, and Ivory Jackson. (Courtesy of the Southern Folklife Collection at the University of North Carolina.)

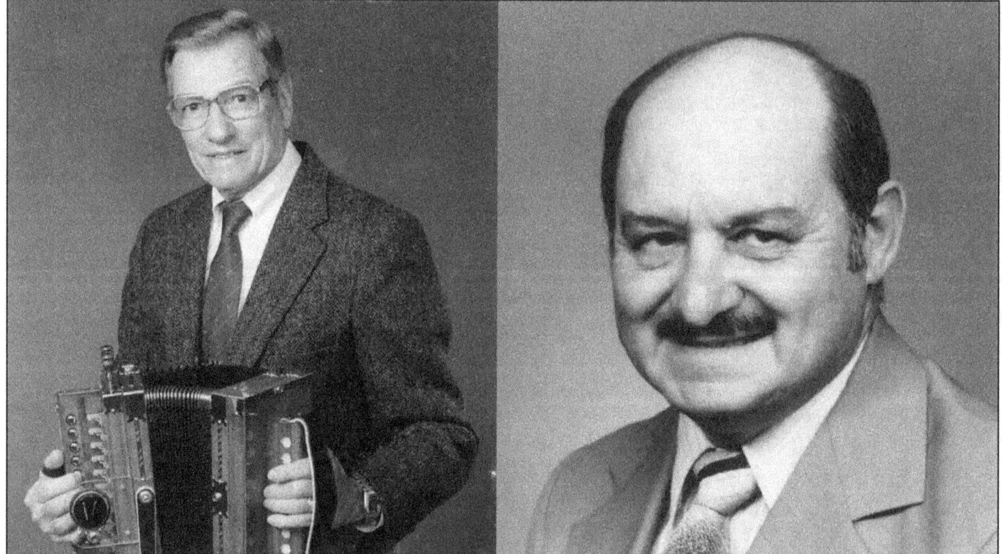

Accordionist Phil Menard (left) and drummer Lesa Cormier (right) are respected Cajun musicians. In addition to playing with local bands, they recorded many songs and albums, preserving a heritage that might otherwise have been lost. Along with Bernadine Thibedeaux LeBlanc, they helped establish the Lake Charles chapter of the Cajun French Music Association in 1987, which sponsors an annual Cajun music festival at Burton Coliseum. (Courtesy of Cajun French Music Association.)

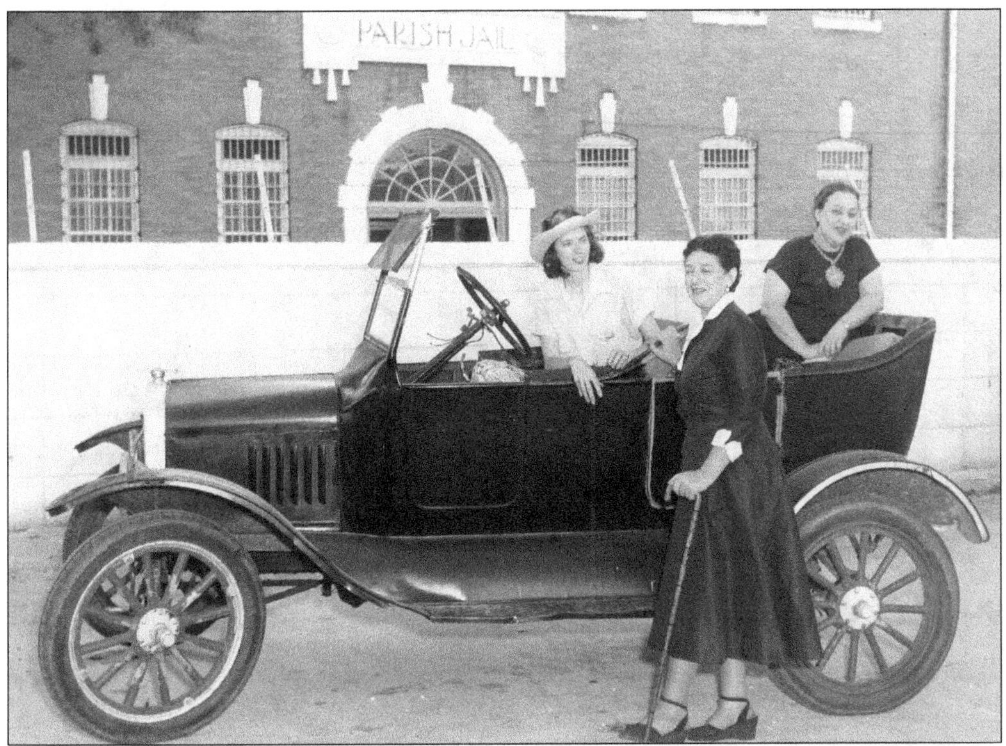

Lake Charles has been home to a thriving amateur theater community since the founding of Lake Charles Little Theatre in 1927 by Rosa Hart. In this photograph, Charlotte Tucker (left) and Hart (right) sit in a car while an unidentified woman stands next to them in front of the Calcasieu Parish Jail. Hart led Lake Charles Little Theatre for 30 years, never accepting payment for her services. The Rosa Hart Theatre, located in the Lake Charles Civic Center Complex, was dedicated in 1982 as a tribute to the cultural leader.

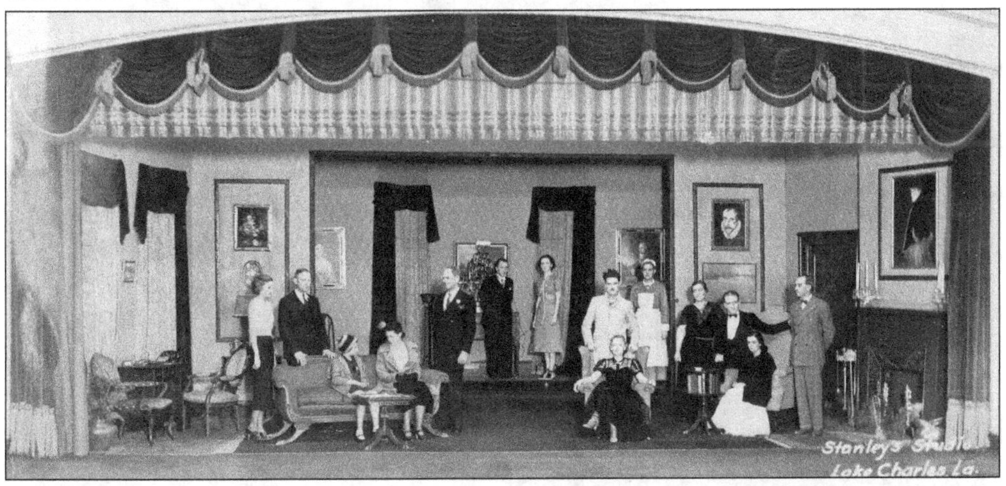

The Lake Charles Little Theatre used several venues for performances through the years. This 1937 performance of *First Lady* occurred in the theater on the second floor of the Masonic Temple on Hodges Street. The following year, the Little Theatre purchased the abandoned Railway Express Company stable at 320 Bilbo Street, which became the home of the Little Theatre until Rosa Hart retired in 1957.

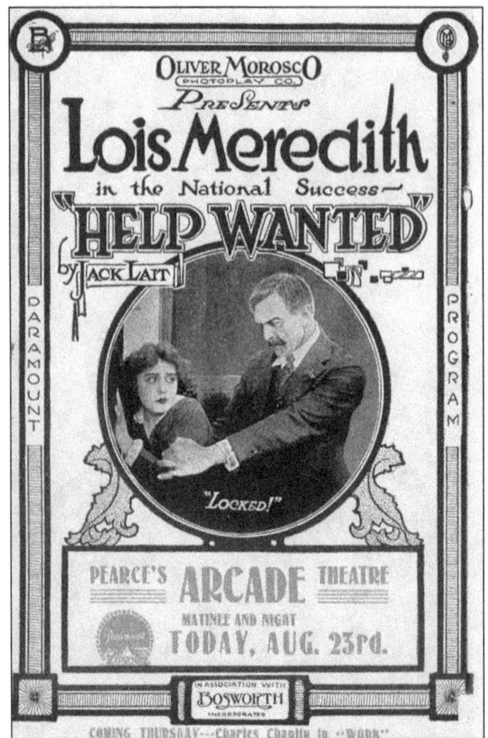

The community raised money to build the Arcade Theatre so that theatrical troupes that performed in New Orleans could play Lake Charles before going on to Houston. It opened on September 26, 1910, just before movies became popular in the 1920s. It got its name from the 60-foot-long corridor through the center of the Miller Building that separated the box office from Ryan Street. This playbill advertises one of many nationally known acts, vaudeville troupes, and orchestras that played here. The resplendent stage and proscenium also served as a community auditorium for high school graduations and other civic events.

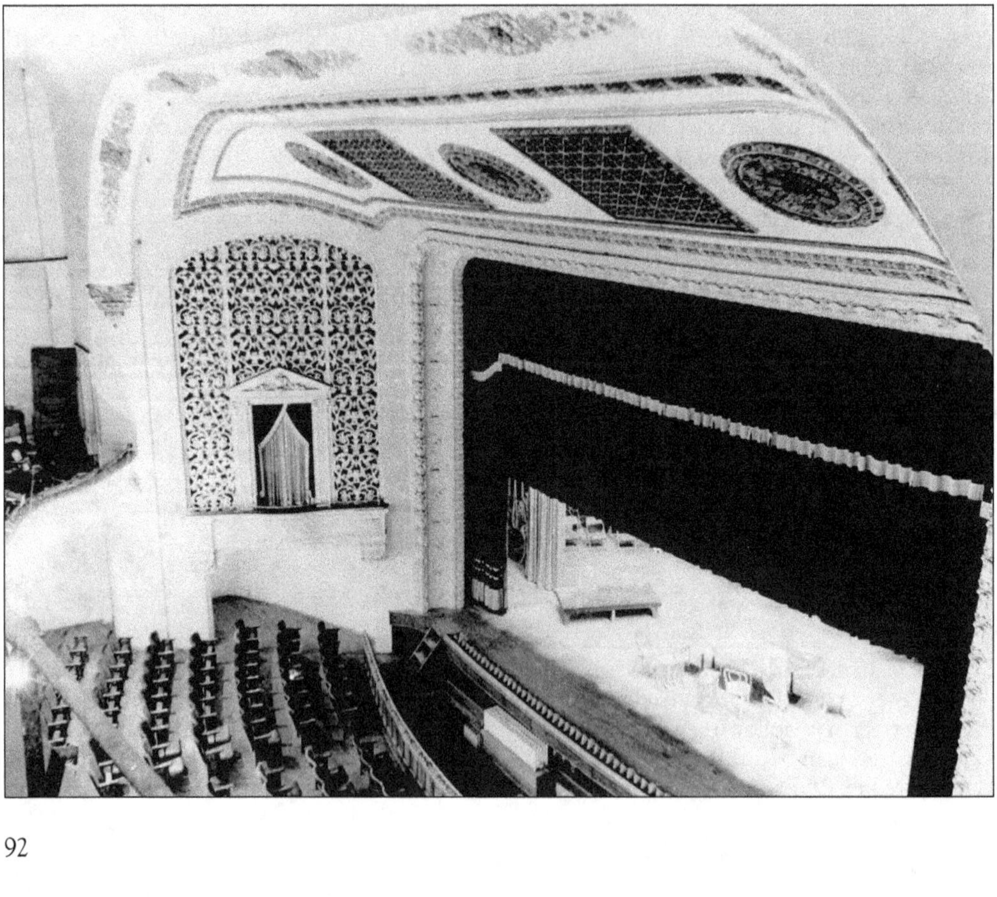

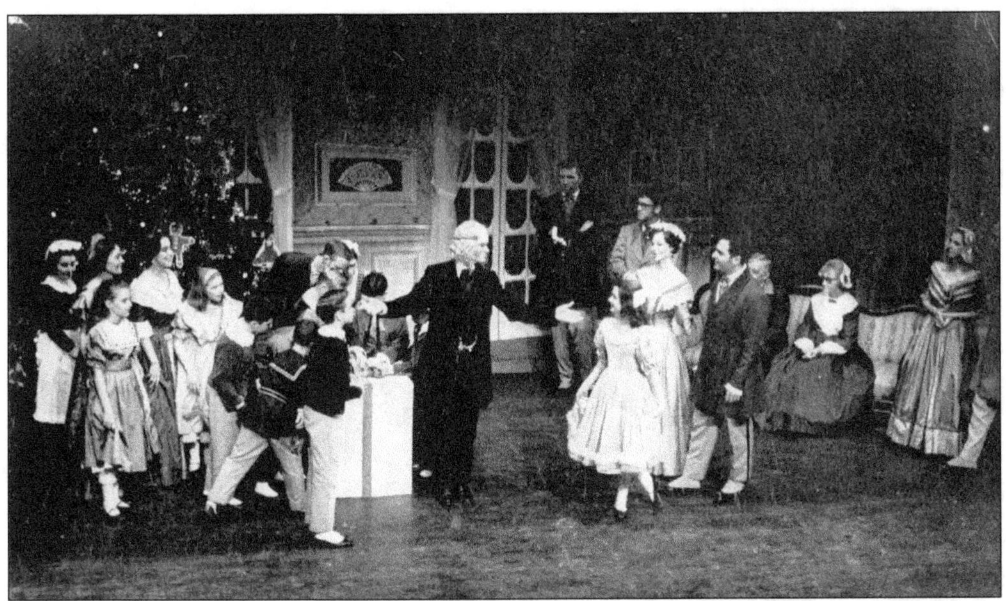

The Lake Charles Ballet Society debuted *The Nutcracker* at the Arcade in 1963, making Lake Charles one of the first cities outside of New York and San Francisco to produce a full-length *Nutcracker*. The Arcade's fly loft made this and other productions possible. Lamar Robertson (at center stage) played Herr Drosselmeyer in the production many times. (Courtesy of Cissie Clarke.)

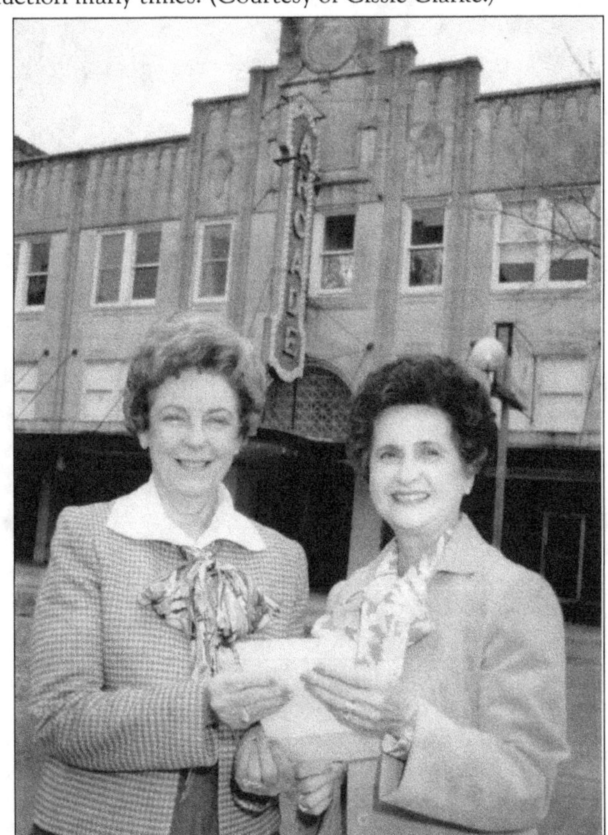

When the Arcade was condemned because of fire code violations in the 1970s, the arts community rallied to restore and save the beautiful and beloved theater. It became southwest Louisiana's first nationally recognized historic site when, because of the efforts of the community and the Calcasieu Historical Preservation Society, it was listed in the National Register of Historic Places in 1978. Perla Baillio Crosby, of Southern Amusement Co., donated the Arcade to Mavis Raggio, as a representative of the Arcade Foundation, in March 1985. Unfortunately, it burned down on Thanksgiving evening that same year. The bricks were saved and used to build the Arcade Pavilion in Bord du Lac Park—a memorial to the enchanted theater.

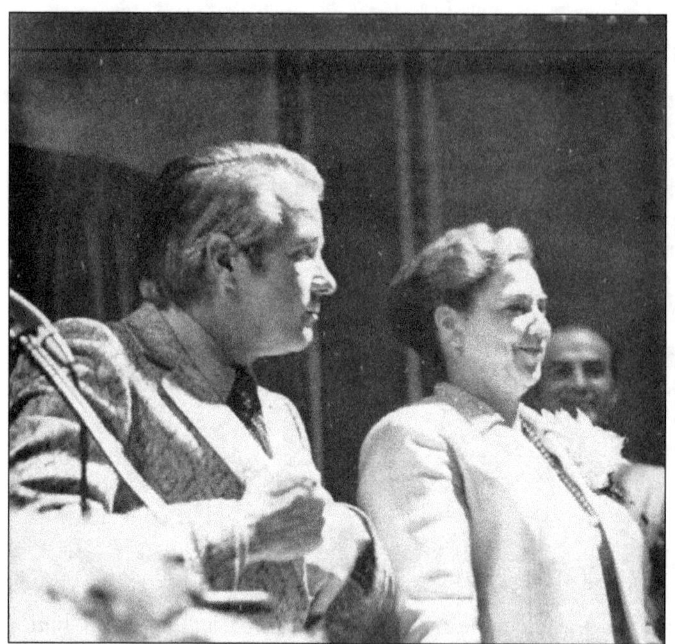

In this 1973 photograph, Ida Winter Clarke stands next to Gov. Edwin Edwards during the closing ceremonies of the Southwestern Regional Ballet Festival, hosted by the Lake Charles Ballet Society. Clarke founded the Lake Charles Ballet Society and served as artistic director from its incorporation in 1963 until her death in 1987; her daughter, Cissie Clarke, served as director from 1987 to 2005. The LCBS brought many professional dance companies to the area and trained performers who went on to professional dance careers around the country. (Courtesy of Cissie Clarke.)

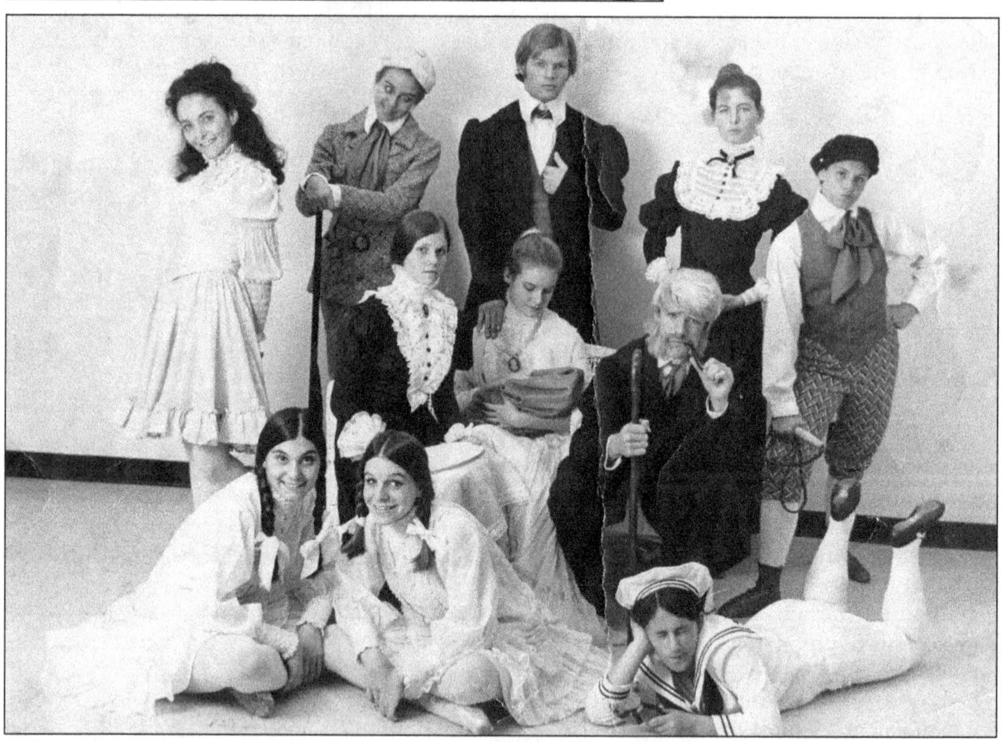

Lady Leah LaFargue Hathaway founded Lake Charles Civic Ballet Company in 1968. This 1969 production of *Daguerreotype*, an original ballet choreographed by Hathaway, was one of many works created by the company. Pictured are, from left to right, (first row, on floor) Thereza DeFelice, Nancy Cagle, and Mary Abate; (second row, seated) Nancy Coldiron, Libby Lovejoy, and Mike White; (third row, standing) artistic director Hathaway, Colleen Hodges, Van White, Martha Kay Reynolds, and Debi Moore. (Courtesy of Lake Charles Civic Ballet.)

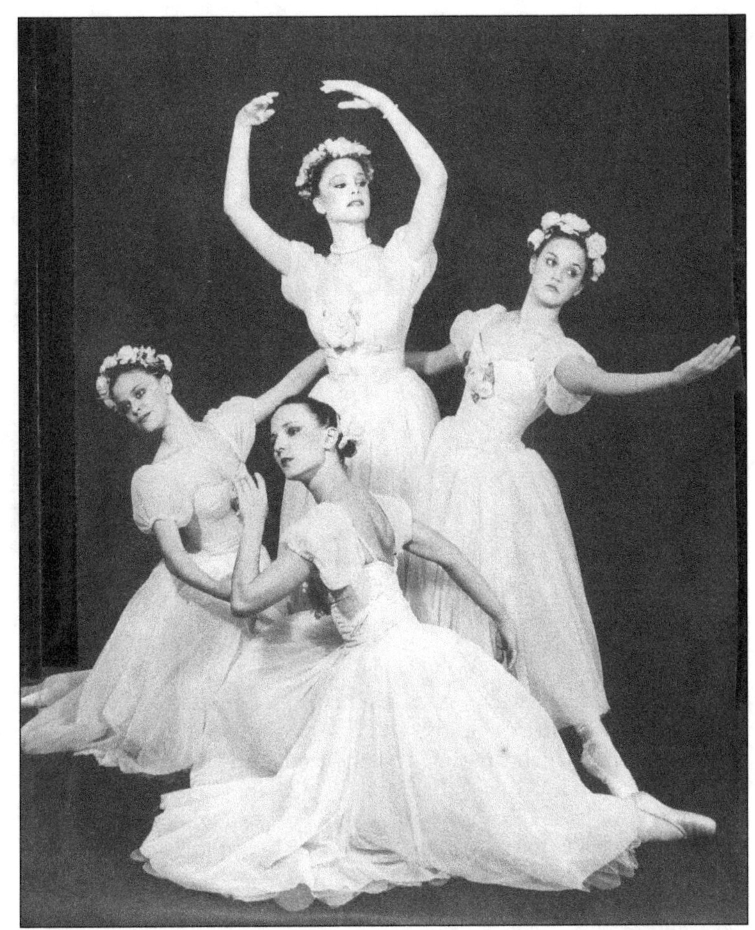

Four of the dancers in Dance Theatre Southwest (DTS) perform *Pas de Quatre.* From left to right: Meg Quinn, Mary Abate, Gambrelle Jones, and Cissy Quinn. Chartered in 1977 under the direction of Sarah Quinn Jones, DTS has produced and choreographed many major works in conjunction with local arts organizations, including *Pulcinella*, *Oklahoma!*, *The King and I*, and, with McNeese Theatre, Keith Gates's *Evangeline.* (Courtesy of Sarah Quinn Jones.)

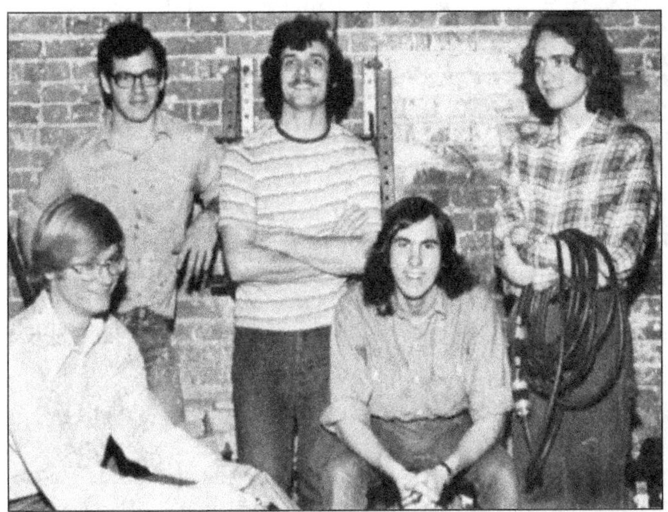

All community arts groups depend upon a great deal of volunteer labor. The backstage crew for the Lake Charles Ballet Society poses in front of the back wall of the Arcade in 1973. From left to right are (seated) Lewis Hawk and Neil Price; (standing) Tim Allured, David Edwards, and David Howard. Today, Allured and his wife, Laura, perform in libraries and elementary schools around the state, and Edwards volunteers backstage with the McNeese Banners Cultural Series.

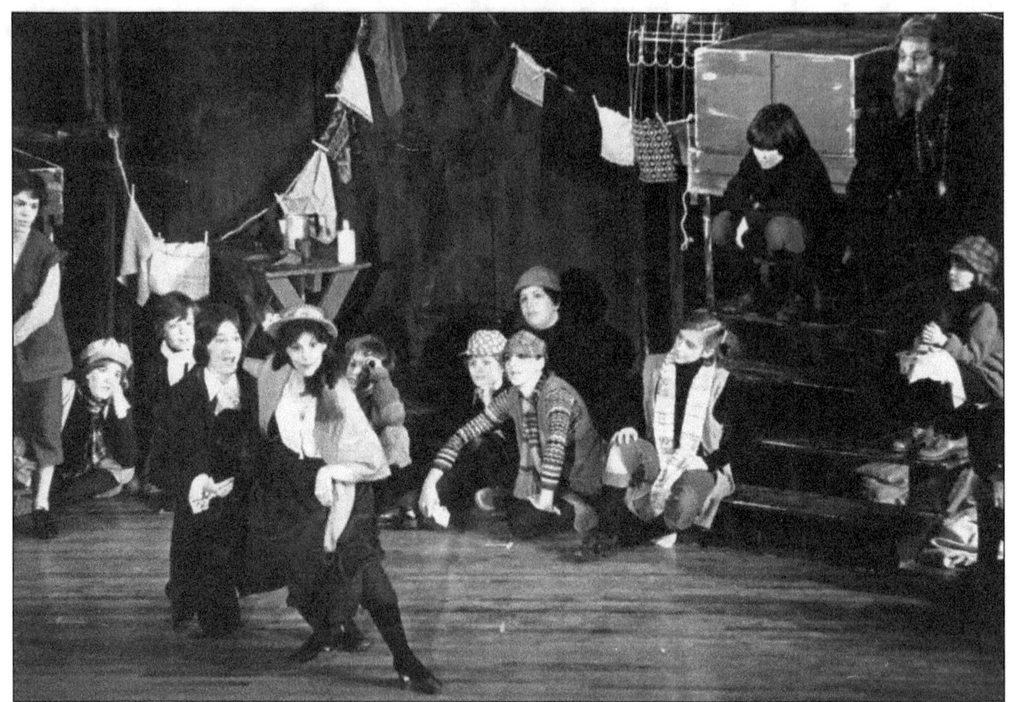

Artists Civic Theatre & Studio (ACTS) was founded by Marc Pettaway, full-time director for 46 years, during which time ACTS produced many Broadway musicals. This 1977 production of *Oliver!* shows Jeff Lyons with Barbara Cox ("Nancy") seated on his knee. This picture was taken on the stage of Lake Charles High School during a school performance. Daniel Ieyoub ("Fagin") stands in the background at right. (Courtesy of Sarah Quinn Jones.)

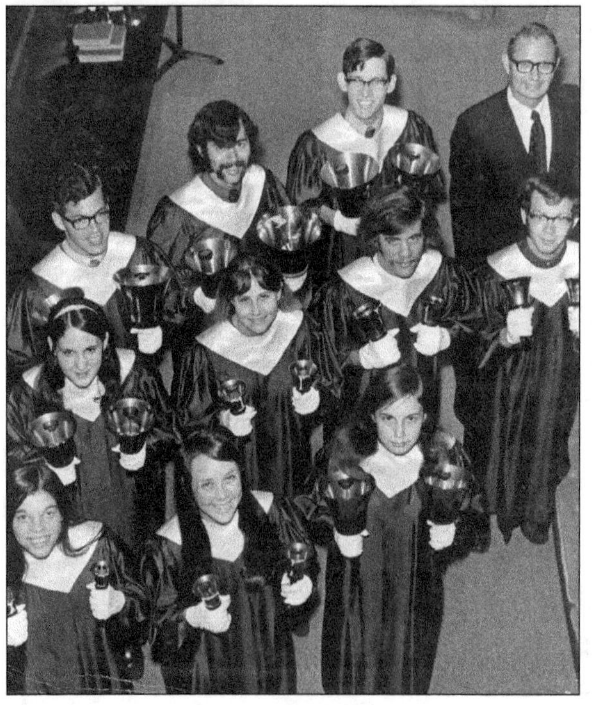

The Wesleyan Bell Choir, directed by Donald Earl Allured, minister of music at First United Methodist Church from 1965 to 1976, became nationally famous and toured the country every summer. A group of amateurs with varying degrees of musical training, their achievement was remarkable. This photograph shows the 1971 choir. Pictured here are, from left to right, (first row) Beth Schmutz Kramer, Marilyn Monk Powers, and Amy Gilham Wallace (who later directed the choir); (second row) Anne Bowman Blume, Nancy Jo Hobbs, James "Jim" Mayo, and Bruce Allured; (third row) Tim Allured, Lee Allured, Bobby Dower (managing editor of the *Lake Charles American Press*), and director Donald Allured. (Courtesy of Marilyn Monk Powers.)

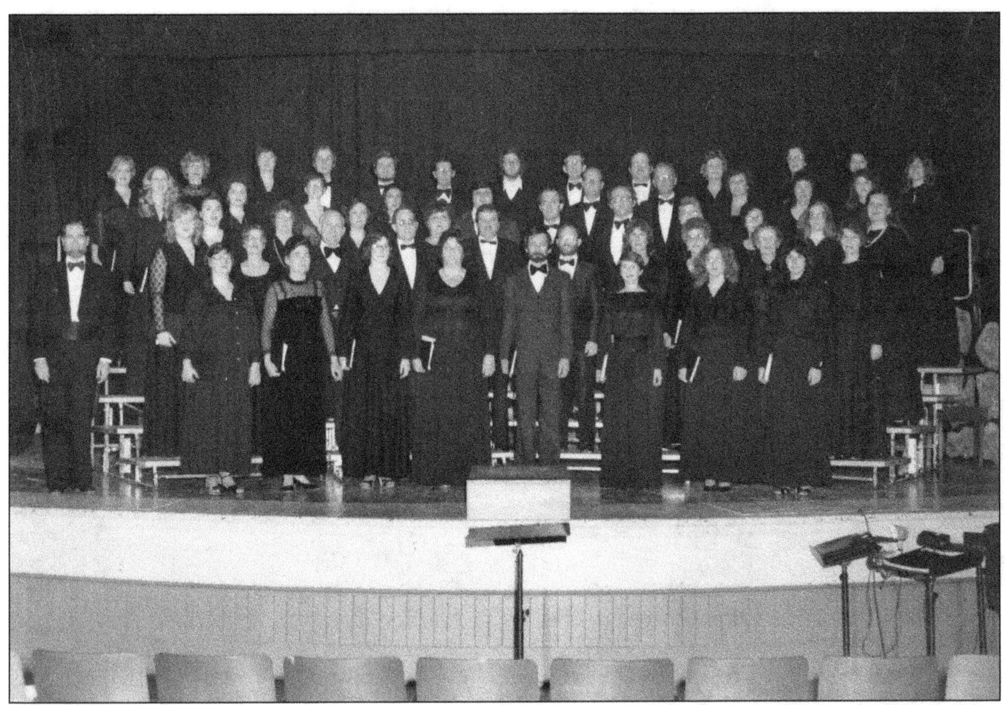

The Louisiana Choral Foundation (above, around 1972) began when Lamar Robertson (at extreme left), choirmaster at University United Methodist Church, and Donald Allured, minister of music at First United Methodist Church, combined the two church choirs to perform Verdi's *Messa da Requiem* as part of the grand opening of the Lake Charles Civic Center. The Masterworks Chorale was directed by Robertson, a Lake Charles native, until his retirement in 2002; he also conducted the children's choir, Les Petites Voix, for many years. The Chorale has been conducted by Dr. Darryl Jones since 2002. With the research help of accompanist and assistant artistic director Abbie Fletcher, the Louisiana Choral Foundation produced *Suite Louisiane* in 1997 to coincide with the opening of Central School as an arts center. In the photograph below, Nathaniel Allured (holding stein) sings lead on "Les Mardi Gras," backed by longtime Chorale members Mike Sober, Tony Palumbo, Bruce Allured, and Ward Fontenot. (Courtesy of Becky Allured.)

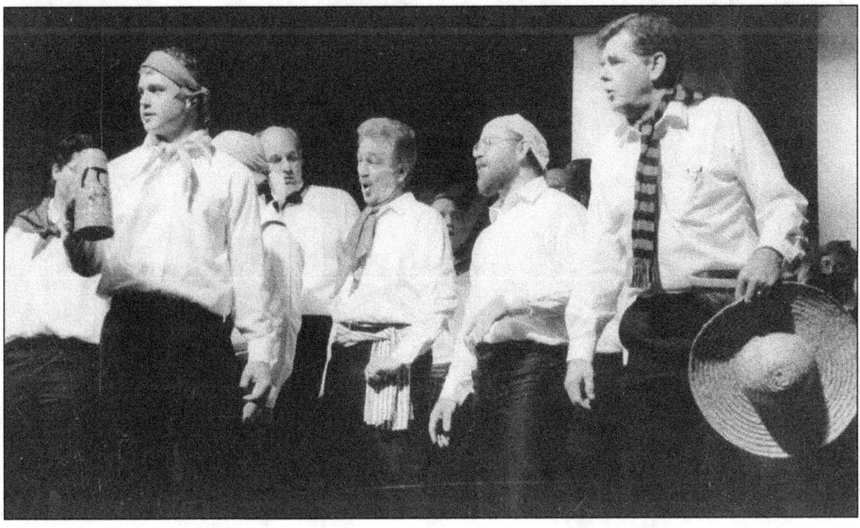

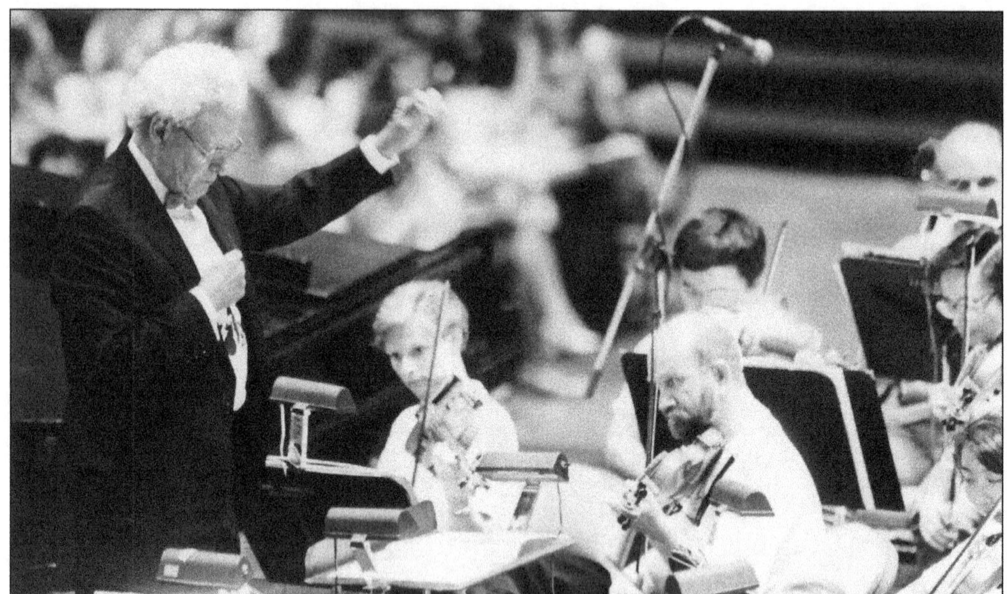

The Lake Charles Symphony, the brainchild of the Junior Welfare League, made its debut in November 1958. Maestro William "Bill" Kushner (above) took over its direction in 1978 and conducted for three decades. Born in Lake Charles in 1924, Kushner graduated from Lake Charles High School and earned degrees from Juilliard and Columbia University, where he met his wife, Sylvia Deutscher, an accomplished musician. The couple's three children, Lesley, Tony, and Eric, also graduated from Lake Charles High School and went on to become internationally acclaimed artists. In the 2005 photograph below, Tony (center) and Eric pose with Eric's wife, Maighread McCann, while visiting family after Hurricane Rita. Tony Kushner is most famous for his epic play, *Angels in America*, which won the Pulitzer Prize in 1993. He has continued to produce award-winning works, and he was awarded the *Chicago Tribune* literary prize for lifetime achievement in 2009. (Above, courtesy of Bill Kushner; below, courtesy of Gloria Wegener.)

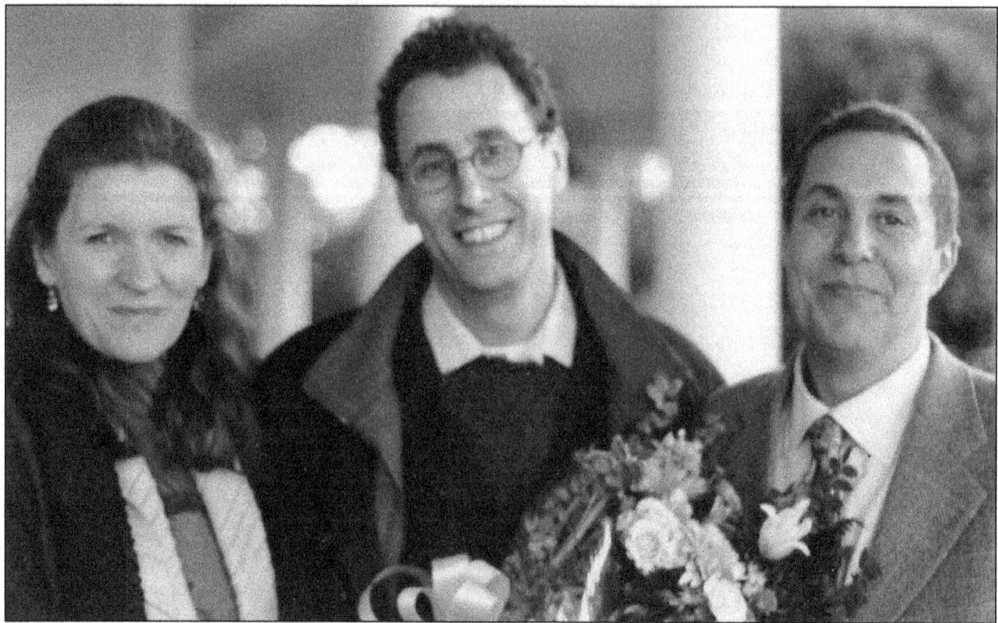

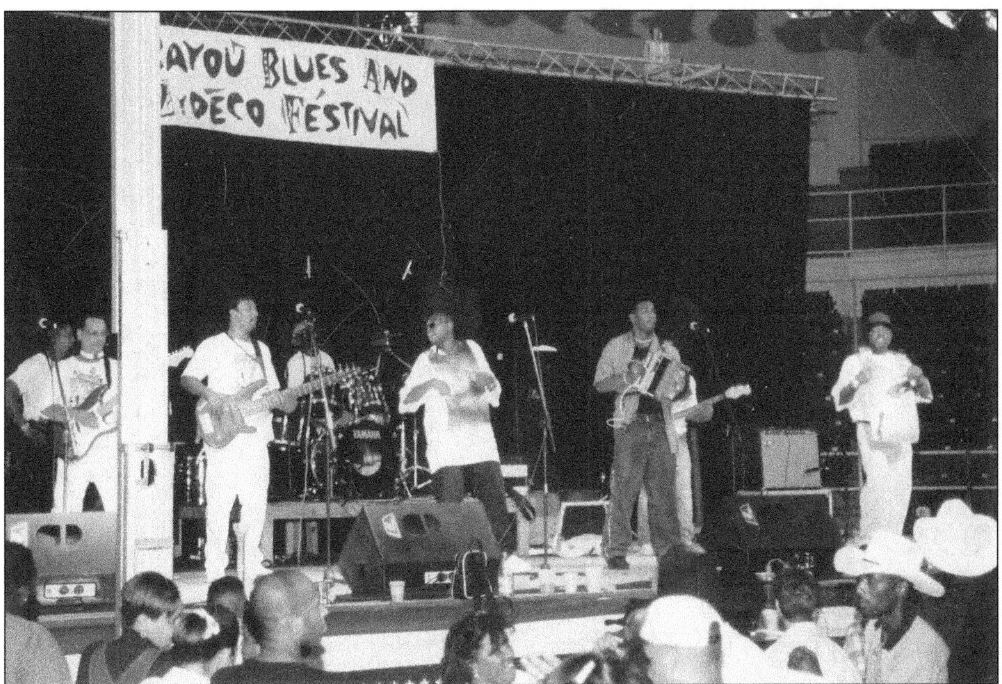

Chris Ardoin and Double Clutchin perform at the Bayou Blues and Zydeco Festival, a joint production of the Black Heritage Festival and the Banners Series held from 1996 to 2001. Ardoin comes from a "tradition of zydeco legends" and is a fourth-generation musician. Ardoin performed at Carnegie Hall at the early age of 10 and is accomplished on the accordion, bass guitar, and the washboard. (Courtesy of Stella Miller, Black Heritage Festival.)

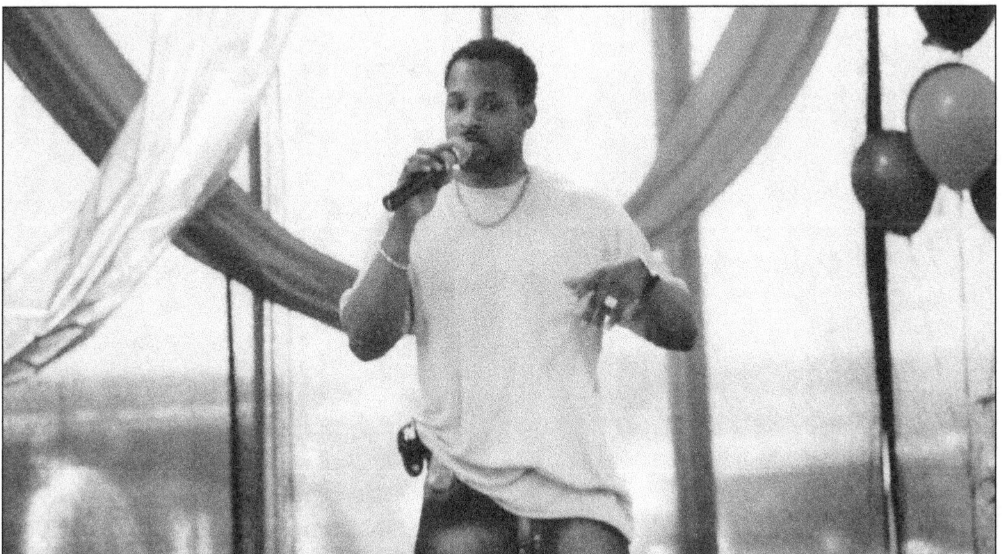

Harold Guillory performed at the 2011 KZWA MLK Family Day at the Lake Charles Civic Center. In 2008, the Black Heritage Festival honored him for his contributions in promoting zydeco music as the host of the television show *Louisiana Live*. The Black Heritage Festival was established in 1987 to present African American culture, performing artists, and educational events. (Courtesy of Stella Miller, Black Heritage Festival.)

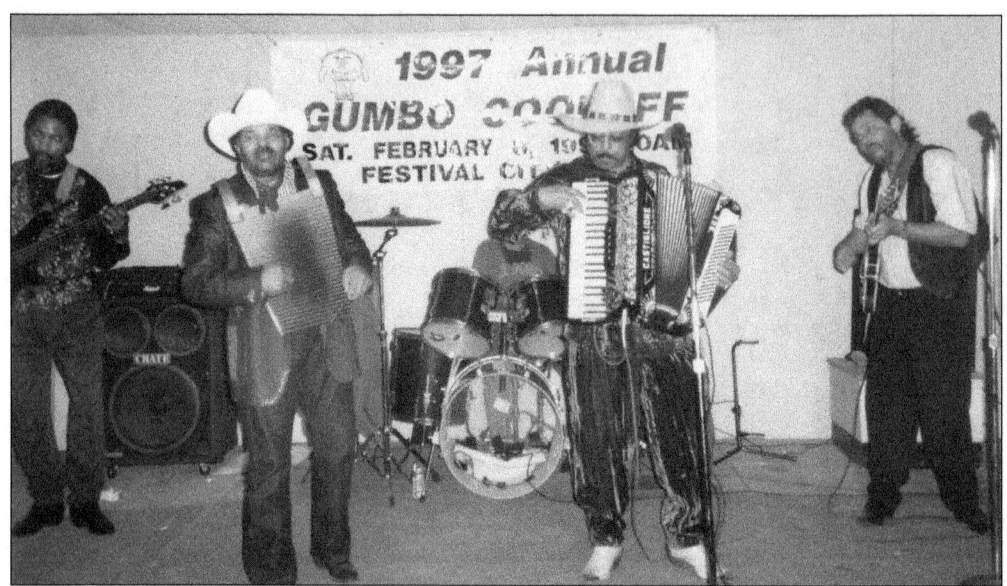

Rockin' Sidney Simien, born in 1938, began his musical career in the late 1950s. While on the Goldband Records label, he "took to wearing a turban" and became known as Count Rockin' Sidney. In the 1970s, he transformed himself into the "zydeco monarch, complete with a crown, cape and gold tooth." His most famous song, "My Toot Toot," won a Grammy and sold over a million copies in 1985. (Courtesy of Lawrence Morrow.)

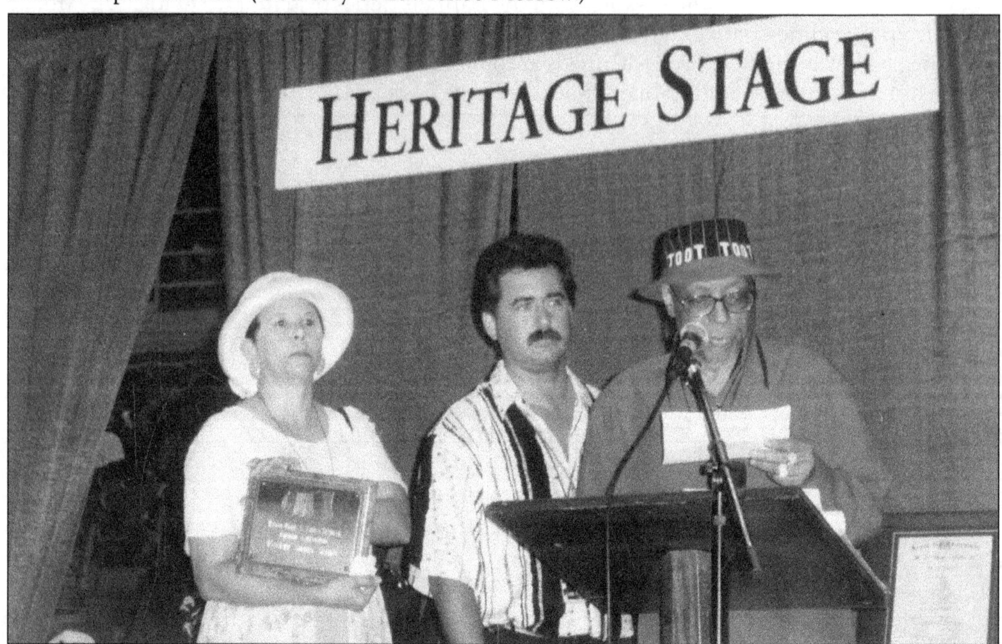

Rockin' Sidney was also an astute businessman. He used royalties from "My Toot Toot" to purchase radio station KAOK-AM and Festival City (a six-acre entertainment complex) in Lake Charles, and started a new label called ZBC Records. Here, he accepts a Lifetime Achievement Award at the 1998 Bayou Blues and Zydeco Festival for his over 30 years of accomplishments in rhythm and blues and zydeco music. Also pictured are Gary Daigle (center) and Sidney's wife, Carol. (Courtesy of Lawrence Morrow.)

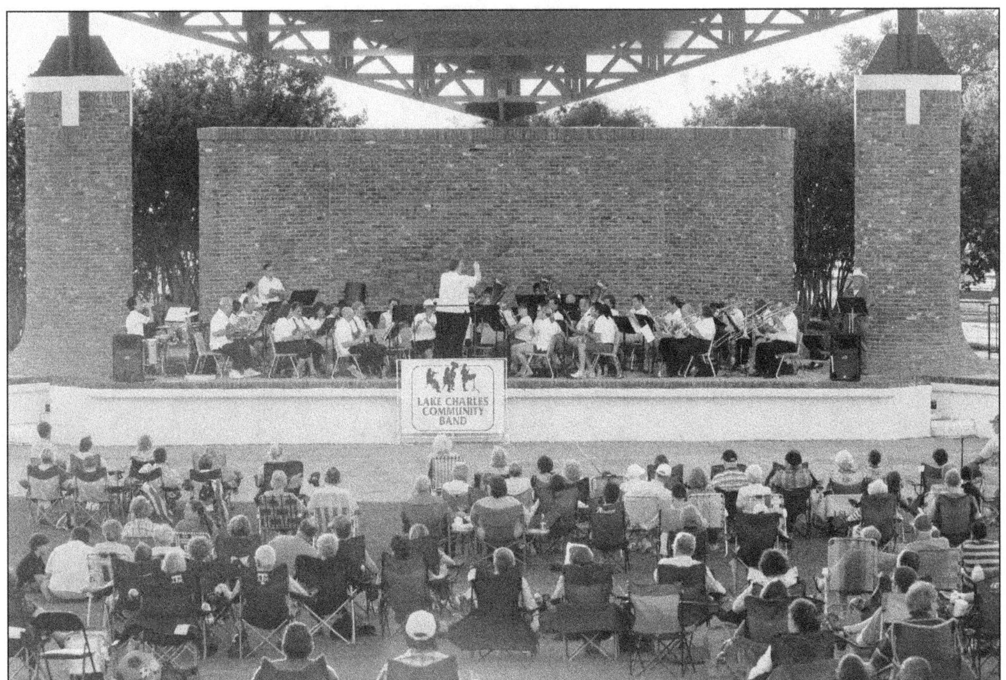

Warrant Officer Herman G. Vincent started the Community Band of Southwest Louisiana in 1979. A graduate of Landry High School, Vincent studied trumpet at Juilliard and later became bandmaster of the Air Force Band at Mitchell Air Force Base in New York. The Community Band is still going strong and is pictured performing at the Arcade Memorial Pavilion on the Fourth of July, conducted by current director Rod Lauderdale. (Courtesy of Dennis Thibodeaux.)

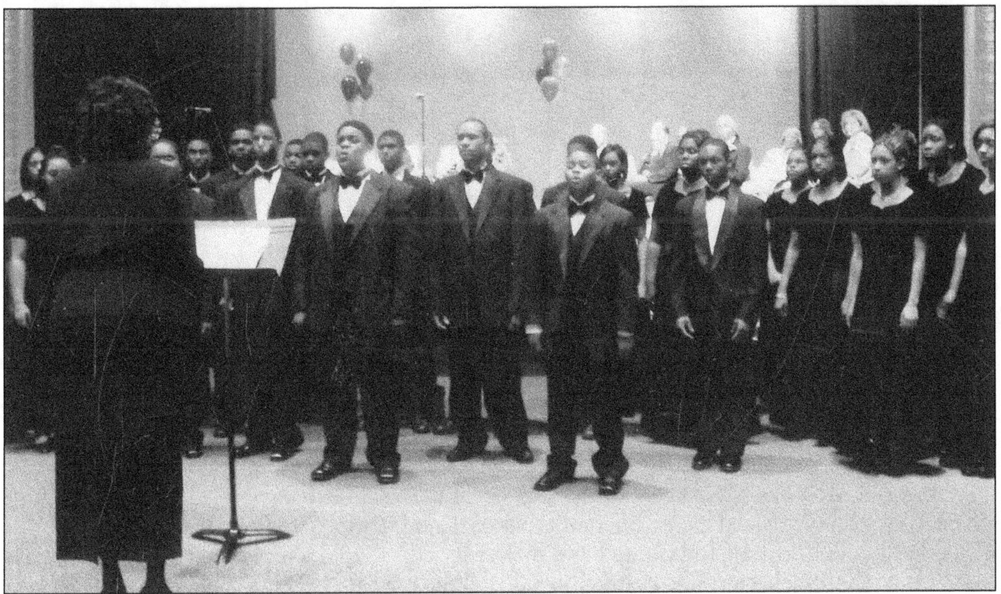

The Washington Marion Magnet High School Gospel Choir performed at the Black Heritage Festival under the direction of Gladys McKnight. The choir regularly performs at other venues and events in the area, such as the Contraband Days Festival and the annual Martin Luther King Gospel Extravaganza. (Courtesy of Stella Miller, Black Heritage Festival.)

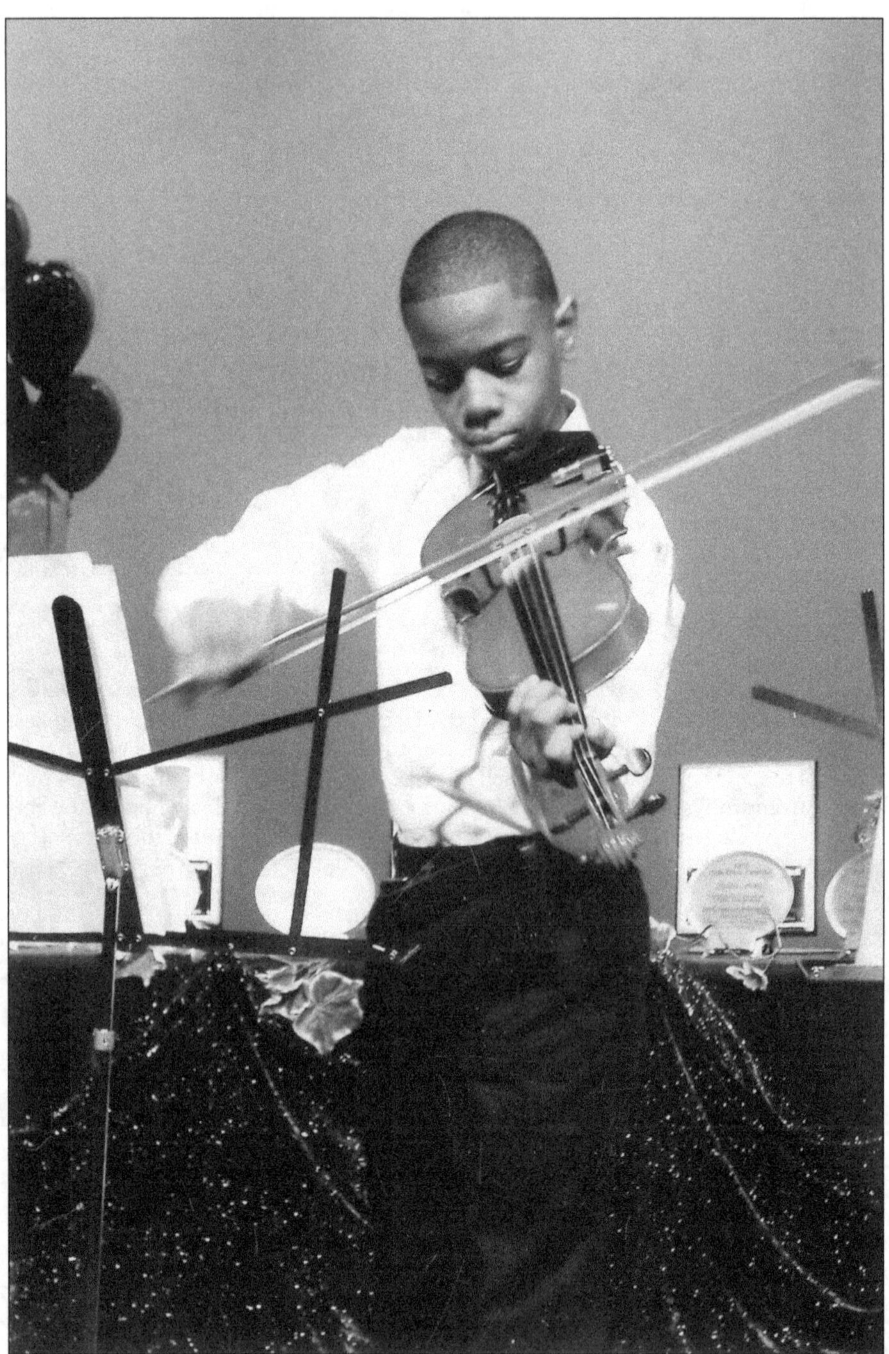

Lake Charles has produced many different types of talented artists, ranging from musicians who learned at home to the highly trained and university-educated. Here, 13-year-old Jairus Daigle performs at the Black Heritage Festival in 2005. The son of Chester Daigle II, a well-known Louisiana blues and jazz musician, Jairus, a classically trained violinist, plays jazz and blues violin professionally. Jairus Daigle is proud to represent the next generation of Lake Charles talent, as indicated by the title of his first album, *It's My Time* (2009). (Courtesy of Stella Miller, Black Heritage Festival.)

Eight

Familiar Faces

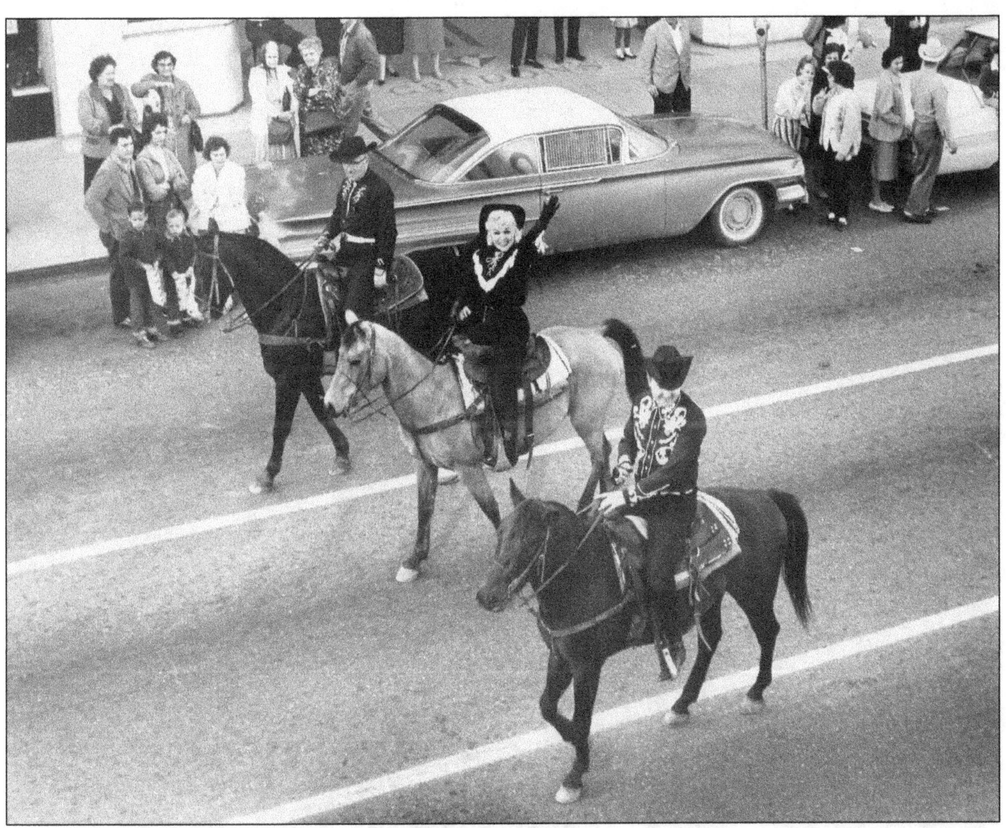

Lee Janot (center) rides down Ryan Street during a rodeo parade. Lenore P. "Lee" Janot Rew had an hour-long afternoon variety show on the KPLC television station during the 1960s. A pioneer for women in broadcasting, Lee started her career at KLOU-AM before moving to KPLC.

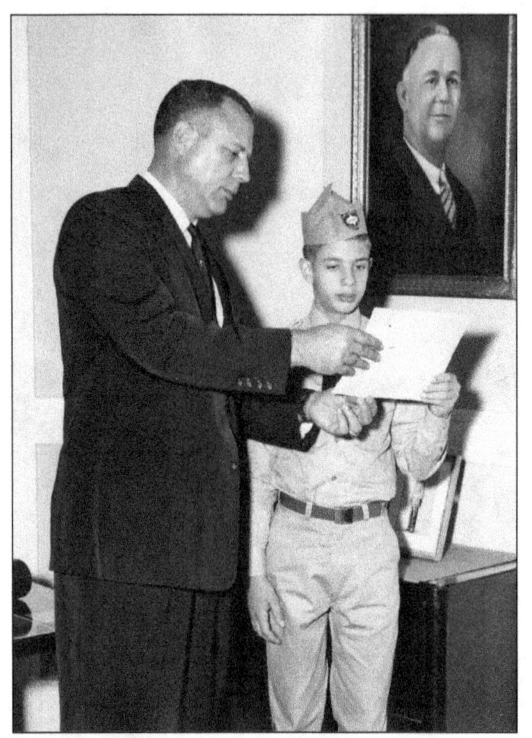

Henry A. "Ham" Reid Jr. was elected Calcasieu Parish sheriff in 1943. He was the youngest sheriff in the nation, assuming office at the age of 21, and was reelected nine times. He is pictured here presenting the Junior Deputy Award to his son, a member of the first junior deputy class in Calcasieu Parish. In the background is a portrait of Henry A. Reid Sr., elected Calcasieu Parish sheriff in 1912 and 1928–1941. The Reid family served Calcasieu Parish in law enforcement for 96 years. (Courtesy of Lawrence Morrow.)

Alvin Dark (center) attended Lake Charles High School and lettered in football, basketball, track, and baseball. He began college at LSU, where he played all four sports. Dark transferred to Southwestern Louisiana Institute to finish his degree, and began his professional baseball career for the Boston Braves in 1948 as their rookie of the year. He later played shortstop for the New York Giants.

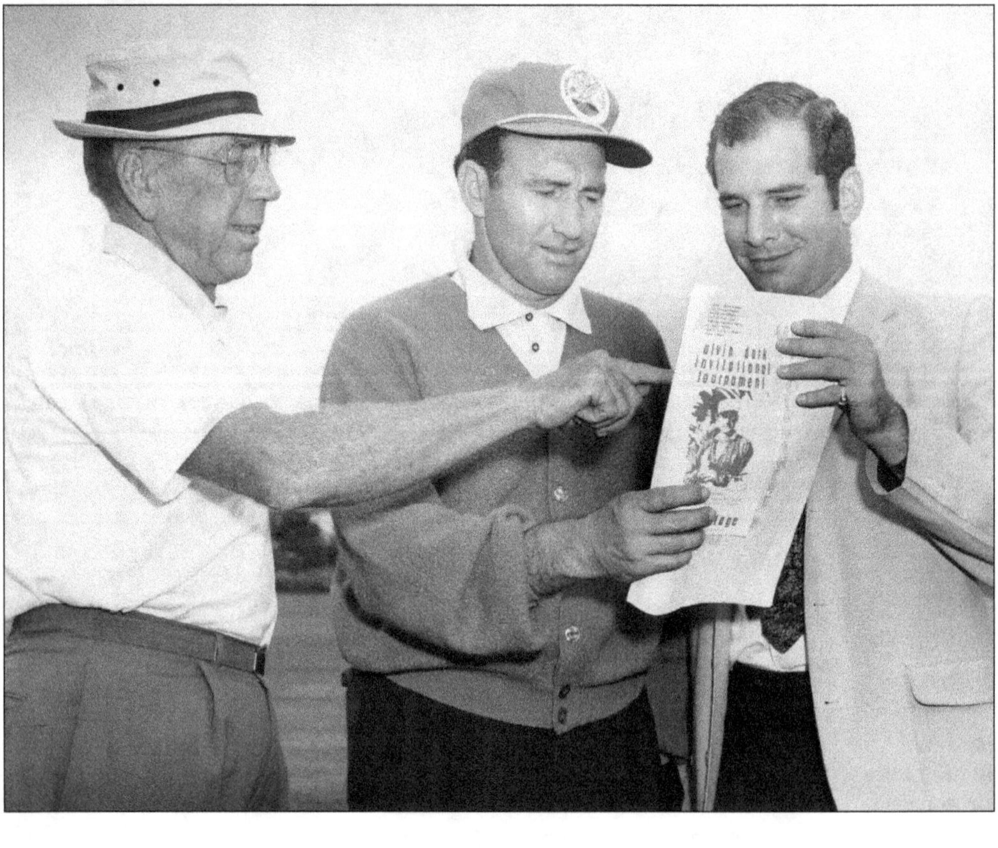

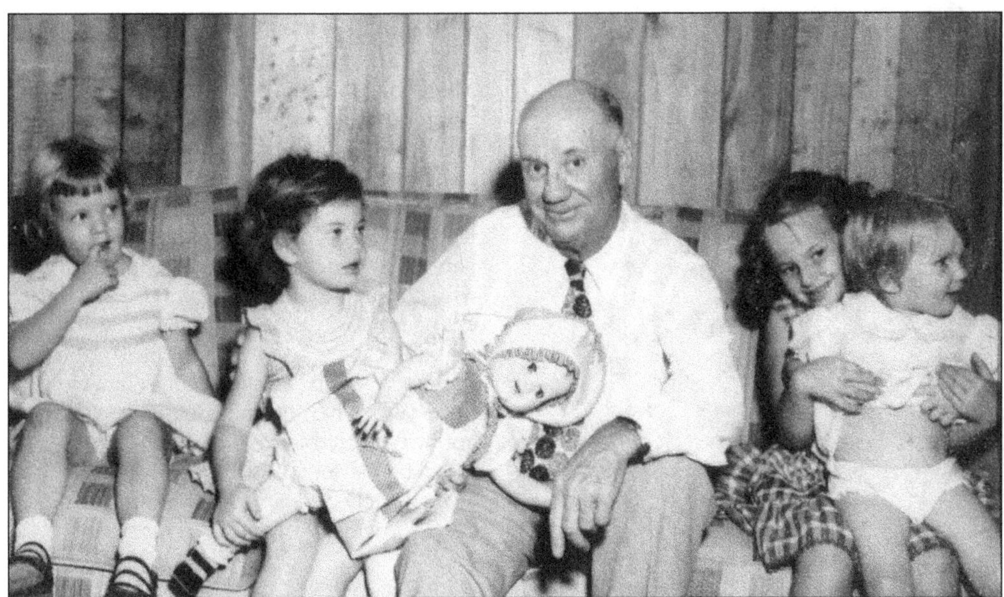

William Thomas Burton (1884–1974) moved to southwest Louisiana from Texas as a teenager and worked in a variety of businesses, including oil and banking. His proudest accomplishment was saving the assets and deposits of countless citizens who had their money in the Calcasieu National Bank, which almost failed during the Great Depression. Securing a loan from the Reconstruction Finance Corporation, he liquidated the old Calcasieu National Bank and rechartered it as the new Cal Marine National Bank, which opened for business in 1934. A noted philanthropist, he contributed generously to his favorite causes, including McNeese State University. He donated the land upon which Burton Coliseum is built. In the c. 1953 image above, Burton sits with several of his great-grandchildren. Pictured are, from left to right, Carolyn Woosley, Linda Lou Lawton Drost, Burton, Evelyn Gay Lawton, and Mary Edith Woosley. Calcasieu Marine National Bank, a three-story, limestone-faced building, is one of a group of buildings in Lake Charles designed by the New Orleans architectural firm Favrot and Livaudais. (Above, courtesy of Carolyn Woosley.)

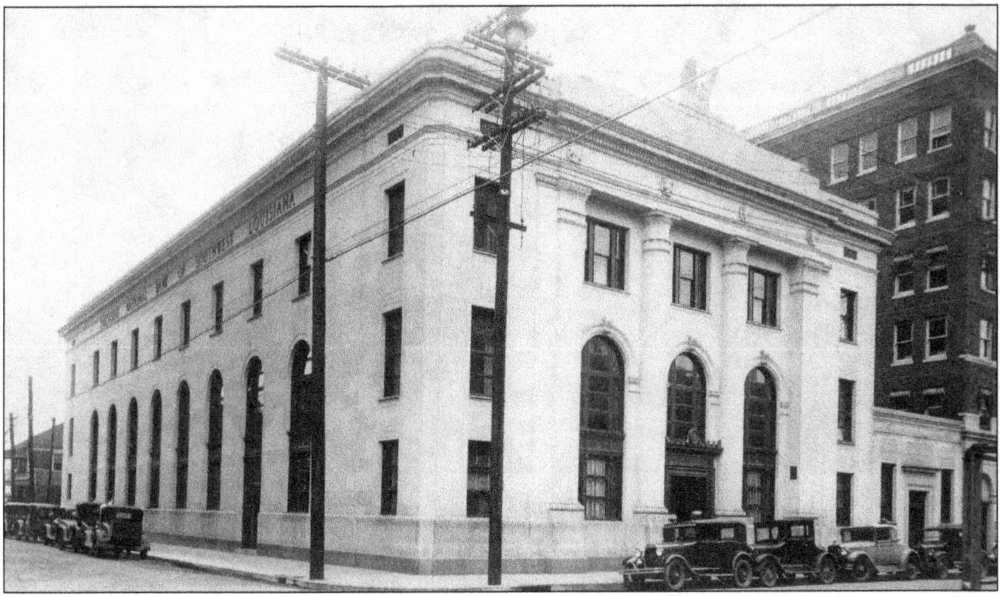

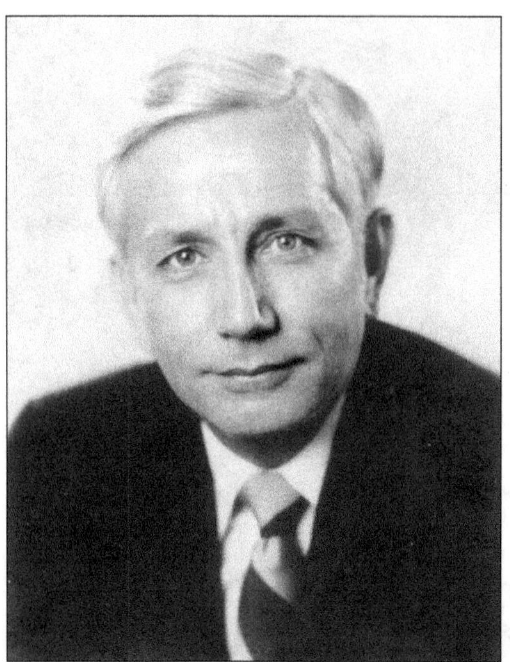

William Lasater "Bill" McLeod Jr. was born in 1931 in Marks, Mississippi. In 1942, McLeod's family moved to Lake Charles, where his father was the minister of the First Presbyterian Church. In 1968, McLeod was elected the state representative from Lake Charles. During the 1968 session of the legislature, several reform-minded legislators banded together to form the "Young Turks," who crafted a series of bills intended to change the way state government operates, making it more accountable to the public. McLeod remained a state representative until 1975, when he became a state senator, and was elected judge of the Fourteenth Judicial District Court in 1990. The annual McLeod Lecture Series at McNeese State University is named in his honor.

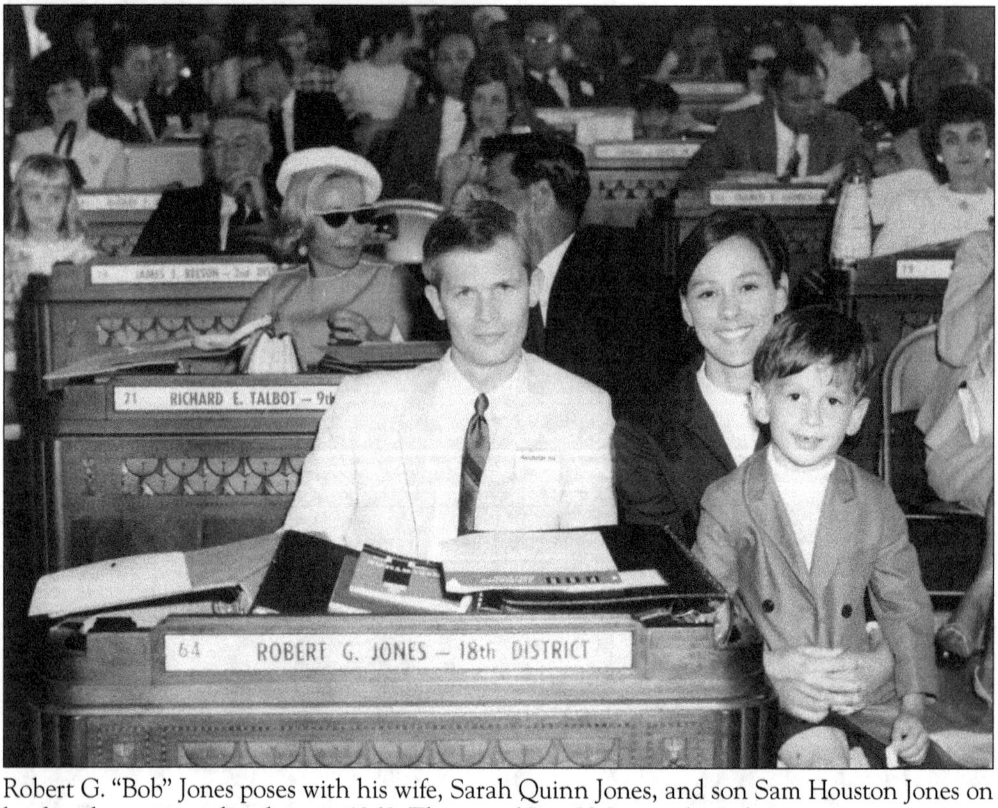

Robert G. "Bob" Jones poses with his wife, Sarah Quinn Jones, and son Sam Houston Jones on his first day as a state legislator in 1968. The son of Sam H. Jones, the only Louisiana governor to hail from Lake Charles, Bob Jones joined Bill McLeod Jr., as one of the "Young Turks." His term in the house was followed by one term in the Louisiana Senate. (Courtesy of Robert G. Jones.)

Reginald Ball Jr. owns one of the most successful black-owned businesses in the state, Reggie Ball's Cajun Foods Inc. The business was founded by Reginald Ball Sr. (1918–1979), who ran Ball's Auditorium (pictured in chapter six) in the 1950s, staging dances and concerts—but the restaurant adjacent to the auditorium became his greatest success. People came from all over to taste the famous fried chicken seasoned with his special concoction of spices, and he soon opened restaurants as far away as Chicago under the name Creole Fried Chicken. The family business now concentrates on the seasonings, and Reggie Ball's Cajun Foods is expanding its markets to include major retail chains around the country.

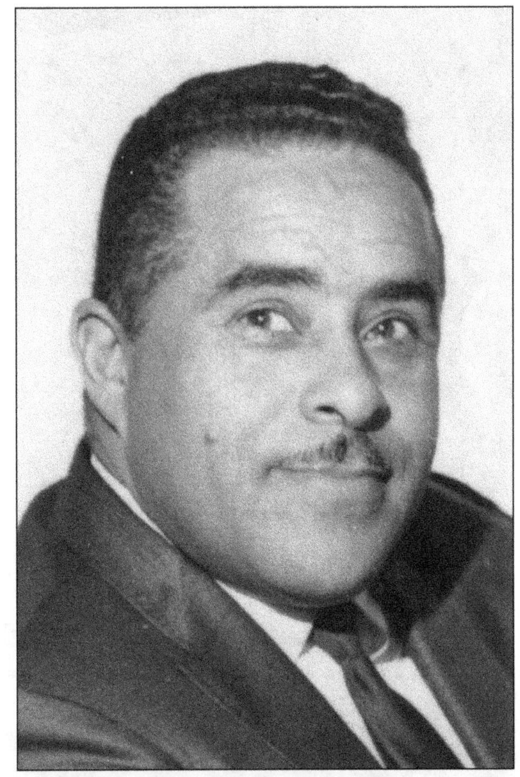

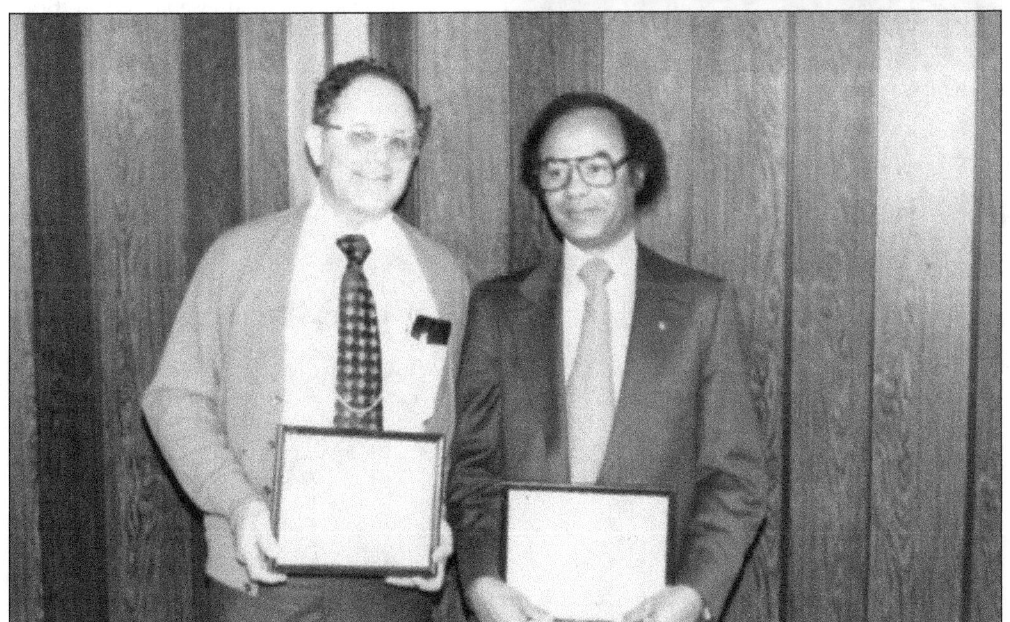

Mack Abraham (left) founded Abe's Food Center. Like many Lebanese, the Abrahams operated family-owned grocery or dry goods stores. The first Abe's Grocery began in 1946 on the corner of Bank and Commerce Streets. Frank Pryce (right) owned Pryce's Pharmacy on Enterprise Boulevard. Pryce's Pharmacy turned 100 years old in 2008, with Pryce serving as pharmacist for 55 years. Frank's grandfather, Dr. George S. Pryce, started Pryce's Pharmacy in 1908.

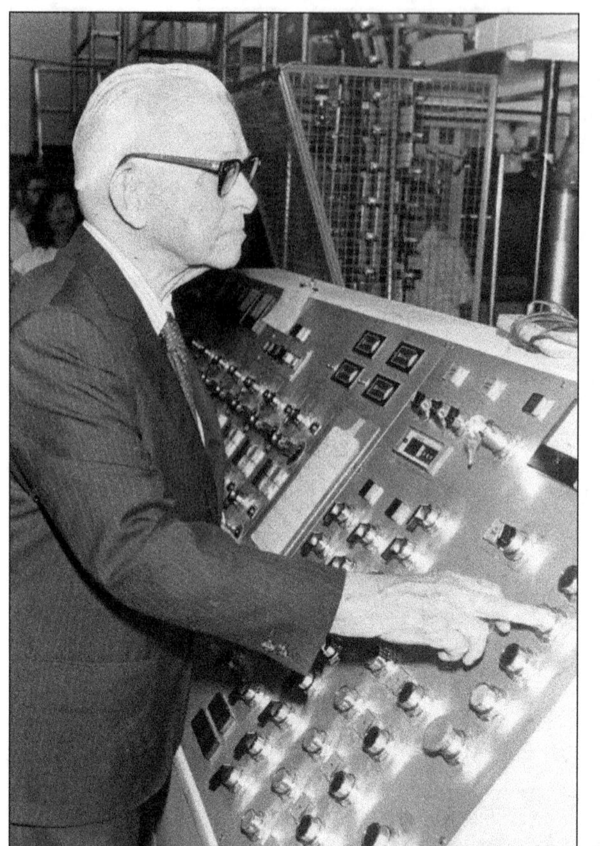

Thomas B. Shearman Sr. is seen around 1985 at the controls of the *Lake Charles American Press*, the longest running newspaper in southwest Louisiana. The *American Press* was created when the *Lake Charles Daily Press* merged with the *Lake Charles Daily American* in 1910. Shearman purchased the paper in 1943 after working several years in national advertising. The Shearman family has contributed generously to the community, particularly in the arts. Three generations of Shearmans have led the newspaper, and its current publisher, Tom Shearman III, has been active in historic preservation in downtown's Charpentier District. (Courtesy *Lake Charles American Press*.)

James C. "Jim" Beam has been with the *American Press* as an editor and reporter since 1961. Though he retired as executive editor in 2000, he continues to cover the Louisiana legislature, a job that takes a good bit of seasoning to do well. His son, Bryan C. Beam, has served as Calcasieu Parish administrator since April 2010.

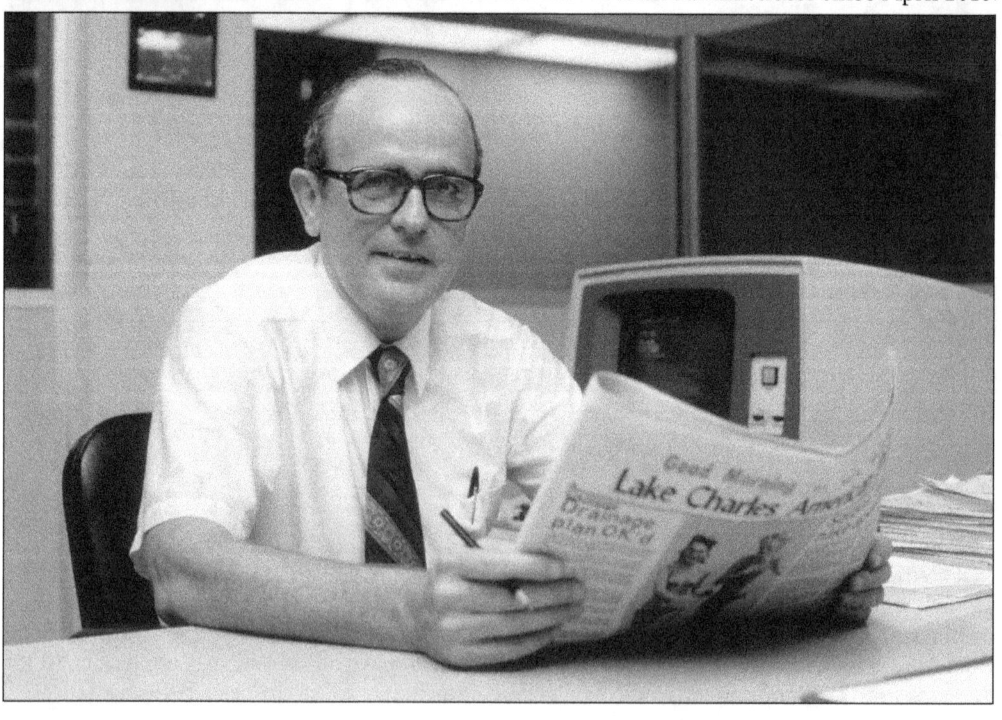

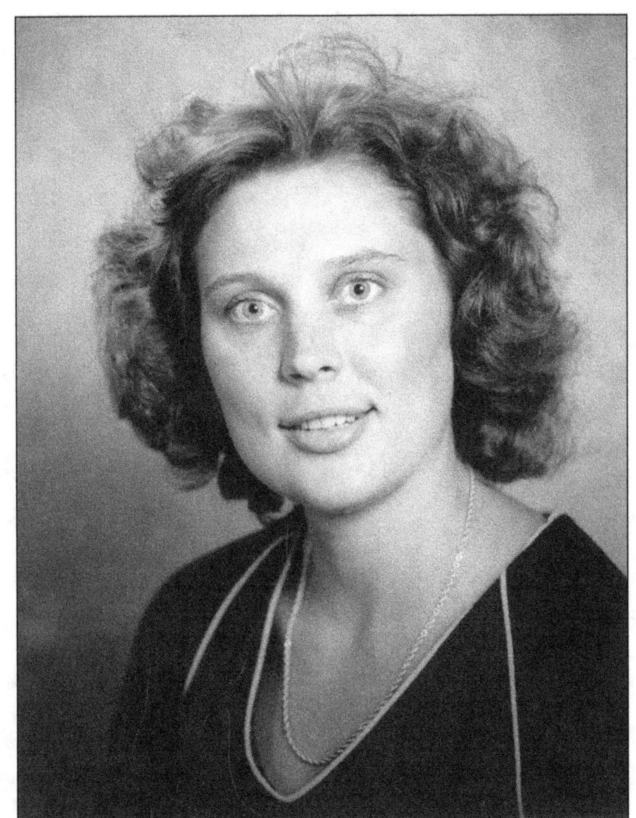

Mary Kay Hopkins, pictured here around 1978, is a pioneering businesswoman in Lake Charles. In 1976, she opened a real estate brokerage, now Mary Kay Hopkins LLC, which was the first small business in the state to receive the Louisiana Quality Award from the Louisiana Quality Foundation. She became one of the first women in the Southwest Louisiana Chamber of Commerce when she joined in 1978, and the Southwest Louisiana Association of Realtors twice named her Realtor of the Year.

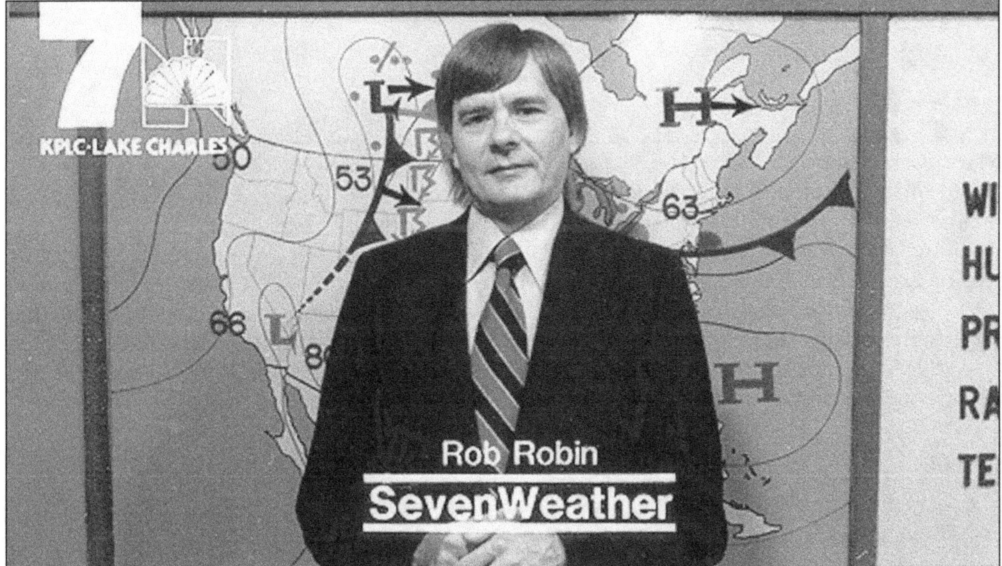

Rob Robin was an icon as the dependable weathercaster at KPLC television station from 1971 to 1987. In those days, being a weathercaster required manual dexterity as well as intelligence and training—Rob drew the weather map behind him by hand. Rob came to Lake Charles from Amarillo, Texas, in 1966 to work at KLOU radio, and returned to his radio roots in 1987 at KYKZ, where he has remained since. (Courtesy of Rob Robin.)

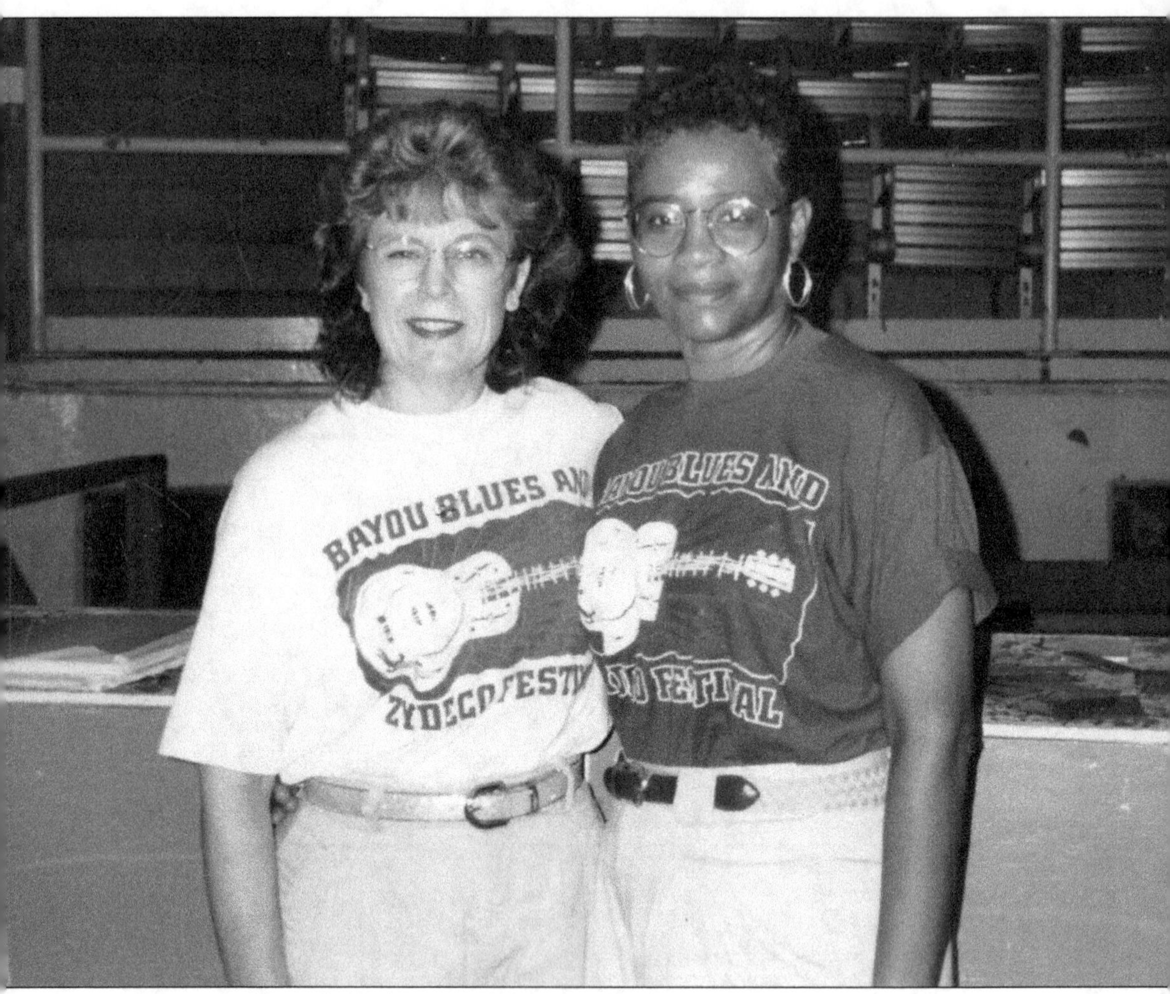

Mary Richardson (left), director of the Banners Series at McNeese State University since it began in 1992, and Stella Miller (right), longtime director of the Black Heritage Festival, take a break from the action at the Bayou Blues and Zydeco Festival in 1996. The festival was jointly sponsored by the two organizations until 2001. The Black Heritage Festival was established in 1987 to promote African American culture and is held every March at the Lake Charles Civic Center. It also sponsors the Black Heritage Gallery, Partners in Education, scholarships for graduating seniors, the Black History Hall of Fame, and educational programs. The Banners Series, founded by McNeese president Dr. Robert Hebert and held each spring, presents more than 20 cultural events for the public and about 60 visiting artist programs for schools.

State representative Elcie Guillory (left) stands with Bishop Jude Speyrer (center) and Chester Jones (right). Guillory served Calcasieu Parish and Southwest Louisiana for more than 30 years. He served 17 years on the Calcasieu Parish Police Jury and was elected state representative in 1993. (Courtesy of Lawrence Morrow.)

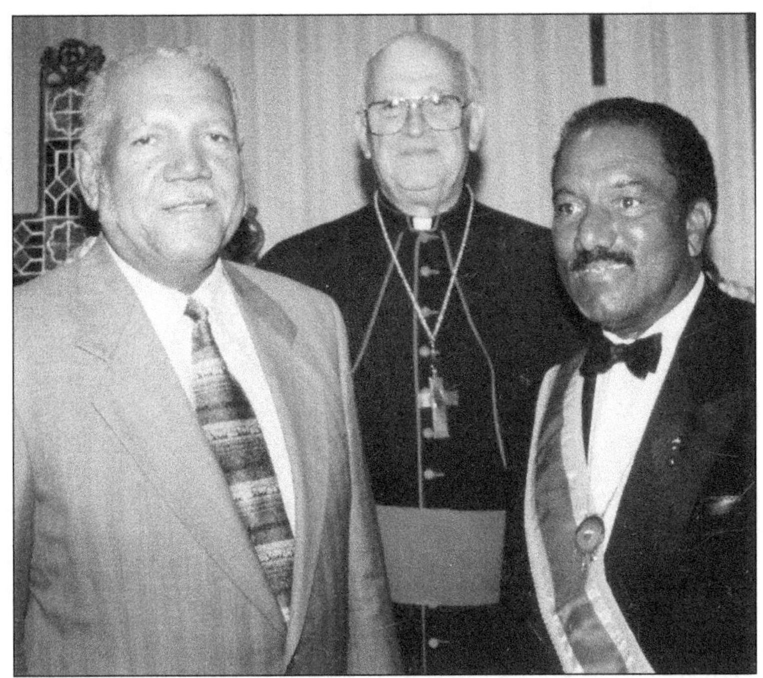

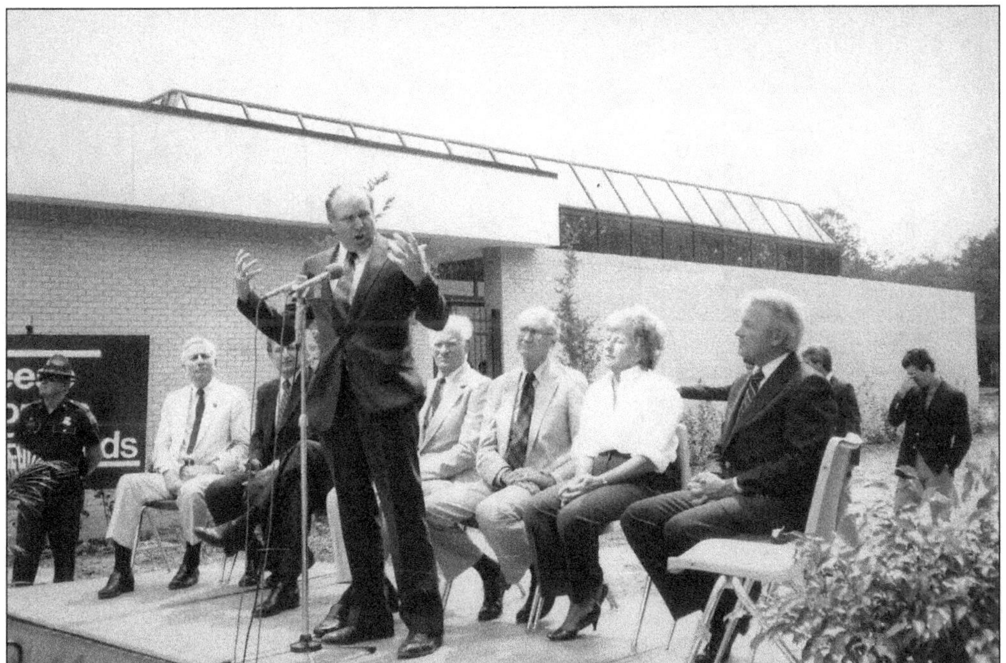

McNeese president Jack Doland (standing) dedicated the new business building in 1984. It was renamed in 1988 in honor of W.T. and Ethel Burton, major benefactors of McNeese. Doland became the head football coach for McNeese in 1970 and left eight years later to run for the Louisiana State Senate. Seated from left to right are Sen. William "Bill" McLeod, Mayor Paul Savoie, two unidentified, Frank Pruitt, unidentified, and Gov. Edwin Edwards.

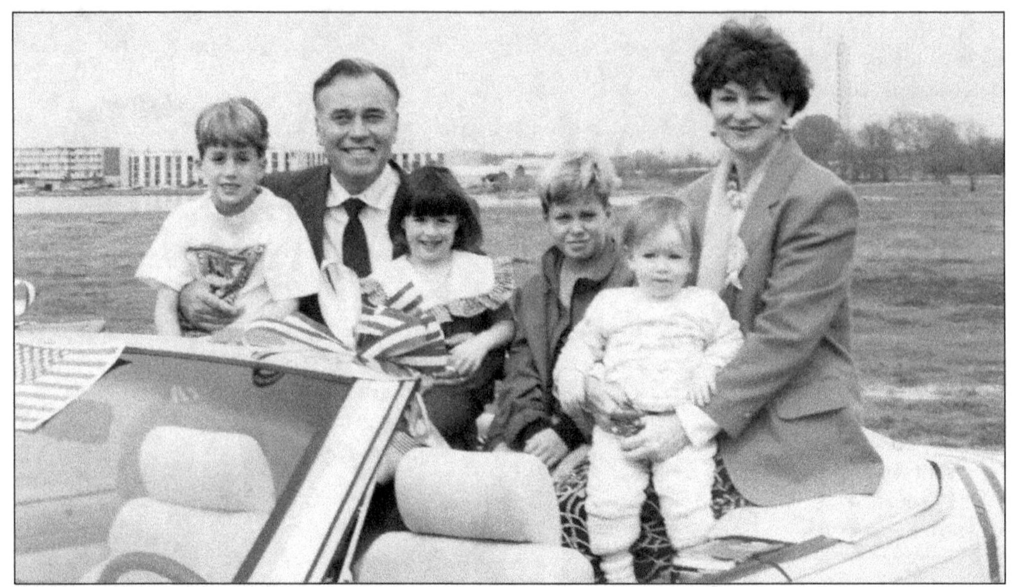

James "Jimmy" Cox, attorney, and Marilyn Cox hold their grandchildren as they prepare to join a Gulf War parade held the day after his election to the Louisiana State Senate in 1991. Harrah's Casino, on the lake in the background, was destroyed by Hurricane Rita in 2005. The children are, from left to right, Shannon Filo, Claire Elise Hodgins, Taylor Filo, and Camille Renee Hodgins. (Courtesy of Jim and Marilyn Cox.)

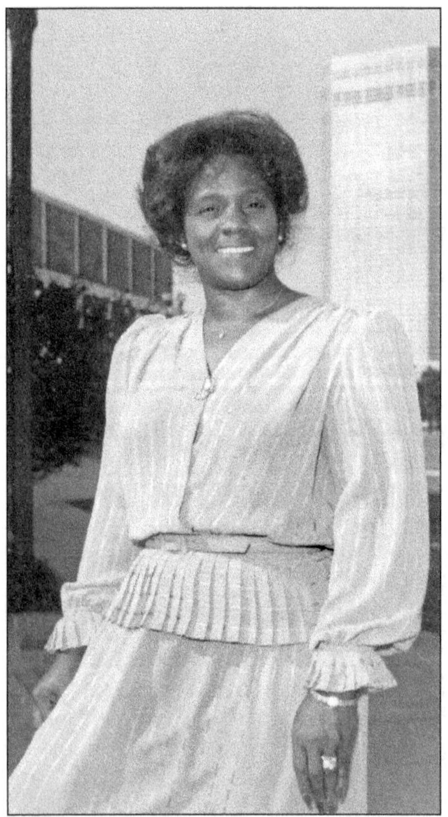

Faye Brown Blackwell is the general manager and co-owner of KZWA-FM radio, which opened in 1994 on Enterprise Boulevard. Blackwell is the founder of the Martin Luther King Coalition, which celebrated its 25th anniversary in 2009. The annual MLK celebrations include a memorial prayer breakfast, festival, parade, and gospel extravaganza. Blackwell serves the community as a member of several civic and social clubs and is a past member of the Lake Charles City Council. (Courtesy of Lawrence Morrow.)

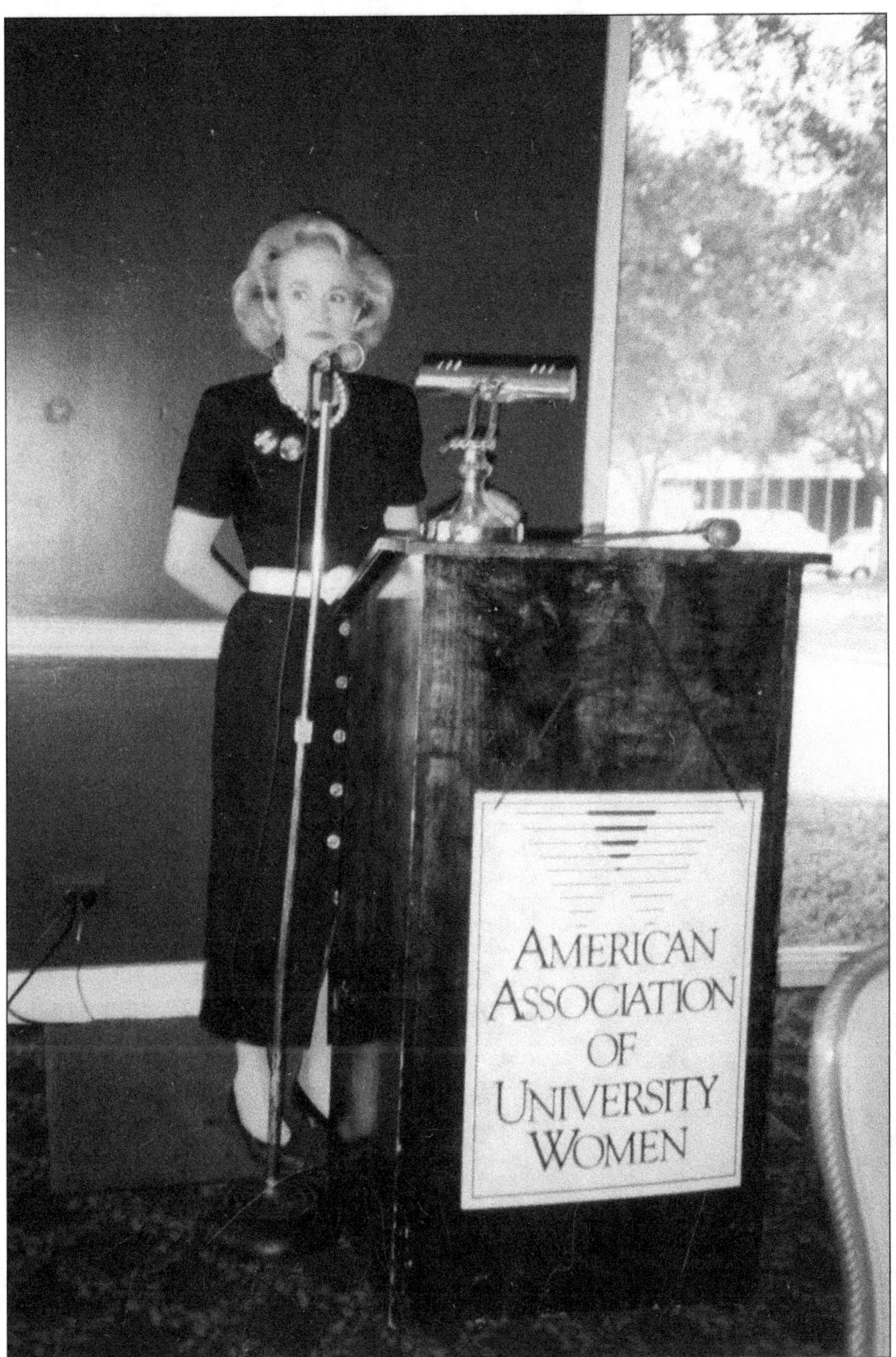

Lake Charles native Willie Landry Mount speaks to the American Association of University Women at their Founder's Day luncheon in April 1994. Mount served for six and a half years as Lake Charles's first female mayor, and in 1999, she was the first woman elected to the Louisiana State Senate to represent District 27.

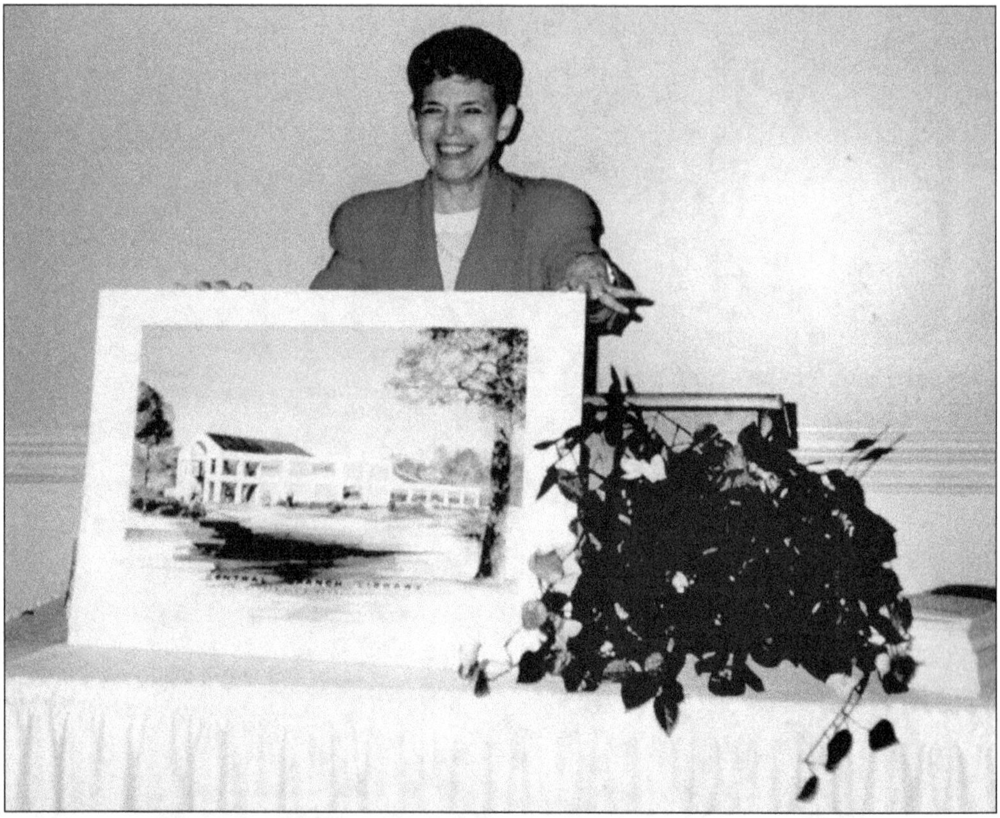

Lynda Carlberg served as the library director of Calcasieu Parish from 1978 to 1997. Under her leadership, Calcasieu was the only system in the nation to simultaneously renovate all of its existing libraries. This 1994 photograph shows her holding a painting of Central Library, which opened in 1995. She was a recognized expert in public librarianship and was deeply admired by her colleagues. The Lynda Carlberg Award is given in her memory to outstanding Louisiana librarians.

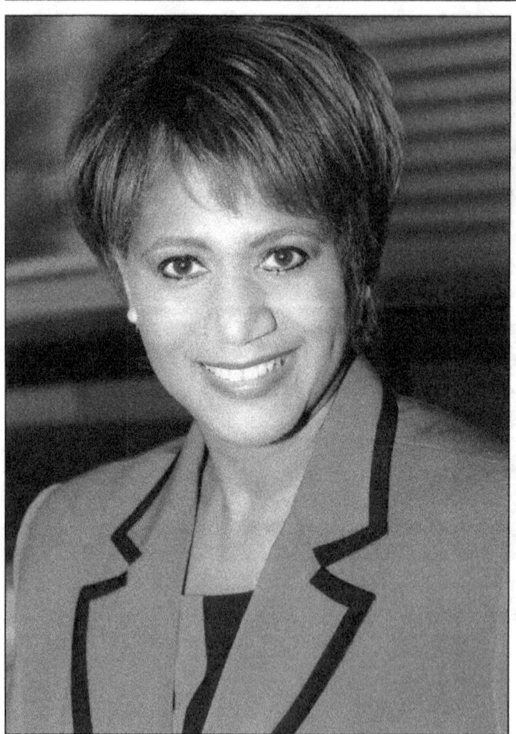

Cynthia Arceneaux has been a fixture in Southwest Louisiana homes for almost three decades as the evening news anchor for the NBC affiliate in Lake Charles, KPLC-TV. Cynthia arrived in Southwest Louisiana in 1981 after graduating from Louisiana State University with a bachelor's degree in broadcast journalism. She was the first African American to anchor the evening news in Lake Charles. (Courtesy of Cynthia Arceneaux.)

Nine

The Modern Era

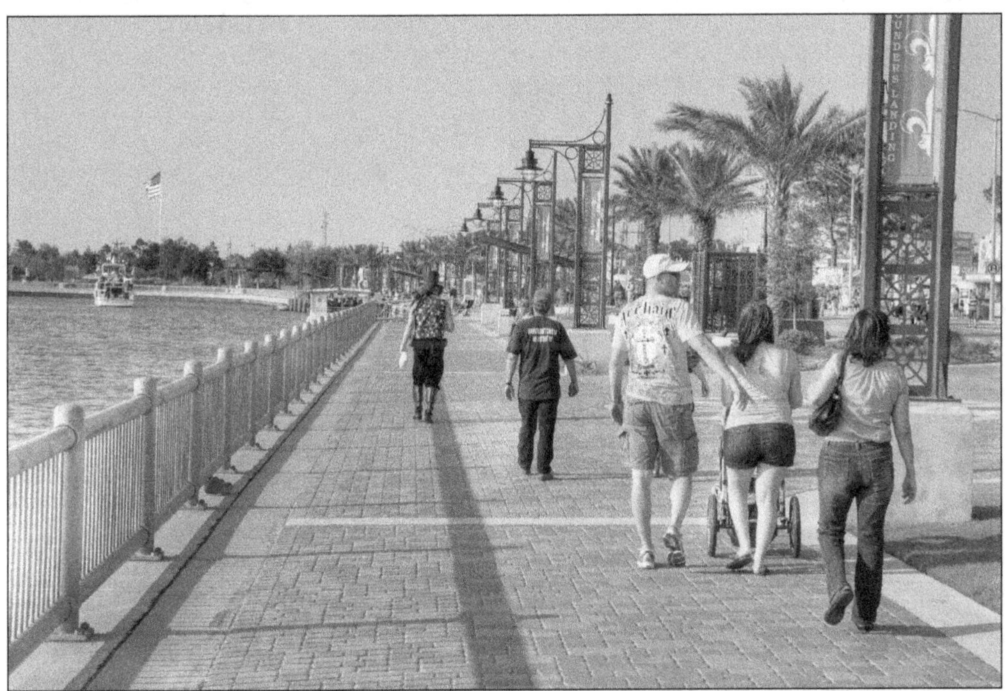

This 2010 photograph shows the Lakefront Promenade in downtown Lake Charles. Following the destruction caused by Hurricane Rita, Lake Charles voters approved a $90 million capital improvement project in 2007 to revitalize the downtown and lakeside districts. The construction of the promenade and the adjoining Bord du Lac Marina was completed in September 2010. (Courtesy of Dennis Thibodeaux.)

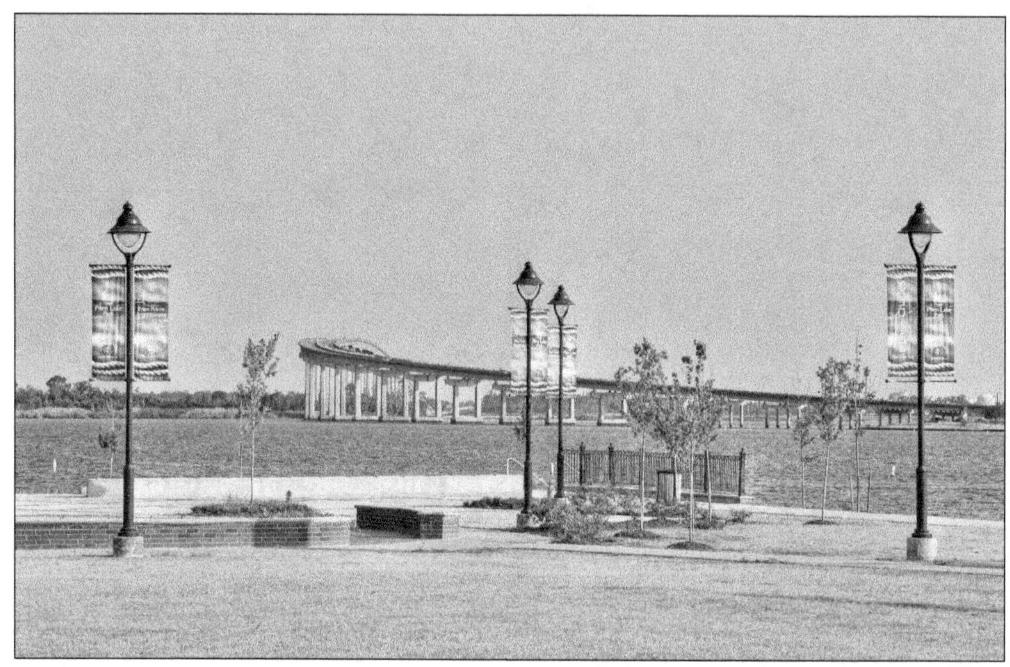

Construction began on Prien Lake Park in 2005, just months before Hurricane Rita put the project on hold. The park, which finally opened in April 2008, features French Colonial–style structures, free wi-fi, canoe and boat launches, and a 100-seat amphitheater. Prien Lake and the Interstate 210 bridge provide a dramatic backdrop for park visitors. (Courtesy of Dennis Thibodeaux.)

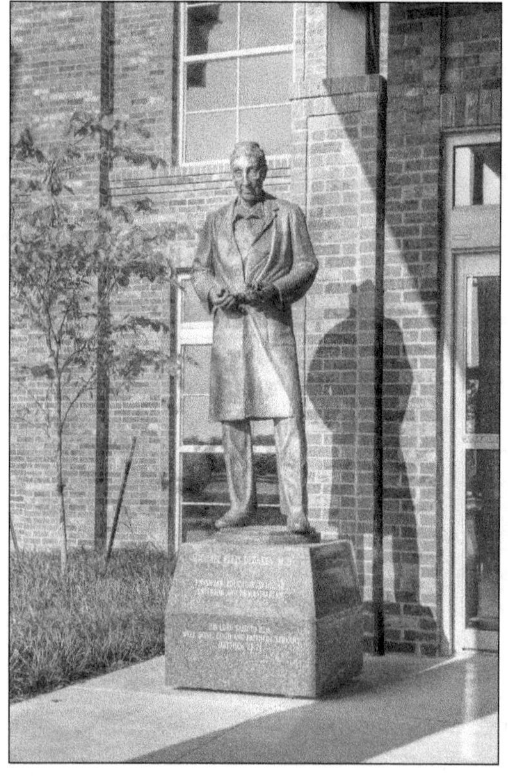

Born in Lake Charles in 1908 to Lebanese parents, Michael DeBakey grew up on Broad Street, graduated from Lake Charles High School, and became a world-renowned cardiac surgeon and medical inventor. He performed the first successful artificial heart surgery in 1966. In his honor, the street that takes visitors to St. Patrick's Hospital and its Heart Center was recently renamed Dr. Michael DeBakey Drive. This life-size monument of DeBakey is located at the new Lake Charles International Airport, built after Hurricane Rita destroyed the old facility in 2005. (Courtesy of Dennis Thibodeaux.)

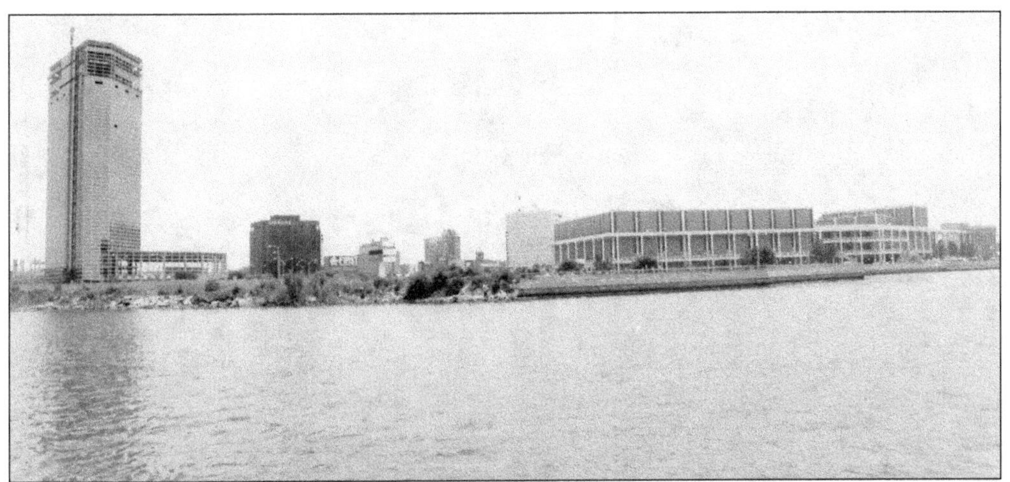

This view of downtown from the lake shows the 1983 construction of the CM Tower at Lakeshore Drive and Broad Street. Originally constructed for the Calcasieu Marine Bank, it rises 21 stories and has an adjoining six-story parking garage. It includes a two-story banking wing and restaurant facilities on the 20th floor. To the right is the Lake Charles Civic Center, home of the minor league football team the Swashbucklers and the Rosa Hart Theatre.

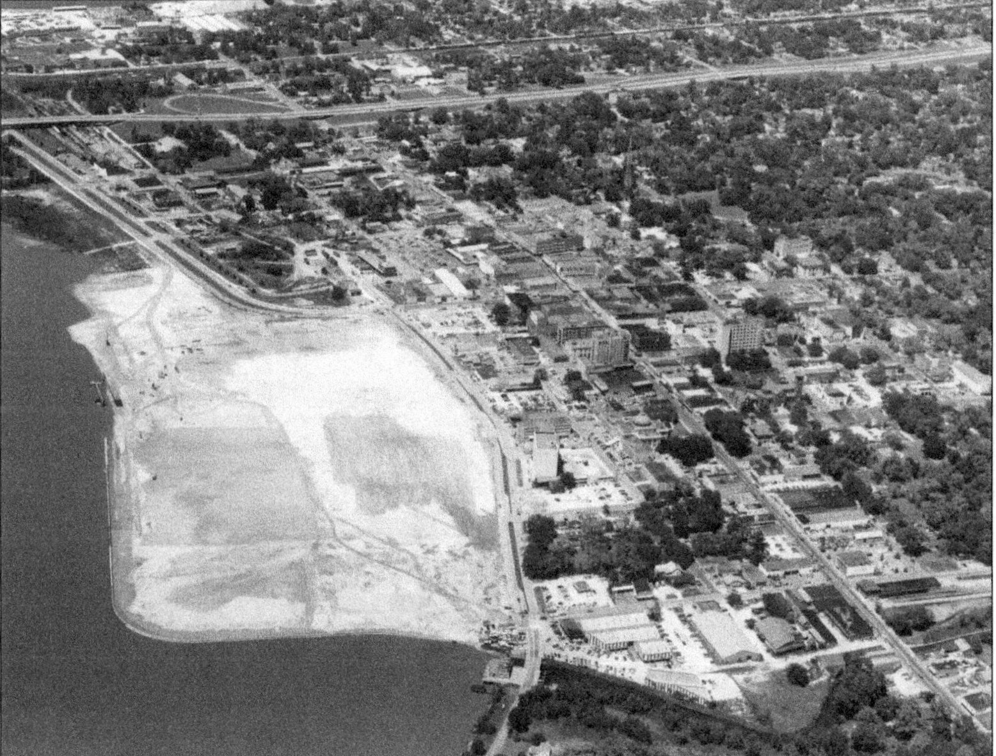

This aerial view of the lakefront shows the first phase of the construction of the Lake Charles Civic Center, which began in November 1969. Builders added 22 acres by constructing a retaining wall from Broad Street to Clarence Street, about 800 feet from the waterfront, and filling the space with sand dredged from the lake. The final project covered 57.5 acres and was completed on September 22, 1972.

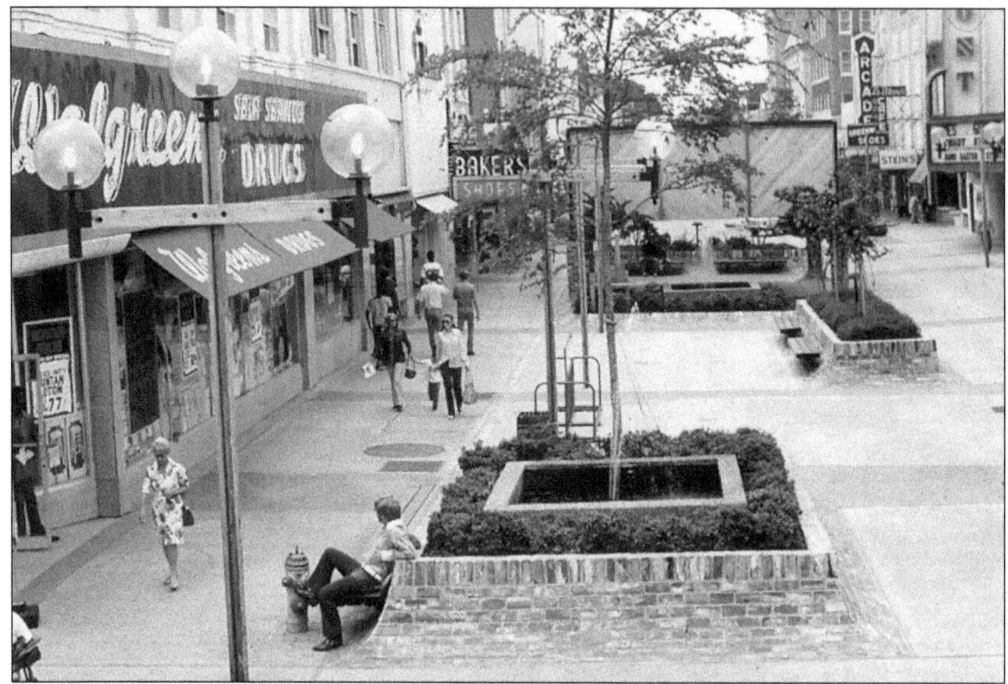

As retail shopping moved away from downtown to residential neighborhoods in the 1960s, Lake Charles mayor James Sudduth and downtown merchants created "Operation Heartbeat" in 1968. Designed to rejuvenate the downtown business district, the proposal involved closing streets and rerouting traffic around a central pedestrian mall on Ryan Street. The venture was unsuccessful, and the city decided to abandon the mall and reopen the streets in 1980.

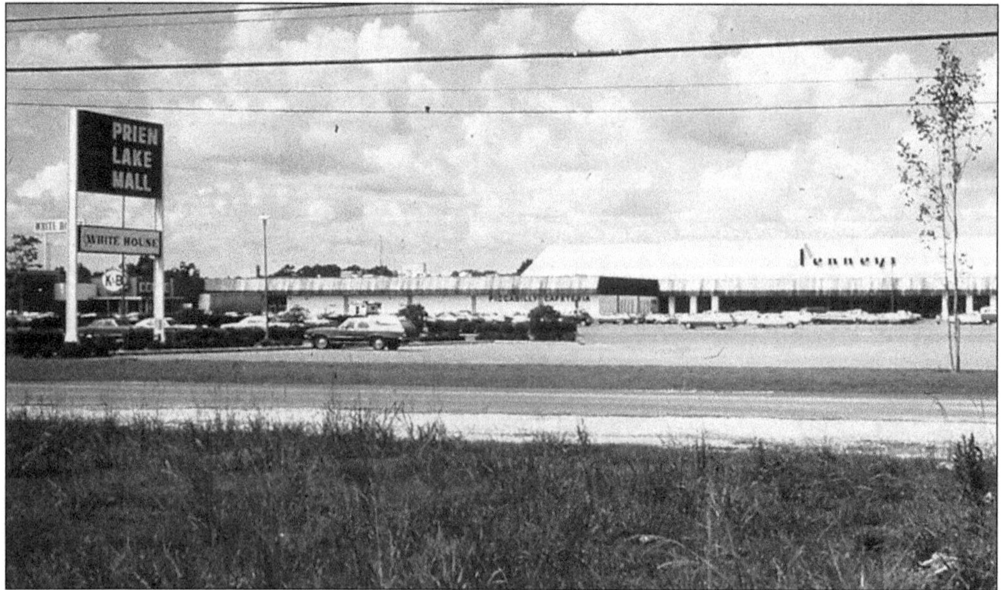

The 450,000-square-foot Prien Lake Mall opened in April 1972. The mall boasted a specially designed climate-control roof that provided springtime shopping conditions all year, thus contributing to the demise of the open-air mall downtown. New stores included The White House, JCPenney, Thom McAn, and Mangel's.

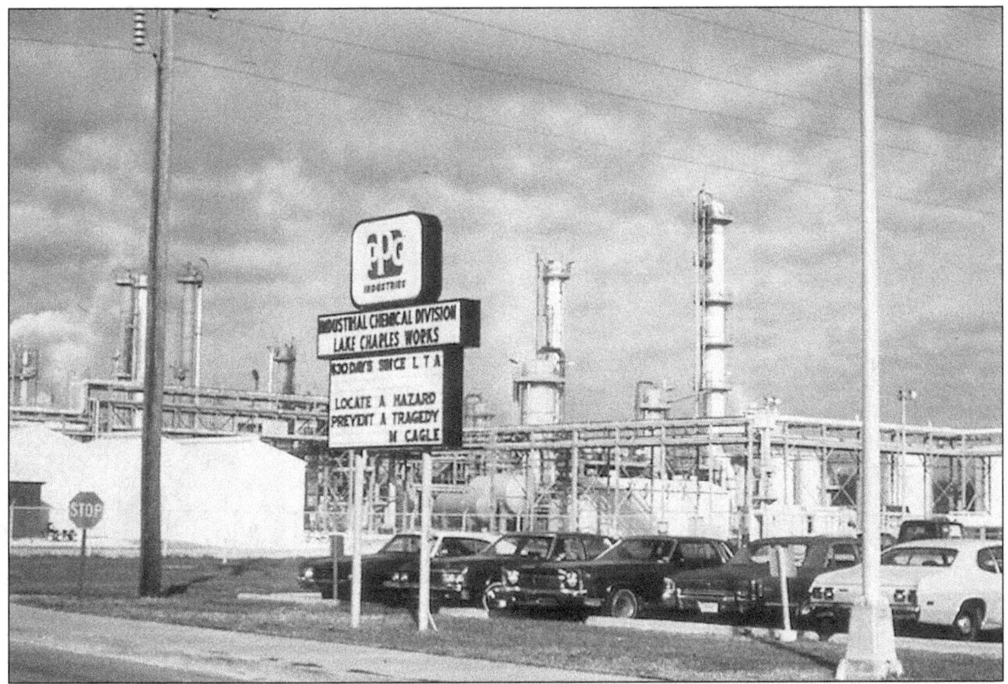

PPG Industrial Chemical Division began operations in Lake Charles in 1942; its plant here is the largest of PPG's worldwide operations. It is but one of many of the petrochemical facilities that located in the area during World War II as part of the vast mobilization of the country's defense. The refineries typically paid good wages, particularly for the semi-skilled, and many job seekers came to Lake Charles from the nearby rural areas. Tensions continue between citizens concerned about industrial pollution and those grateful for the employment.

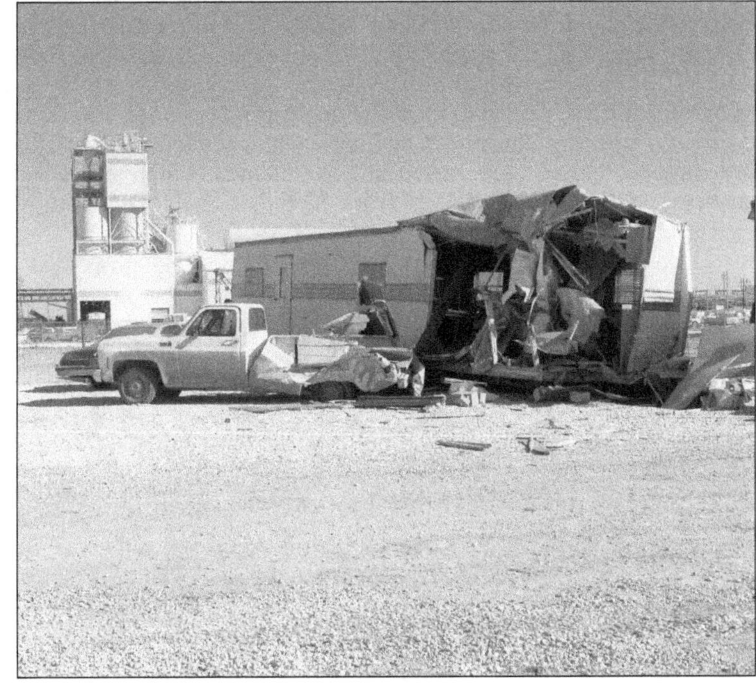

On January 15, 1976, a dispute between labor unions and independent contractors erupted into violence at the building site of the Jupiter Chemical Company on Pete Manena Road. A mob of 75 to 100 men stormed the site and fired several hundred shots. One person, Joe Hooper, was killed, and five others were injured. The violence spurred efforts in the Louisiana legislature to pass a right-to-work bill later that year.

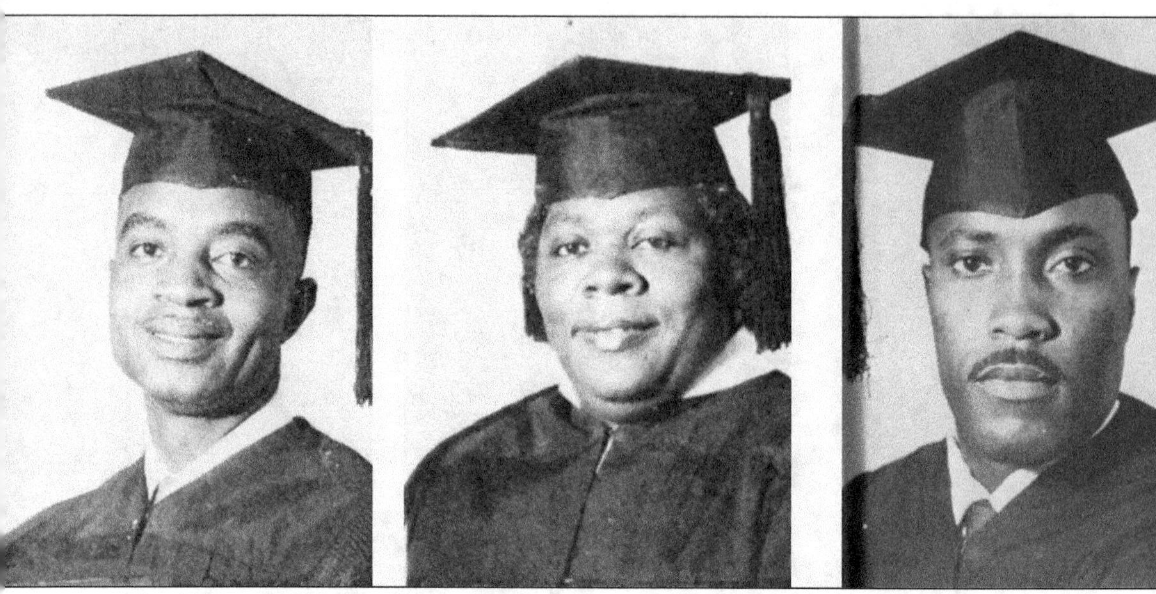

The 1950s and 1960s saw the beginning of massive social change as segregation was dismantled. The local NAACP, led by Lawrence Conley and Doretha Combre (owner of Combre Funeral Home), sued McNeese State College in 1953 when black students were denied admittance because of Louisiana's segregation laws. The parties to the suit were Joyce Richard, Leonora Chandler, Hattie Coleman, Frances Fondel, Ruthie Fondel, Barbara Fruge, Mary Jane Silas, Florence Cooper, Thelma Phelmpugo, Lucille Kane, Delorious Toussand, Marva Thibodaux, and Marshall McGovern. The NAACP's lead attorney on the case, whose name was on many similar lawsuits against other state colleges, was A.P. Tureaud. Tureaud was assisted by Thurgood Marshall, later the first African American Supreme Court justice. The federal judge hearing the case was Edwin Hunter, for whom the Federal Building in Lake Charles is named. He ruled in favor of the plaintiffs, who were duly registered. While many other schools around the South saw riots when blacks were admitted, McNeese's president, Lether Frazar, handled the situation skillfully by enlisting the student leadership to help him keep order. He called a meeting of male student leaders and told them that he "was not going to have any trouble." Firm leadership made an enormous difference in how the campus reacted when black students appeared for the first time. More than 20 registered in 1955. Pictured here from left to right are some of the first graduates: Solimn Webb, class of 1956; Sammie Cleodia Bergeron, class of 1957; and Charles Herrigan, class of 1955.

Under a federal mandate, the formerly all-white public schools began to integrate. The Lake Charles High School class of 1967 included three black students. Brenda Ball is pictured here in a senior photograph, second from left on the bottom row.

Festive Occasion

ABRAHAM, TIM—Football 1; Basketball; FBLA 4; Key Club 1, 2, 3, 4; Debate Club 1, 2, 3, 4; Pelican State 4; National Forensic League 2, 3, 4; Rally 3; Student Council 4

AIRHART, MELBA—Kilties 1, 2; FTA 4; FBLA 4

ALLURED, ROSS—Band 1, 2; Football 1, 2, 3

ARABIE, AUSTIN—Key 2, 3, 4; Industral Arts Club 4

BABIN, LYNN—FTA 4; FHA 4; FBLA 4

BAKER, MARGARET—Library Club 1, 2, 3, 4; FTA 3, 4; FHA 1, 2; FBLA 4; Debate Club 1; Glee Club 3

BALWIN, STANLEY—Basketball 1, 2, 3, 4; FTA 4; FBLA 4; LC Club 3, 4

BALL, BRENDA—FTA 4; FHA 4

BALL, CHARLOTTE—Kilties 2, 3, 4; Library Club 4; FTA 3, 4; FBLA 3, 4; Basketball Boosters 2, 3, 4

BARNES, PAT—Band 1, 2, 3; FBLA 3, 4; Debate Club 2, 3, 4; Mu Alpha Theta 3, 4; NHS 4; Radio Club 3, 4; National Forensic League 2, 3, 4

BATCHELOR, SHARON—FBLA 4; Glee Club 1, 2, 4; Chorus 1, 2, 4

Tim Abraham
Ross Allured
Lynn Babin

Melba Airhart
Austin Arabie
Margaret Baker

Stanley Balwin · Brenda Ball · Charlotte Ball · Pat Barnes · Sharon Batchelor

School organizations integrated more slowly than athletic teams, but by 1975, St. Louis High School's Speech Club included several black students. Pictured here are, from left to right, (first row) Kathy Pitts, Angela Sigur, Julie Dalgleish, Elisa Prejean, and Pat Webb; (second row) Carter Watson, Mark Johnson, Pat Yoder, Nanette Noland, Maria Barker, Susan Combre, and Yolande Beaco.

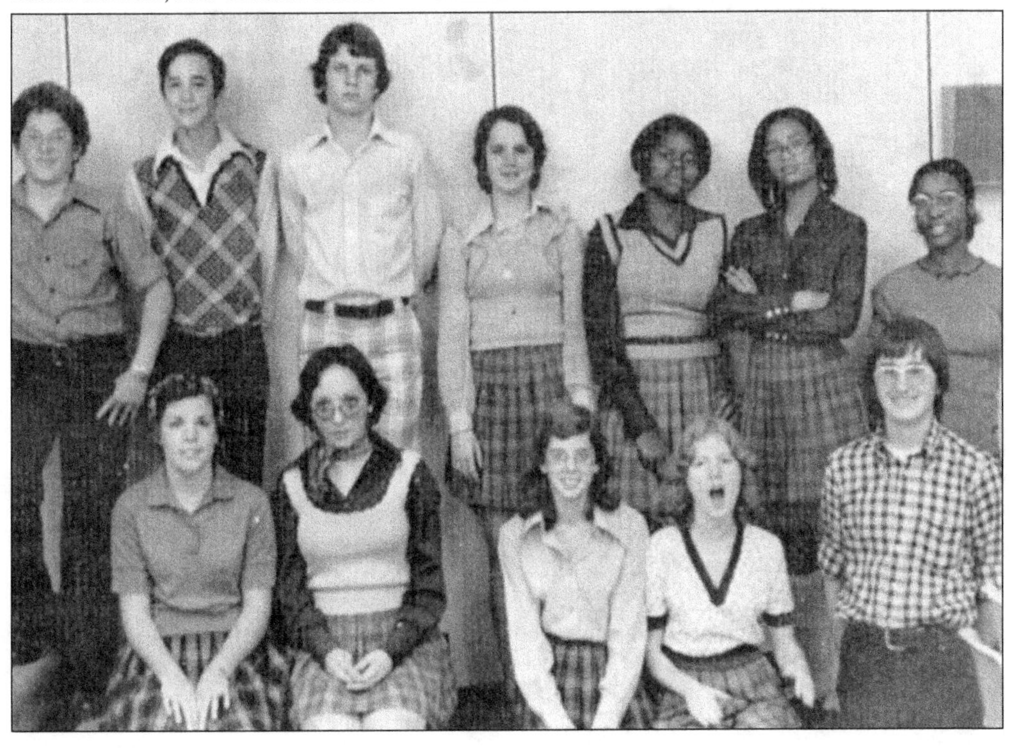

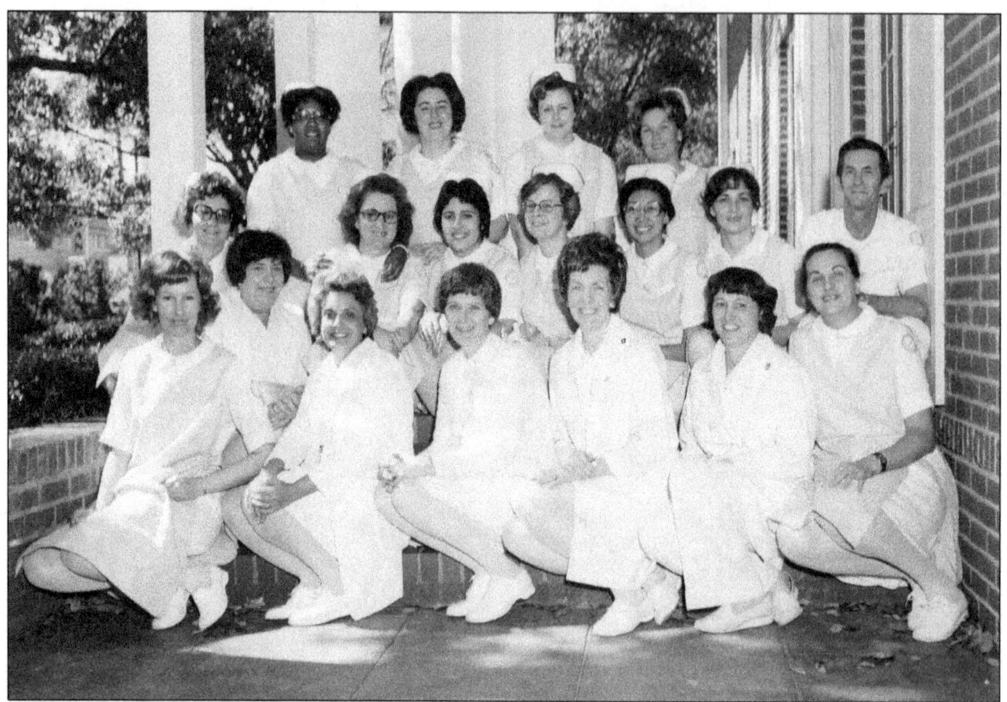

Sowela Technical Community College desegregated in 1962 following an NAACP lawsuit against the five white trade schools in the state. This photograph, showing two of the first black women to complete the nursing program, was taken at Sowela's old location on Broad Street, now occupied by Delta Tech.

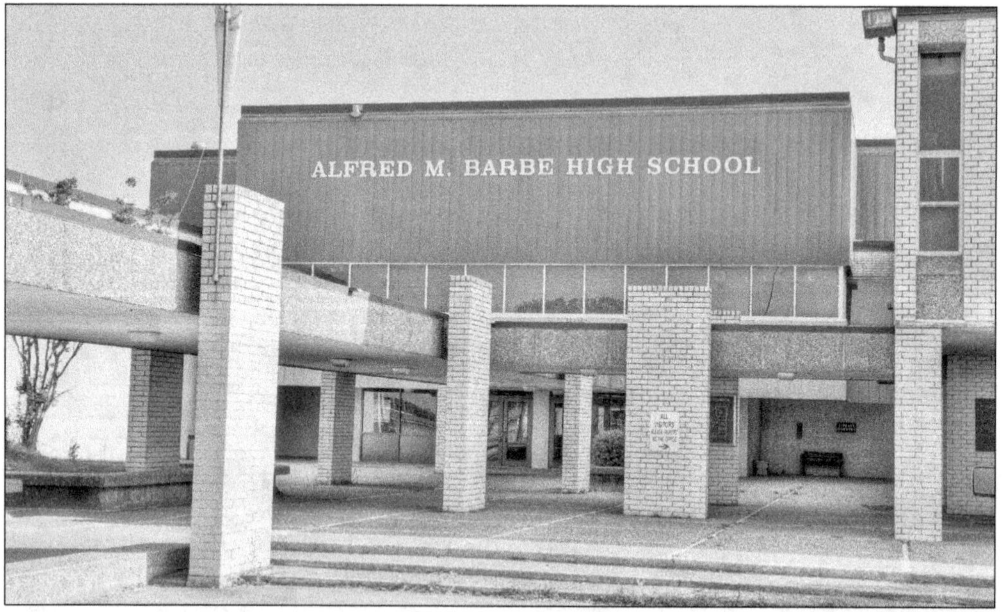

As the city's population shifted south, new schools became necessary to accommodate the growing student population. Alfred M. Barbe High School opened in 1971 with 12 buildings, 60 faculty members, and 1,000 students. Located in Southwest Lake Charles, Barbe is named after Judge Alfred M. Barbe, a benefactor to public education. (Courtesy of Dennis Thibodeaux.)

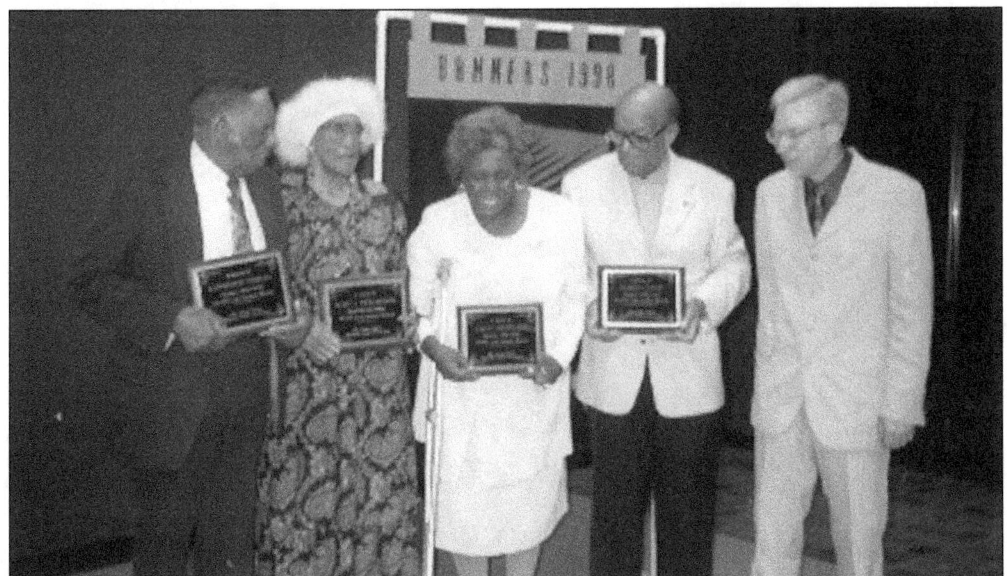

In 1998, four local NAACP pioneers were honored following a Banners Series lecture by Prof. Adam Fairclough based on his book about the NAACP in Louisiana, *Race and Democracy*. Pictured here are, from left to right, Florce Floyd, past president (late 1960s); Nancy Shepard, past president (1980s); Mary Richardson, charter member who joined in 1936; Lawrence Conley, past president (1947–1965); and Adam Fairclough.

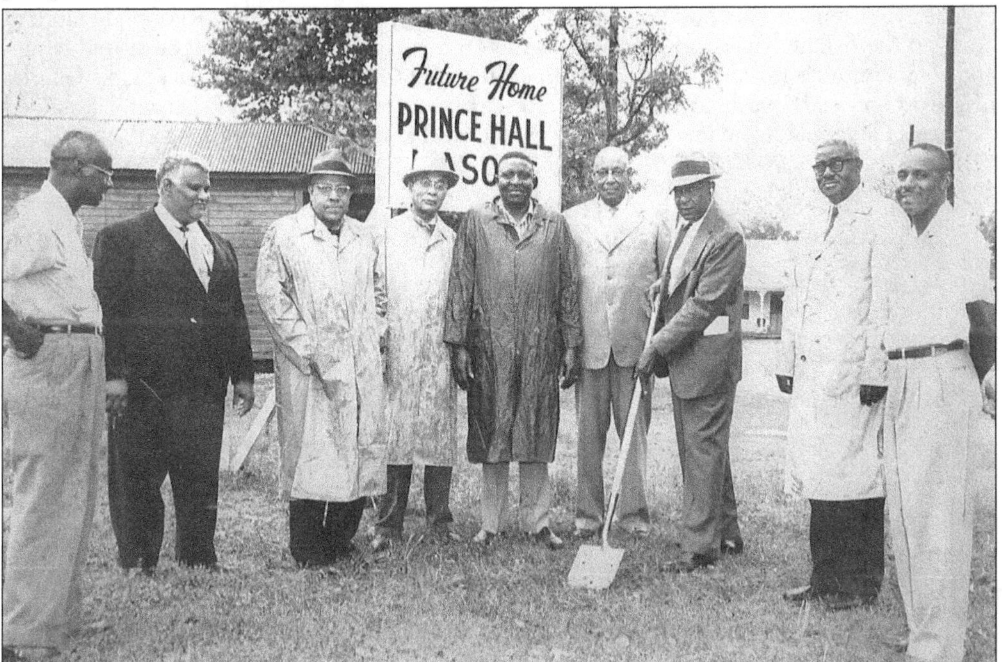

Attending a ground-breaking ceremony for M.W. Prince Hall Grand Lodge of Louisiana are, from left to right, E.H. Walker, Walter Gowdy, John G. Lewis, Ulric W. Pryce, Bartis Abraham, ? Polk, Willie Bell, Rudolph V. Kirk, and William Walker. In 1952, Kirk became the first African American to serve as deputy sheriff in Calcasieu Parish, a position he held for over 15 years. (Courtesy of Cheryl Kirk-Duggan.)

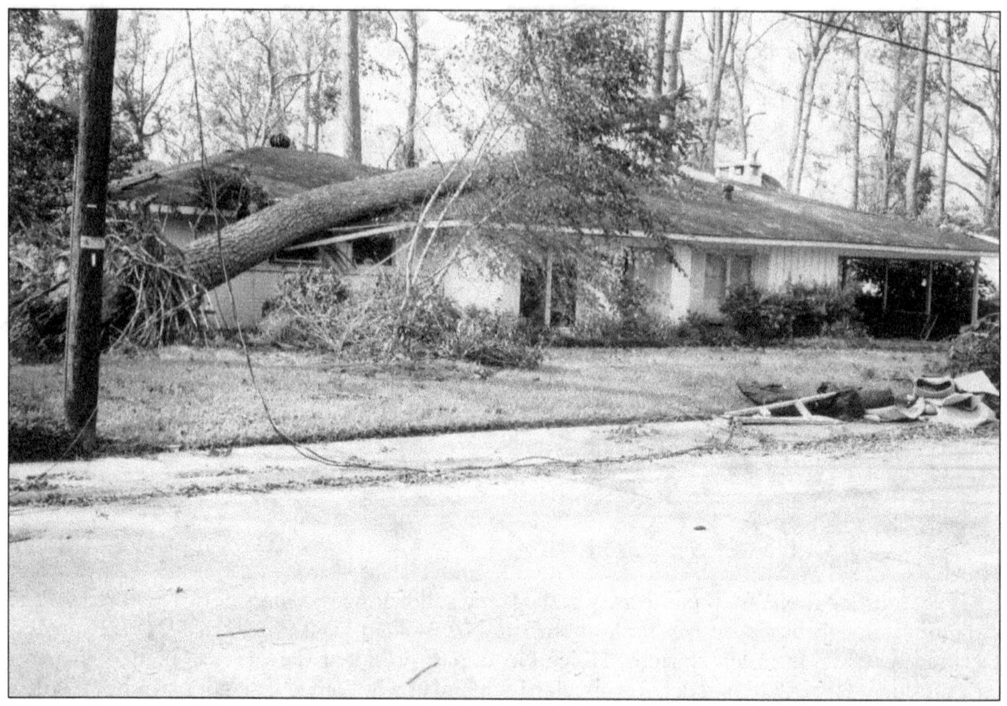

During the weeks following Hurricane Katrina, Lake Charles absorbed hundreds of New Orleans evacuees before facing its own evacuation in the face of Hurricane Rita. Rita made landfall between the Sabine River and Johnson's Bayou on September 23, 2005, and destroyed homes and communities across Southwest Louisiana. These photographs depict a typical Lake Charles neighborhood in the weeks after the storm. Residents and business owners faced wind and flood damage, fallen trees, and damage to the city's electrical grid. (Courtesy of Brenda Bachrack.)

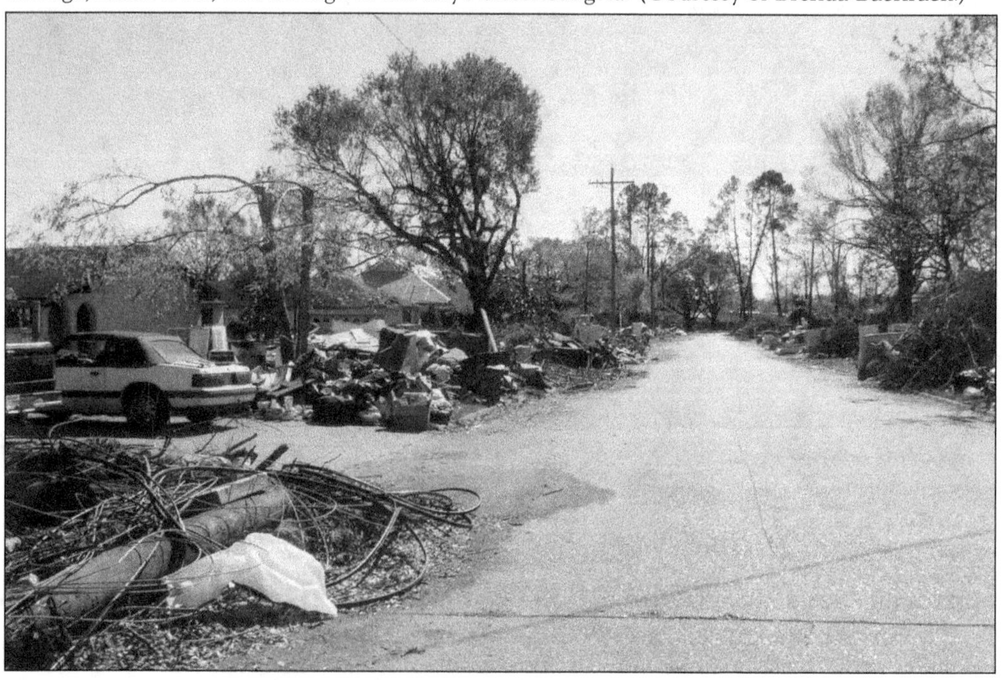

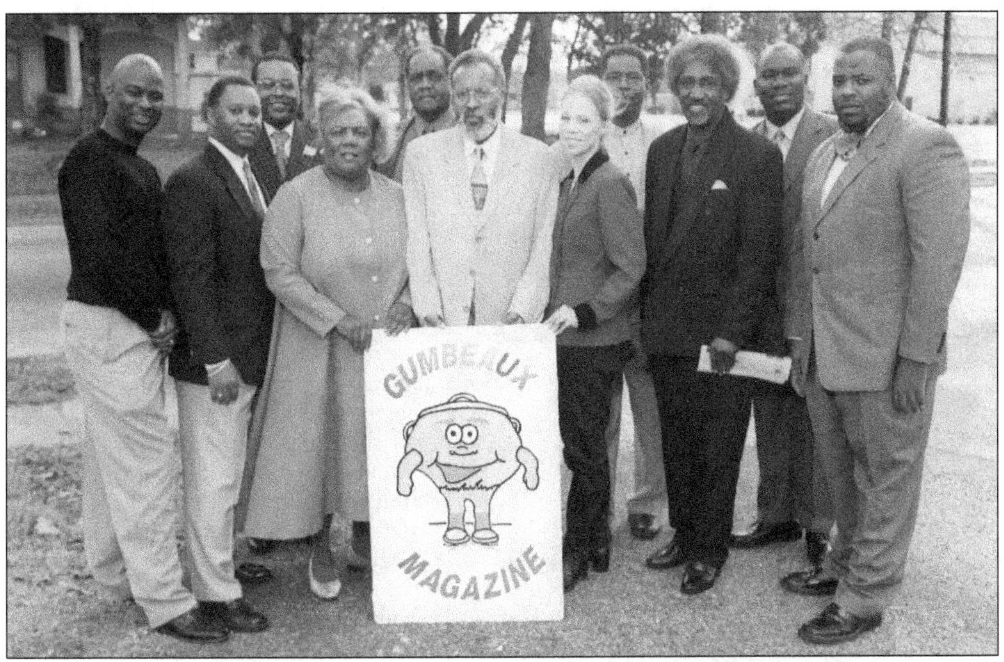

Gumbeaux Magazine began in 1993 and is the only tabloid news publication for African Americans in Southwest Louisiana. Gumbeaux Media includes the "gumbolive" television talk show and a "gumbolive" Internet radio show. Pictured here are, from left to right, (first row) Mark Ned, Michael P. Ned, Dr. Nancy Shepard, founder Lawrence "Gumbo" Morrow, office manager Marcie Sealy, Bobbie Celestine, and investigative reporter Bryan Beverly; (second row) Donald Roy, Ozie "Zeke" Rideaux, Joe Mimms, and Larry Robinson. (Courtesy of Lawrence Morrow.)

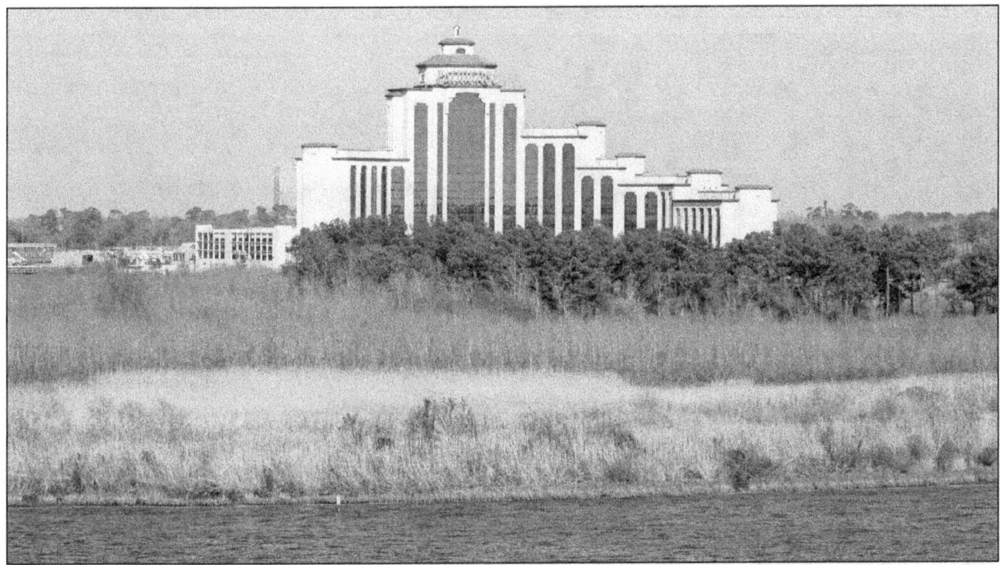

The L'Auberge du Lac casino and resort opened in May 2005, just months before Hurricane Rita hit. The resort closed for 16 days after the storm, and it has since become a popular regional vacation destination, concert venue, convention facility, and local nightlife hotspot. It is the tallest building between Houston and Baton Rouge, and it features an 18-hole golf course designed by Tom Fazio. (Courtesy of Dennis Thibodeaux.)

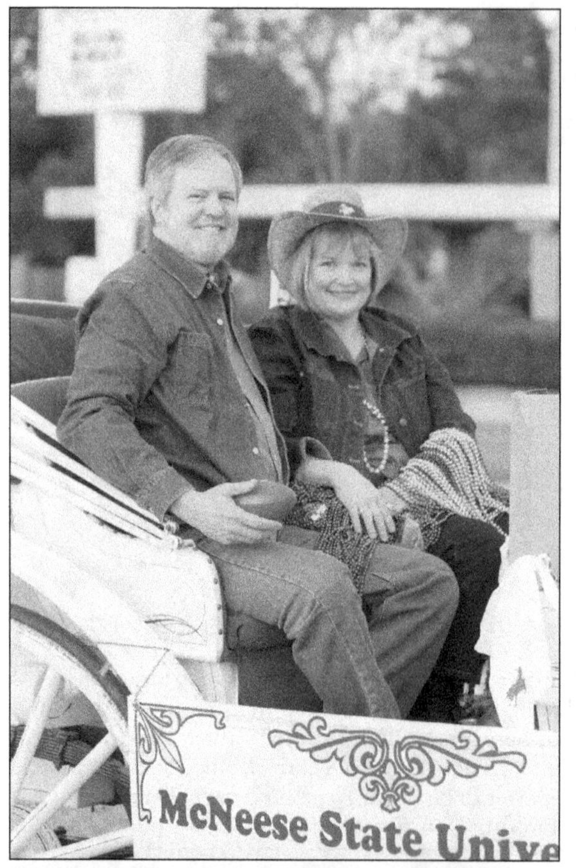

Dr. Phillip Williams and his wife, Sandra, share a carriage ride in the 2011 McNeese Homecoming Parade. Dr. Williams became McNeese's sixth president in 2010, following the retirement of Dr. Robert Hebert. Dr. Williams is the first McNeese president to come from outside the university. (Courtesy of Dennis Thibodeaux.)

Mayor Randy Roach opened ceremonies for a fundraising walk for the local chapter of the National Alliance on Mental Illness. Behind him are State Senator Willie Mount (left) and Gigi Kaufman (right), of Gigi's Fitness centers. Roach, mayor since 2000, was in office when Hurricane Rita hit the parish in 2005. He helped preside over a smooth evacuation of citizens before the storm, and a major recovery process afterward. Under his leadership, the city improved infrastructure and developed a downtown and lakefront improvement plan. (Courtesy of Dennis Thibodeaux.)

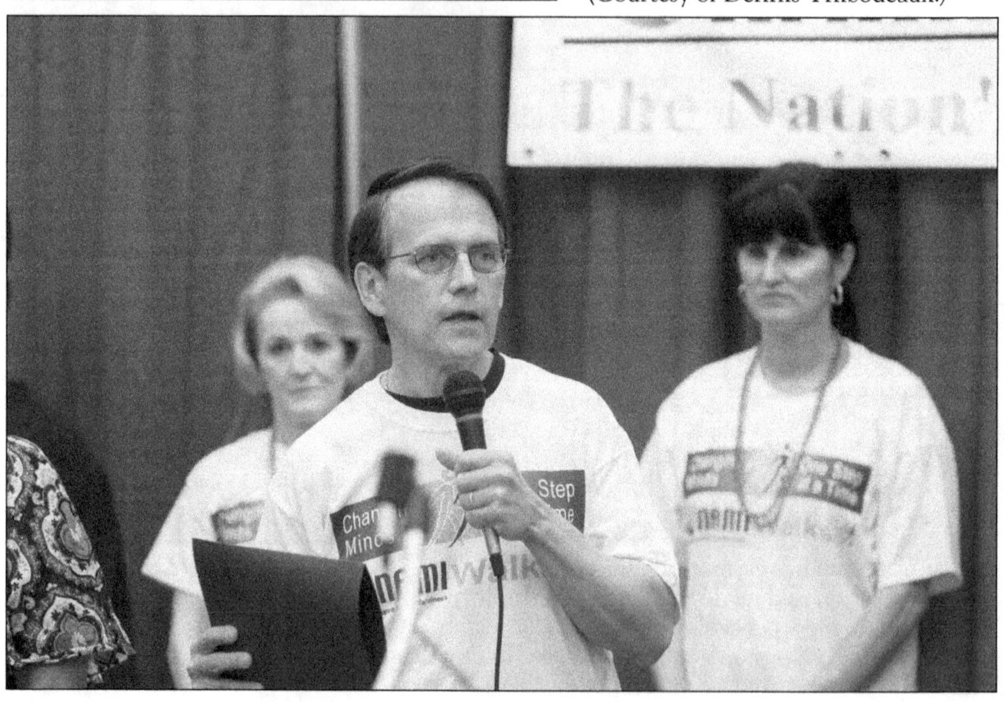

INDEX

www.ingramcontent.com/pod-product-compliance
Lightning Source LLC
LaVergne TN
LVHW081546100826
845153LV00004B/318
9781531661403